Language Games: Innovative Activities for Teaching English

Edited by Maureen Snow Andrade

Maria Dantas-Whitney, Sarah Rilling, and Lilia Savova, Series Editors

TESOL Classroom Practice Series

 TESOL Teachers of English to Speakers of Other Languages, Inc.

Typeset in ITC Galliard and Vag Rounded
by Capitol Communication Systems, Inc., Crofton, Maryland USA
Printed by United Graphics, Inc., Mattoon, Illinois USA
Indexed by Pueblo Indexing and Publishing Services, Pueblo West, Colorado

Teachers of English to Speakers of Other Languages, Inc.
700 South Washington Street, Suite 200
Alexandria, Virginia 22314 USA
Tel 703-836-0774 • Fax 703-836-6447 • E-mail tesol@tesol.org •
http://www.tesol.org/

Publishing Manager: Carol Edwards
Copy Editor: Jean House
Additional Reader: Kelly Graham
Cover Design: Capitol Communication Systems, Inc.

ISBN 9781931185530
Library of Congress Control No. 2008910203

Language Games: Innovative Activities for Teaching English

LANGUAGE GAMES:
INNOVATIVE ACTIVITIES FOR TEACHING ENGLISH

Curriculum Reference Chart

Chapter	Other Purposes/Skills	Level/Age
Reading/Writing		
2. Storyboarding for the Oscars	• vocabulary • grammar	advanced+ young adult/adult
3. WARTS	• technology • vocabulary • grammar	beginning+ young adult/adult
4. What Is It?	• English for specific purposes (technical writing)	intermediate+ young adult/adult
5. Who's the Best Detective?	• listening/speaking • culture	high intermediate+ young adult/adult
6. Pass It On! Writing Games	• grammar • vocabulary • reading	high beginning+ young adult/adult
Listening/Speaking		
7. In the Director's Shoes: Bridging Meaning and Pleasure in an ELT Game	• writing • technology • vocabulary	intermediate+ young adult/adult
8. Tabletop Role-Playing Games	• reading • writing	intermediate+ young adult/adult
9. Podquests: Language Games on the Go	• technology • reading • vocabulary • culture • grammar	intermediate+ young adult/adult
10. The Survey Game	• vocabulary • culture • grammar • writing	intermediate+ young adult/adult
Vocabulary		
11. Let's Go Shopping	• speaking • grammar	beginning+ children/adult
12. Collocations in the Foreseeable Future	• reading • writing • listening/speaking	intermediate+ young adult/adult
13. Urban Myths: Fact or Fiction?	• reading • writing • listening/speaking	intermediate+ young adult/adult

Chapter	Other Purposes/Skills	Level/Age
14. Speaking Through Art	• speaking • critical thinking • culture • content-based • speaking	intermediate+ young adult/adult
15. Define Your Terms	• speaking • reading • writing • grammar	intermediate+ adult/young adult
Grammar		
16. Treasure Hunting With Grammar	• writing • reading • vocabulary • critical thinking	beginning– intermediate children
17. Nice Tower, But It May Fall Down: A Game for Teaching Modals of Probability	• speaking	intermediate children/adult
18. The Teacher's Choice Game	• speaking • vocabulary	intermediate+ young adult/adult
19. What's the Problem?	• problem-based learning • critical thinking • speaking	high beginning+ children/young adult
Game Templates		
20. Pass the Clothespin	• review • vocabulary • listening/speaking • grammar • writing • reading	beginning–advanced children/adult
21. On-the-Spot Games from Learner Content	• speaking • vocabulary • grammar/writing	intermediate+ children/adult
22. Energizing yet Educational Games	• practice • review • vocabulary • listening/speaking • grammar	beginning+ children/adult
23. Do-It-Yourself Games	• listening/speaking • grammar • vocabulary • reading • writing • culture • review • collaborative • learning	intermediate+ young adult/adult

Chapter	Other Purposes/Skills	Level/Age
Get Acquainted		
24. Bingo	<ul><li>speaking</li><li>grammar</li><li>content review</li></ul>	high beginning+ young adult/adult
25. Flags of Ourselves: Language Practice Using Student-Generated Props	<ul><li>listening/speaking</li></ul>	beginning+ young adult/adult
Content-Based Instruction		
26. Add, Mix, and Shake: Science, Grammar, and Games in the Language Classroom	<ul><li>speaking</li><li>grammar</li><li>vocabulary</li></ul>	intermediate children
27. Using Common Language Games in a Science and Technology Curriculum	<ul><li>speaking</li><li>vocabulary</li></ul>	low intermediate+ young adult/adult
28. The Business Apprentice	<ul><li>speaking (presentations)</li><li>vocabulary</li><li>culture</li></ul>	high intermediate+ young adult/adult
Critical Thinking		
29. Logical Use of Logic Puzzles	<ul><li>reading</li><li>vocabulary</li><li>grammar</li></ul>	high beginning+ children/adult
30. Three Games to Exercise the Brain	<ul><li>listening/speaking</li><li>writing</li><li>reading</li><li>creative thinking</li><li>problem solving</li></ul>	beginning+ children

Table of Contents

PART 1: SKILLS FOCUS

A. Reading and Writing

B. Listening and Speaking

C. Vocabulary

D. Grammar

Chapter 17

Chapter 18

Chapter 19

PART 2: BEYOND SKILLS

A. Game Templates

Chapter 20

Chapter 21

Chapter 22

Chapter 23

B. Get Acquainted

Chapter 24

Chapter 25

C. Content-Based Instruction

D. Critical Thinking

Series Editors' Preface

The TESOL Classroom Practice Series showcases state-of-the-art curricula, materials, tasks, and activities reflecting emerging trends in language education and in the roles of teachers, learners, and the English language itself. The series seeks to build localized theories of language learning and teaching based on students' and teachers' unique experiences in and out of the classroom.

This series captures the dynamics of 21st-century English for speakers of other languages (ESOL) classrooms. It reflects major shifts in authority from teacher-centered practices to collaborative learner- and learning-centered environments. The series acknowledges the growing numbers of English speakers globally, celebrates locally relevant curricula and materials, and emphasizes the importance of multilingual and multicultural competencies—a primary goal in teaching English as an international language. Furthermore, the series takes into account contemporary technological developments that provide new opportunities for information exchange and social and transactional communications.

Each volume in the series focuses on a particular communicative skill, learning environment, or instructional goal. Chapters within each volume represent practices in English for general, academic, vocational, and specific purposes. Readers will find examples of carefully researched and tested practices designed for different student populations (from young learners to adults, from beginning to advanced) in diverse settings (from pre-K–12 to college and postgraduate, from local to global, from formal to informal). A variety of methodological choices are also represented, including individual and collaborative tasks and curricular as well as extracurricular projects. Most important, these volumes invite readers into the conversation that considers and so constructs ESOL classroom practices as complex entities. We are indebted to the authors, their colleagues, and their students for being a part of this conversation.

ESOL teachers use language games to increase motivation, provide authentic and meaningful language practice, increase student engagement, and infuse the classroom with fun. This volume describes a variety of innovative games used today in language classrooms around the globe, reflecting different contexts and cultures. Chapters in this book demonstrate how both theory and practice inform our teaching approaches. While some of the games focus primarily on the four traditional language skills, reading, writing, listening, and speaking, as well as the supporting areas of vocabulary and grammar, other games clearly have a different emphasis, such as critical thinking and content-based language instruction. Yet other chapters focus on objectives such as getting acquainted, or provide ideas for game templates that teachers can adapt for various purposes and types of content.

This book stands apart in that the contributions reflect multiple classroom uses. Themes evident throughout the volume reflect pedagogical goals and practices for language learning such as communicative competence, interaction, authenticity, skills integration, content emphasis, and collaboration.

Maria Dantas-Whitney, Western Oregon University
Sarah Rilling, Kent State University
Lilia Savova, Indiana University of Pennsylvania

CHAPTER 1

Language Games—
In Celebration of Creativity!

Maureen Snow Andrade

THE UNIVERSAL APPEAL OF LANGUAGE GAMES

Many of us can remember holidays, sick days, or long winter evenings when we passed the time by playing card games and board games around the table with family and friends. Most of us also have played social games that liven up a party, help guests become better acquainted, and make everyone present feel comfortable. More recently, computer games have emerged on the scene, generating a dedicated following. Watching game shows on television is another common pastime, and reality shows are replete with competitions featuring common yet highly skilled mortals battling it out for glory or huge cash prizes.

Games certainly have not gone out of fashion, although they have evolved to encompass an enormous range of possibilities. Recently, games have become characterized by the use of technology. Some computer games may involve solitary players or individuals engaged with competitors who are hundreds or even thousands of miles away. In this respect, playing some games is solitary, yet global. The universal appeal of games makes them highly attractive to language teachers who can implement them in the classroom for a variety of purposes. Although factors such as culture, age, proficiency level, and curricular goals vary, teachers can find a game to enhance almost any aspect of language learning.

The wide range of games, competitions, contests, and challenges also creates difficulty in defining the term *game*. Some researchers have identified challenge as an essential component to a game while acknowledging that competition is not necessary and can have negative learning effects (Shameem & Tickoo, 1999; Wright, Betteridge, & Buckby, 2006). Many games, in fact, require cooperation to accomplish a common goal. In this volume, games are conceived of in their broadest sense, encompassing individuals or teams and ranging from puzzles and self-challenges to team competitions or projects, role playing, and debates. They engage the learner, stimulate discovery, and involve interaction.

Part of the appeal of games is that they lend themselves to a variety of learning styles to support and develop students' interpersonal, intrapersonal, linguistic, spatial, musical, logical-mathematical, and bodily kinesthetic predilections (Gardner, 1983). Some language teaching methodologies, such as total physical response, for example, are based on the idea that movement helps learners absorb and retain language (e.g., see Larsen-Freeman, 2000). For example, in this book one of the games described in the chapter "Add, Mix, and Shake: Content, Vocabulary, and Games in the Language Classroom," by Lan Hue Quach and Scott P. Kissau, involves students in creating the materials for the game by cutting out and gluing circles. Students receive bean bags for correct answers and then toss them at targets. Movement, which supports a bodily kinesthetic learning style, is but one possible element of a game.

Other games in the volume support alternate learning styles. "Logical Use of Logic Puzzles," by Kurtis McDonald, supports the logical-mathematical form of intelligence, whereas Mary E. Hillis' get-acquainted bingo game focuses predominantly on intrapersonal intelligence as students interact with each other, and also visual intelligence as students see a visual representation of the information they collect by visiting with their peers and filling in bingo cards. Because learners (and teachers) have different learning styles, not everyone will like every game. Learners have multiple learning styles and may vary in their preferences at any given time. Games can be designed to accommodate a variety of learning styles and preferences, and if used consistently, can become an integral feature of the language classroom.

The universal appeal of games—and the influence of teachers' own cultures, education, experiences, talents, skills, and teaching–learning preferences—means that, among any group of teachers, an extremely diverse set of games for the English as a second language (ESL) or English as a foreign language (EFL) classroom can be realized. As evidenced by the chapters in this volume, using games for language learning is limited only by one's imagination.

GAMES AND LANGUAGE LEARNING

Using games in the ESL or EFL classroom contributes to lowering the affective filter (Krashen, 1981). In other words, factors that might negatively impact language learning, such as inhibitions, doubts, low self-esteem, and lack of motivation, are ameliorated. When students can relax, have fun, and focus on the purpose of a game, their anxiety is lessened and defenses lowered; they begin to have more confidence in using the language and increased motivation. By sustaining learners' interest, games also lessen some of the hard work involved in learning a language (Wright et al., 2006). Games potentially encourage students to take risks and learn by trial and error as they experiment with the language. Experimentation leads to language development (Oxford, 1990). Risk-taking, a natural component of many games, generally is considered a positive factor in language learning. In the classroom, risk-taking occurs in a safe environment with trusted peers and teacher.

By going beyond structured, teacher-centered talk to create meaningful, student-initiated interaction, games generate opportunities for interaction, which plays a critical role in language learning. As students negotiate meaning in peer–peer communication, they receive the comprehensible input necessary for language development (e.g., see Krashen, 1985), but also may be pushed slightly beyond their current levels through exposure to new vocabulary and structures, particularly if more proficient students are grouped with those less proficient. Teachers must be aware of students' actual level of target language compared to their potential level and emphasize meaningful interaction and relevant content for second-language development. Through the use of games, learning may occur incidentally without the student even realizing it (Rinvolucri & Davis, 1995; Shameem & Tickoo, 1999) as peers work with each other to solve problems and construct meaning.

One advantage of incidental learning is its support of language acquisition as opposed to language learning. Krashen (1982) views language acquisition as a natural process in which items pass through the affective filter and become internalized. In contrast, learned items such as grammar rules are conscious and become part of a monitor. They are used only if they are simple, if the learner is focused on form, and if the learner has enough time to apply the monitor. However, it is difficult to monitor output in the flow of discourse. Classroom contexts can provide formal instruction as well as input that is comprehensible and relevant, thereby supporting language acquisition.

When games present situations in which students must communicate with each other to accomplish a goal, the language of the classroom becomes more authentic. Rather than teachers asking students inauthentic questions to which they already know the answers, games can be used to create opinion gap situations to approximate more relevant language exchanges (Wright et al., 1983). Through games, teachers can create realistic contexts for language to be practiced—situations that require learners to understand each other, express their own viewpoints, and provide information (Wright et al., 1983, 2006). Games often have repetitive elements that are similar to language drills but more meaningful (Wright et al., 1983, 2006). When language is meaningful, it will be better remembered. Communicative activities should assist students in learning new language features and also practicing those already acquired (Shameem & Tickoo, 1999). Teachers can design games to focus on practicing communicative language, reviewing vocabulary and structures already presented, and introducing new language features. Creating situations that bring language to life through pictures, dramatization, and stories helps link language to action (and to communication), and work and play merge (e.g., see Lee, 1979).

The use of games for language learning is based largely on a constructivist approach in which knowledge is developed through active learning (e.g., see

Richard-Amato, 2003). Students can ask questions, search for answers, collaborate, identify multiple solutions to problems, take charge of their own learning, play the role of the teacher, and engage in thought-provoking activities to use language and create knowledge. Vygotsky's (1978) theory of the Zone of Proximal Development is the foundation of the constructivist movement in education. The latter suggests that learning is a social process that is a step ahead of development. Learners move from their actual level of development to their potential level through problem-solving, guidance, and collaboration with slightly more advanced peers.

Games and activities that take into account students' current levels of proficiency can be designed to push learners beyond these levels to create optimal learning environments, supporting Vygotsky's (1978) theory. This active learning process also involves fostering collaboration as team members help each other and work toward a common goal. When students are engaged socially in a fun, interactive activity, learning will occur (Shameem & Tickoo, 1999). Teachers should use techniques to create good feelings and build a community of learners. A friendly atmosphere should prevail, even when games involve competition and players are involved in surpassing others and improving their own performance (e.g., see Lee, 1979).

Teacher Considerations

Teachers need to acknowledge that some people like games more than others and that students may be focused on learning English for a specific purpose, such as increased employment opportunities, and resist games (Wright et al., 1983). Teachers must focus on learning objectives rather than incorporating games solely to have fun (although this may be appropriate occasionally) or use up class time. If the latter occurs, students will rightly view games as largely a waste of class time. When games are clearly tied to objectives and appropriate to the focus of the lesson, and teachers demonstrate their usefulness, they will be more successful. So learners will perceive it as legitimate, the rationale for the game or activity must be explained because it may not be readily apparent (Shameem & Tickoo, 1999).

Other considerations for using games are: preparation time, the value of the game in accomplishing curricular aims, the time needed to set up the game in class, and the students' perceived interest (Wright et al., 1983). Teachers also need to ensure that learners have the vocabulary and linguistic structures to play the game and that the instructions are clear. Teachers can write out the instructions to the game to develop students' reading skills and enable them to refer back to the instructions if they have questions as they play, give the instructions in a dictation format, or provide minimal instructions and allow students who understand the rules to help others as the game is played (Rinvolucri & Davis, 1995). These ideas reinforce language learning on a number of levels, add variety to class procedures, and demonstrate creativity. Depending on the level of the students, a demonstration by the teacher or other students may be needed before play begins.

Teachers need to be aware of their students' personalities and abilities and not set up a game in any way to disadvantage students with lower levels of proficiency. If students are not comfortable participating in a game, they can be assigned other responsibilities, such as keeping time or tracking the score. As much as possible, however, teachers should design games that will be accessible and of interest to all students and create a positive classroom rapport so that students will feel comfortable playing and be willing to try something new. Similarly, cultural contexts must be considered and games adapted not only to respect students' cultures but to be of high interest. The aim of most games is to allow students to interact, make mistakes, work to communicate, and to provide some sense of challenge. Teachers should allow this authentic language use to occur naturally without overly structuring the activity, correcting students, or giving too much help.

ABOUT THIS BOOK

The range of purposes for using games in the language classroom led to some difficulty in organizing this book. Whereas some of the games focus primarily on the four traditional language skills—reading, writing, listening, and speaking—as well as the supporting areas of vocabulary and grammar, other games clearly have a different emphasis, such as critical thinking and content-based language instruction. Yet other games focus on objectives such as getting acquainted, and can be adapted for various purposes and types of content. The nature of the games led to dividing the book into two parts. The first, "Skills Focus," concentrates on traditional skills and language components (reading and writing, listening and speaking, grammar, vocabulary) while the second part, "Beyond Skills," features game templates, get-acquainted games, and games used for content-based instruction and critical thinking development. The two categories make the book easy to use and indicate primary areas of focus.

In Part 1: Skills Focus, the games are divided into skill and subskill areas including reading and writing, listening and speaking, grammar, and vocabulary. Five authors contribute games related to reading and writing. Shane Dixon's "Storyboarding for the Oscars" involves students in creating storyboards to help them brainstorm and organize a piece of narrative writing. Students share their storyboards and vote for those that should receive "Oscar" awards. Next, in "WARTS (Writing Activities Require Time and Satisfaction)," Nancy Tarawhiti describes two writing games. In the first game, which emphasizes brainstorming and fluency, students choose an item from a box and write about it for a set time period, after which they share and vote on their favorite. In the other game, students work in groups to complete the various stages of the writing process, resulting in a thesis statement and topic sentences. These are discussed as a class, and one is selected as the best model. Next, Belinda Ho shares a team guessing game, "What Is It?," designed to elicit the defining characteristics of an object, which leads to definition writing. "Who's the Best Detective?," by Nancy Ackles, helps students develop argumentative writing skills as they determine who committed a fictitious murder. Those who solve the mystery win the game. Finally, in "Pass It On! Writing Games," Robb Mark McCollum explains the steps to participating in a collaborative writing game that involves drawing and sentence writing to reinforce the importance of clarity.

Also in Part 1, four authors share games related to listening and speaking skill development. Vander Viana demonstrates how students can improve their communicative abilities in a competition that involves creating a movie using a free online tool in his contribution, "In the Director's Shoes: Bridging Meaning and Pleasure in an English Language Teaching Game." "Tabletop Role-Playing Games," by Johansen Quijano, suggests ways to enhance students' participation as they interact in a collaborative narrative involving dice rolling and character creation. Next, Hayo Reinders and Marilyn Lewis explore creative ways to use MP3 players. "PodQuests: Language Games on the Go" explains how to engage students in a competition involving following directions, answering questions, and gathering, recording, and sharing information. Finally, Kevin Cross and Patricia Pashby share "The Survey Game," in which students gather cultural information from their classmates, compare responses, reach consensus, and make guesses about the most popular answers to survey questions as they build listening and speaking, vocabulary, and cross-cultural skills.

Vocabulary learning is the focus of the next five chapters in the volume. Hyacinth Gaudart involves students in a role-playing game in "Let's Go Shopping." Students learn vocabulary by "purchasing" items such as vegetables or furniture using teacher-produced illustrated playing cards. "Collocations in the Foreseeable Future" highlights three games—variations of crossword puzzles, concentration, and tic-tac-toe—created by Rachel Adams Goertel and Carole Adams to familiarize students with the meaning and use of frequently used collocations. Students practice and strengthen knowledge of target vocabulary as they read and retell stories and determine whether or not the stories are true in "Urban Myths: Fact or Fiction?" contributed by Timothy Doe. Barnaby Ralph's "Speaking Through Art" shares a series of activities with competitive elements that require students to rank, describe, discuss, and write about works of art, thereby contextualizing vocabulary study within a content-based approach. In "Define Your Terms," a guessing game by Michael Shehane and Michael Moraga, after students learn practical phrases for explaining a definition of a word, they give their teammates clues about specified vocabulary. Each team attempts to identify more vocabulary items than the opposing team.

The final area of focus in Part 1 demonstrates how games are effective in reinforcing knowledge and use of grammar. Writing clues to lead their classmates to a treasure is the aim of "Treasure Hunting With Grammar." Xiao Lan

Curdt-Christiansen explains how the game teaches specific grammatical structures by requiring children to incorporate them into their clues. In Mark Wolfersberger's game, "Nice Tower, But It May Fall Down: A Game for Teaching Modals of Probability," students complete to build the highest tower, commenting on the process using modals of probability and learning to distinguish variations in their meanings. Karen Hilgeman addresses the problematic area of teaching participial adjectives in "The Teacher's Choice Game." Students make playing cards with words and phrases. The student playing the role of the teacher determines which of the words or phrases is the best match for a specific participial phrase. The last game in this section, "What's the Problem?," is contributed by Leong Ping Alvin. Working collaboratively in this game, students solve a puzzle in order to discover the usage of various grammatical structures.

In Part 2: Beyond Skills, the games are organized into four categories: game templates, get-acquainted games, games involving content-based instruction, and those that encourage critical thinking. First, for game templates, Amanda A. B. Wallace illustrates how a clothespin and a coin are used to generate excitement in a team competition called "Pass the Clothespin: Cleaning Up in the ESL Classroom." The purpose of the game is to review a given teaching point or topic of study. Next, Kevin McCaughey helps students review grammar, practice vocabulary, and gain speaking practice in "On-the-Spot Games From Student Content." Students supply the content for the game by identifying and describing an object or a topic and creating guessing cards; other students must guess what is being described. Karen Hilgeman describes eight games for review and practice of instructional points in her contribution, "Energize and Educate!" The games are adaptable to any content, learner level, or age, and they involve activities as diverse as relay races, line-ups, tic-tac-toe, bingo, and sportscasting as well as tools such as dice, flashcards, and drawings. Last, Susan Kelly presents "Do-It-Yourself Games," in which students create their own games and teach them to the class. This technique involves students in presenting the game to the class for oral skills practice and/or creating written rules. Through their involvement, students gain autonomy and practice target grammar and vocabulary.

At the beginning of each teaching term, teachers regularly look for creative ideas to help students become acquainted with each other. Mary E. Hillis' "BINGO: Building Interest and Negotiation Through Games From the Outset" does just that. Students create their own bingo cards with questions they would like to ask their classmates. Then, as the teacher calls out students' names, they share the information they have collected and mark off squares on their cards to get a bingo. In a similar type of activity described in "Flags of Ourselves: Using Student-Generated Props in the Classroom," Chad Kallauner asks students to create colorful flags representing different aspects of their lives. Through sharing their flags, students practice their English, learn about each other, and create community in the classroom.

To enhance content-based instruction, Lan Hue Quach and Scott P. Kissau contribute the chapter "Add, Mix, and Shake: Content, Vocabulary, and Games in the Language Classroom" to introduce the next series of games—those that support both content and language learning objectives. The authors demonstrate how three different games can be used to review science content and engage students in expressing their understanding of topics. The games involve the use of visual aids and cue cards, a bean bag toss, and an identity-guessing activity. Lindsay Miller and Samuel Wu also share a game for reinforcing content knowledge in "Using Common Language Games in a Science and Technology Curriculum." Even university-level students studying science and engineering can benefit from such straightforward games as crossword puzzles, hangman, and oral presentation competitions. These games can be used to learn content-based terminology, recognize the differences between oral and written text, and improve speaking and presentation skills. Finally, Kimberly S. Rodriguez and Susan M. Barone build on a popular reality television show in their game, "The Business Apprentice." Business students work in groups to create a marketing campaign for a product, after which they are judged by business professors. The competition is language intensive, developing oral skills (particularly using language for negotiation) as well as business skills and cultural knowledge. All of the games in this section are adaptable for a variety of content areas.

The final section in the volume consists of two contributions, both focused on the development of critical thinking skills. First, in "Logical Use of Logic Puzzles," Kurtis McDonald shows how giving students a story scenario and requiring them to piece together clues to solve a puzzle can promote mental engagement, increase motivation, and provide reading comprehension and vocabulary practice. Then, Alexander Sokol, Edgar Lasevich, and Marija Dobrovolska share games for developing critical thinking skills in "Three Games to Exercise the Brain." To Take Into My House, Feature Constructor, and The Most Useful Thing in the World involve learners in critical thinking, vocabulary practice, and authentic communication scenarios as they collaborate to discuss objects and their features and uses.

Although the games have been organized in the volume by their primary focus, it should be noted that none has a single focus. Each game clearly lends itself to addressing multiple language objectives, and many could be considered to integrate a variety of skills and support diverse curricular aims. Because of this wide range of possible uses, I have created a chart (p. iv) in which the games are categorized by their primary emphasis, with other areas of focus also listed. To use this book most effectively, I recommend referring to the chart to get an idea of the skill or curriculum areas potentially addressed by a particular game and then reviewing the game itself to see how it lends itself to a particular instructional purpose. Readers should keep in mind that the chart provides a guide only. It is important to recognize that almost any game can be adapted to suit a teacher's objective, content, or context. One needs but a little imagination and ingenuity to adapt a game for a particular purpose.

The chart (p. iv) also notes the most applicable proficiency level and age for playing each game. Once again, however, the games are adaptable to different levels and ages. If the chart denotes a beginning level and the teacher is instructing advanced-level students, it still is likely that the game can be adapted to be relevant. In most cases, the authors of the games share variations for adjusting the games to different levels and contexts. Similarly, the age categorizations in the chart represent a general age group. In reality, each game may be appropriate for higher or lower ages or may be modified to be suitable. Young adult–adult is descriptive of a secondary or tertiary education level and also would include adult education programs. Games designated as appropriate for children are aimed at those of primary school age (i.e., 6–12). Games appropriate for youth (i.e., middle school students, ages 12–14) may be found in both the child and young adult categories.

The book goes beyond the typical recipe book approach, which generally involves little more than a listing of materials, briefly stated procedures, and a designation of the applicable skill and appropriate proficiency and age level. Each game in this volume is characterized by an in-depth discussion including rationale; learning objectives; a description of ideal and alternate contexts; detailed procedures; variations for materials, procedures, content, skill, and/or curriculum emphasis; Web resources; cultural notes; language-learning and interaction tips; and reflections on the success and uniqueness of the game, including student response. The chapters also feature illustrations, diagrams, pictures, worksheets, templates, handouts, drawings, visuals, and other teaching aides to ease teacher preparation.

Because the games are contributed by a number of authors, they reflect many different contexts and cultures. A range of authors' voices describe their teaching experiences using games. Although the chapters follow similar formats, variations are evident and support the diversity of our profession. When integrating the games suggested in the pages of this volume into a specific language curriculum, consideration must be given to the learning context, including factors such as the age, background, proficiency level, and purpose of the learner, and adjustments made as needed.

This book also stands apart in that the contributions reflect multiple classroom uses. Themes evident throughout the book reflect pedagogical goals and practices for language learning such as communicative competence, interaction, authenticity, skills integration, content emphasis, and collaboration. The games focus on developing students' English skills, but more than that they focus on students learning language and content, engaging in collaboration, becoming active learners, and utilizing technology. They have been inspired by traditional games, cultural games, television shows, board games, party games, and card games, but they go beyond these to demonstrate how teachers are inspired by a number of sources and contribute their own unique talents and interests to their teaching. They represent creative methods for fulfilling curricular objectives.

The contributions also support and demonstrate the application of theoretical concepts such as problem-based learning (Barrows & Tamblyn, 1980), the zone of proximal development (Vygotsky, 1978), active learning (Cummins, 2000), vocabulary acquisition (Nation, 2001), and learning collocations (Lewis, 2000). They demonstrate how both theory and practice inform our teaching approaches.

The purpose of this book is to encourage the enjoyment of learning. As each of the contributors has been inspired by a variety of sources and experiences, so can each of us be inspired to try out and adapt new techniques for the ESL–EFL classroom as we benefit from what our colleagues have shared in this volume.

REFERENCES

Barrows, H. S., & Tamblyn, R. M. (1980). *Problem-based learning: An approach to medical education.* New York: Springer.

Cummins, J. (2000). Academic language learning, transformative pedagogy, and information technology: Towards a critical balance. *TESOL Quarterly, 34,* 537–548.

Gardner, H. (1983). *Frames of mind: The theory of multiple intelligences.* New York: Basic Books.

Krashen, S. (1981). *Second language acquisition and second language learning.* Oxford, England: Pergamon Press.

Krashen, S. (1982). *Principles and practices in second language acquisition.* Oxford, England: Pergamon Press.

Krashen, S. (1985). *The input hypothesis: Issues and implications.* London: Longman.

Larsen-Freeman, D. (2000). *Techniques and principles in language teaching* (2nd ed.). Oxford: Oxford University Press.

Lee, W. R. (1979). *Language teaching games and contests* (2nd ed.). Oxford: Oxford University Press.

Lewis, M. (2000). *Teaching collocation: Further developments in the lexical approach.* Hove, England: Language Teaching Publications.

Nation, I. S. P. (2001). *Learning vocabulary in another language.* Cambridge: Cambridge University Press.

Oxford, R. (1990). *Language learning strategies: What every teacher should know.* New York: Newbury House.

Richard-Amato, P. A. (2003). *Making it happen: From interactive to participatory language teaching* (3rd ed.). New York: Pearson Education

Rinvolucri, M., & Davis, P. (1995). *More grammar games.* Cambridge: Cambridge University Press.

Shameem, N., & Tickoo, M. (Eds.). (1999). *New ways in using communicative games in language teaching.* Alexandria, VA: TESOL.

Vygotsky, L. S. (1978). *Mind in society.* Cambridge, MA: Harvard University Press.

Wright, A., Betteridge, D., & Buckby, M. (1983). *Games for language learning.* Cambridge: Cambridge University Press.

Wright, A., Betteridge, D., & Buckby, M. (2006). *Games for language learning.* (3rd ed.). Cambridge: Cambridge University Press.

Maureen Snow Andrade is an associate professor and department chair at Brigham Young University Hawaii, in the United States, where she teaches ESL and courses in teaching ESOL. Maureen is also editor of the TESL Reporter. *Her professional interests include English for academic purposes, content-based language instruction, program assessment, and adjustment issues for international students.*

Part 1: Skills Focus

A. Reading and Writing

CHAPTER 2

Storyboarding for the Oscars

Shane Dixon

INTRODUCTION

Many English as a second language (ESL) professionals believe in the value of narrative writing for ESL students. It can give students a much needed break from more form-driven essays and allow them to learn rhetorical techniques that are less common in other kinds of academic discourse. DiPardo (1990) argues that, in the case of college-bound students, narrative still composes a large portion of university writing assignments, and Spack (1988) argues that it prepares students for future tasks such as writing personal statements and scholarship applications. In addition, Elliot (1995) argues that there are strong reasons to teach narrative to basic writers, including the development of metacognitive skills, a sense of authenticity, and the ability to convey the nonrational.

Narrative writing, however, does have its limits in training students for academic discourse. For one, because it is a different kind of academic discourse, it lends itself to the teaching of rhetorical features such as building to a climax and creating tone. Further, students often have difficulty creating structures without some sort of guide or background such as the template writing asked of them in a compare-contrast or five-paragraph essay prompt. As MacDonald (1987) states, students must learn to write "composing with an undefined problem, with a writer forced to create a problem for him- or herself" (p. 328).

In short, to write a good narrative, one of the biggest challenges for students is to see this unfamiliar form as familiar. It may be helpful to allow students to think of their short stories as movies. Students generally have a tacit familiarity with popular movies and thus can think of their own stories in terms of cinematic presentation. Furthermore, novice narrative writers commonly forget to add proper description of place, time, and characters. (e.g., a common mistake is for the narrator to fail to describe himself).

Storyboarding is a technique that invites students to imagine the story pictorially in order to describe those elements that are often forgotten. The art of storyboarding is most often associated with movie screenplays. In many big budget films (and sometimes even minor films), the use of storyboards helps a director get a sense of what the movie will look like. In like manner, many students, even with the use of simplistic figures, can enhance the visual aspect of their writing by first laying out basic drawings in small framed boxes. These boxes form a design template that can guide their writing much like an outline or brainstorm. Unlike outlines, however, storyboards offer a fresh, creative way to organize a story. Finally, a storyboard contest invites students to expand their idea of audience by including classmates and also gives students a chance to explain their storyboards, thus using speaking techniques such as hedges, clarifications, and elaborations that prepare them more fully for the writing task. Additionally, a storyboarding contest invites students to think of their stories as something that requires "shaping."

CONTEXT

This activity originally was given to college-bound ESL students at Selnate International, an intensive English program. Because I argue that narrative writing is common in college, this activity seems well suited for advanced, adult ESL students. However, since the concept of telling stories is universal, the assignment is likely adaptable for all levels and ages.

CURRICULUM, TASKS, MATERIALS

Getting Started

Materials needed include the "If This Were a Movie!" worksheet, a sample storyboard, a blank template (see Figure 1), and an "Oscar Voting" worksheet (see Appendixes A–C). Students will storyboard their short stories using blank templates. The storyboards will guide their future writing. A sample storyboard can serve as a model and as a guided practice. These activities should follow explanations of narrative writing and the gathering of story ideas. The teacher must already have explained to students what a narrative is and given examples of stories that fit the structure. Also, the teacher should already have invited students to think of a story they wish to share.

Procedures

1. Invite students to ask each other questions using the "If This Were a Movie!" worksheet (Appendix A). This questioning may be done formally with a time limit and/or required written responses, or as a conversation without a time limit.

2. Give an example storyboard (see Appendix B). The storyboard is numbered so that students can follow it chronologically.

Figure 1. Blank Template for Storyboarding

3. Beneath the storyboard, include examples of narrative writing that "follow" each panel.

4. Leave the last panel without an example of narrative writing. Invite students to write their own ending to the storyboard and share their work. This exercise allows them to verbally describe the final panel and can help a teacher instruct students on how to bring a picture to life with words (e.g., using action verbs, descriptions, or dialogue).

5. Give students the blank template to storyboard their own stories and inform them that pictures can be basic sketches that bring life to the setting. Ask them to pay special attention to what the characters and surroundings look like. Also, tell students that they will share their storyboards in a contest format. Students will vote for the best storyboards. Inform them that classmates will give "Oscars" for the best storyboards. Teachers may wish to time the assignment (15–30 minutes) to ensure that students do not think of this as an art assignment but as an outlining activity. Teachers who wish to maintain anonymity should instruct students not to write their names on their storyboards.

6. Tape or tack each storyboard on the wall or whiteboard. If storyboards are anonymous, write numbers on the corner of each storyboard. Then have students view each storyboard and vote for their favorite by filling out the worksheet "Oscar Voting" (see Appendix C).

7. Invite students who win the Oscar voting to share their storyboard story with the entire class. Students should explain each panel and what the overall story's message will be. Afterward, the winners can elaborate or clarify by answering questions from the teacher or students.

8. All students are then invited to turn their pictures into a written story, paying attention to elements of setting and climax. The teacher can use any of the storyboards to elicit ideas from the students about how to express a particular picture.

Variations

To increase the game aspect of the activity, teachers may wish to have students share their stories in groups of four and then choose a winner. Each group winner, in turn, can compete in front of the entire class and an overall winner can be chosen. A more creative variation involves fiction writing. In this variation, students switch storyboards and make up a story that goes with their partner's storyboard.

REFLECTIONS

Students enjoy this activity because it forces them to think of how to represent a visual picture in words. In this light, they become craftspeople who can shape and artistically display their work for an audience. They also are able to see that sharing stories can be fun and interesting.

REFERENCES

DiPardo, A. (1990). Narrative knowers, expository knowledge. *Written Communication, 7*(1), 59–95.

Elliot, N. (1995). Narrative discourse and the basic writer. *Journal of Basic Writing, 14,* 19–30.

MacDonald, S. P. (1987). Problem definition in academic writing. *College English, 49,* 315–331.

Spack, R. (1988). Initiating ESL students into the academic discourse community: How far should we go? *TESOL Quarterly, 22,* 29–51.

Shane Dixon is an ESL teacher at Selnate International School in Utah, in the United States, where he teaches preparation courses for the Test of English as a Foreign Language and the Graduate Record Exam–Graduate Management Admission Test.

APPENDIX A: IF THIS WERE A MOVIE!

1. If this were a movie, who would be the main characters?
2. If this were a movie, what would be the most important scene?
3. If this were a movie, what kind of music would you use throughout?
4. If this were a movie, who would you choose to be the main actors?
5. If this were a movie, in what places would you film it?
6. If this were a movie, how would you show the message of the story?
7. If this were a movie, would there be characters in real life that you would eliminate or edit in the movie?
8. If this were a movie, would there be unimportant details in real life that you would eliminate in the movie?
9. If this were a movie, what kind of body movements would each character have?

10. If this were a movie, would each of the characters have catchphrases or special ways of speaking?

11. If this were a movie, how would you show the emotion of each character?

APPENDIX B: STORYBOARD EXAMPLE

Prewriting Practice: Storyboards

Storyboarding is a technique that allows movie directors and writers to create images that will work well for film. Some writers believe that having a good idea of the visual images will help you to write better. Because you are not making a film, however, you have to make pictures with your words. Notice how this writer tries to make us see the storyboard with our minds. See if you can finish the story by narrating an ending.

1. Bob and Frankie decide to finish the game.	2. The crowd is surprised.	3. The jailed inmates are cheering.

1. Bob held out his fist and pointed a finger. They had to show the police that they were not losers. He had to stop them from laughing at them. So what if they were prisoners? They were men. And he knew they could win this game, even if the officers were cheating.

   "We're not going to lose," he said. Frankie stood with his mouth open, staring at Bob's determined face. He knew Bob was serious. He felt the sweat on his face and nodded to Bob.

   "Let's finish, then." Frankie clapped his hands together and got back into the huddle.

2. The crowd stopped cheering. The faces of the wives of the police officers changed. They no longer were smiling. Why were the prisoners still determined to win? Didn't they know better? The quiet of the crowd of more than 200 people filled the air.

3. And then the quiet stopped. There was a cheering, but not from the bleachers. The sound came from the prison building. The men were beginning to cheer. They were cheering for Frankie. They were cheering for Bob. These two men had tried to kill each other, but now they were united with one purpose. They needed to show the world that they were

not useless. They were prisoners, maybe they were even sinners, but they were men.

4.

Use a separate piece of paper and write an exciting conclusion to this storyboard. What do you see in this picture? What would be a satisfying ending for you? Will you end it happily? Tragically? In another way? Write for 10 minutes and create an exciting ending!

APPENDIX C: OSCAR VOTING

1. Best Drawing: "These are my favorite pictures."

    _____

2. Most Action: "These drawings really show me what is going on in the story."

    _____

3. Most Compelling: "This is the storyboard I want to know about the most."

    _____

4. Most Thought-Provoking: "This storyboard makes me think."

    _____

5. Other possible categories (optional)

    Category   Person or Number You Want to Vote For

    _____   _____

    _____   _____

CHAPTER 3

WARTS
(Writing Activities Require Time and Satisfaction)

Nancy Tarawhiti

INTRODUCTION

Students have expressed to me their frustration with second-language writing. This has motivated me to take time preparing innovative and stimulating writing activities. This chapter shares two fun activities using peer collaboration that help stimulate ideas, encourage fluency, and assist the writing process. The first activity captures the thoughtful essence of descriptive writing, and the second relates to the outlining process of academic writing in a collaborative environment. Both of these activities give students opportunities to share their writing and be confident in doing so.

The rationale for the first activity is to provide an alternative to conventional brainstorming, which piques students' interest and helps them develop their writing. Students choose an item from a box, write for 20 minutes, read what everyone else has written, and then choose their favorite essay for recognition. The foundation for this activity is Cole's "Class in a Box" (Campbell, 1998). The second activity is a result of students' frustration with creating an outline and writing a five-paragraph essay. It helps students stimulate their thinking within a time limit to outline an essay in a collaborative learning environment.

ACTIVITY ONE

CONTEXT

This activity can be used in a variety of English as a second language (ESL) settings including intensive English-language programs, private language schools, and adult community classes. There is no level restriction for this activity. I have used this activity in an intensive English-language program setting with students at an advanced English proficiency level. These students ranged in ages from 20–40 years old, but they all had a similar proficiency of English. I have used this activity only when every student had a computer, and the computers had headphones, Internet access, and word-processing software. This environment allowed me to use artifacts such as CDs for each student to listen to, which may be difficult in another type of classroom setting.

CURRICULUM, TASKS, MATERIALS

The materials teachers will need for this activity are

- A box: Teachers may be as creative as they want regarding the size and shape of the box, but it must be big enough to hold enough items for the number of students in the class.

- Writing materials: The teacher will need a computer and/or pen and paper.

- Artifacts: The teacher should first select a writing theme, and then use artifacts that connect well to the theme. Some examples may be found in Table 1.

PROCEDURES

In brief, students choose one artifact, write about it for 20 minutes, read the other students' writing, and then choose their favorite writing, excluding their own. This activity is best accomplished when modeled creatively so that the

Table 1. Materials for Class in a Box

Writing Theme	Examples of Artifacts
Opinion Writing	A variety of music CDs
Descriptive Writing	Random artifacts from the teacher's office, including gifts, ornaments, supplies
Compare-Contrast Writing	An assortment of candy bars
Narrative Writing	Selection of pictures from magazines
Summarizing	Reading passages from textbooks and/or tapes, CDs, or other storage devices containing listening passages (e.g., podcasts)
Test of English as a Foreign Language (TOEFL) Writing	TOEFL topics on strips of cardboard or paper so students have something to pull out of the box

anticipation of what is in the box motivates students. When I am dramatic about what may be in the box, students' intrigue is heightened, which makes them eager to write.

1. The teacher tells the students the writing theme (e.g., opinion writing). Then the teacher explains to the students that they will:

    - select a CD from the box

    - brainstorm ideas while listening to the CD for 5 minutes

    - write their opinion of the CD (with supporting statements) for 20 minutes and then stop

    - change computers (or papers) and read their peers' writing

    - choose their favorite writing from among their peers' samples

2. The teacher determines the order in which students will select items from the box (e.g., shortest to tallest, birthday months). The teacher holds the box in a way that students are unable to view what they are selecting. Students randomly select a CD from the box.

3. Students take 5 minutes to listen to their CD, brainstorm, and record ideas while listening.

4. Students type for 20 minutes and write their opinion of the CD they selected, supporting their opinion with examples and details.

5. At the end of 20 minutes, students stop typing. Students now need to read their peers' papers. Students move in a clockwise direction from computer to computer, taking 2–3 minutes to read what their peers have written. The teacher should monitor time at each computer to ensure that students are continuously moving and that every paper is read by every student. On occasion, I have had students use the reading skill of skimming when we have been pressed for time.

6. When students have read all of their peers' papers, on slips of paper students vote for their favorite papers and explain why.

7. The teacher tallies the results, and the paper with the most votes wins.

8. The winning paper (or papers) is printed and distributed in the following class period, when the teacher reads the essay and gives the reasons why it was students' favorite.

Variations

Class in a Box can be modified for different levels and purposes.

- **Beginners:** Have students write only a sentence about the artifact taken from the box and have classmates choose the sentence that best describes the artifact.

- **Vocabulary:** Have students identify synonyms and antonyms that are related to the artifact and then place all the artifacts in front of the class. Have students guess the artifact that the vocabulary words match.

- **Part of Speech:** Students choose their artifact and for 3 minutes write as many adjectives as possible about it. The student with the most words wins.

REFLECTIONS

I have used this activity with diverse proficiency groups, and it has always had a positive impact on the students' writing. Students were excited to see what was in the box and what theme they were going to write. Writing suddenly became more exciting and fulfilling, as opposed to daunting, and this reaction fed directly into their academic writing by motivating them to be better writers.

I believe this game is successful because there is an unknown factor. It is not considered mundane because every week students are wondering what is in the box. I love to see the students' initial reactions when choosing their artifacts because of the motivation that the artifacts create, which, in turn, is reflected in their writing.

ACTIVITY TWO

CONTEXT

As with the previous activity, this activity can be used in a variety of ESL settings, including intensive English-language programs, private language schools, and adult community classes; however, it is better suited for high-intermediate to advanced levels. I have used this activity in an intensive English-language program and a community class setting with students at a high-intermediate to advanced level of English proficiency. These students were from diverse cultural backgrounds, but they all had a goal of pursuing higher education. No technology is required for this activity, so a classroom setting is suitable.

CURRICULUM, TASKS, MATERIALS

The materials necessary for this activity are:

- large sheets of white paper (preferably 11 x 17) for each group

- colored markers with fine tips

- timing device (watch, classroom clock)

The following colored headings may be handwritten on the large sheets of white paper:

Brainstorming: Brainstorm about the topic given. (Red)

Narrowing: From the brainstorming, narrow your topic. (Blue)

Introduction: From the narrowing, write a thesis statement. (Green)

Body Paragraph 1: From the thesis statement, write a topic sentence. (Orange)

Body Paragraph 2: From the thesis statement, write a topic sentence. (Purple)

Body Paragraph 3: From the thesis statement, write a topic sentence. (Black)

Conclusion: Rewrite the thesis statement. (Pink)

Students, in groups of three, will come up with ideas and sentences to put under a specific given heading. After 4 minutes, they will pass their paper to the next group on their right. Groups will continue to write under the next heading based on what the previous groups have written.

Procedures

1. Groups are seated in such a way that they can easily pass papers to each other.

2. Each group selects a person to write while the other two will verbally give input.

3. The teacher gives each group a sheet of white paper with preprinted headings (as shown previously) and a colored marker.

4. The teacher gives the class a topic according to proficiency level, and all the groups use the same topic.

5. Groups then have 3–5 minutes to begin brainstorming as a team, and they write their ideas under the heading "brainstorming."

6. After 4 minutes, the teacher will say "change," and teams will pass their sheet to the next group on their right.

7. Each team will change the writer (so everyone has a turn scribing), and they then begin writing under the "narrowing" heading. Once again, one person in the group writes and the other two people give verbal input.

8. Each team narrows the topic based on what the previous team has written under the heading "brainstorming," not what the team wrote on its original sheet.

9. This process continues, and each group will use the previous groups' input until all the headings are completed. Each heading explains what is required (e.g., "write a topic sentence," "write a thesis statement").

10. The teacher's role is to monitor time and circulate among the groups during the activity to ensure they are on task and everyone is participating.

11. Once all the headings are completed, the teacher collects the sheets and displays them side by side at the front of the classroom.

12. Depending on the classroom and class size, there may be many students who need to view the sheets from a distance. Markers are used so the writing is easier to read.

13. The teacher reviews each heading with the class collectively and has the class select the best input under each heading and explain why. The teacher also may give input and ensure the best example of each heading is correctly selected.

14. The teacher writes an outline using the best selections and distributes copies to students to use as a model. When writing future essays, students can refer to this model outline.

REFLECTIONS

This game can be very competitive, which enhances writing productivity. Sometimes talkative students dominate the discussion, which is why everyone has a turn at being scribe. Teachers know their class best, so groups can be randomly selected or prearranged. Students sometimes find this task overwhelming on their own, but when it is done in a competitive collaborative environment they see how they could, in fact, accomplish it on their own.

REFERENCE

Campbell, C. (1998). *Teaching second-language writing: Interacting with text.* Boston: Heinle & Heinle.

Nancy Tarawhiti, a native of New Zealand, is a master's graduate of Brigham Young University, in the United States, where she is a full-time faculty member. Her primary interest is second-language learning strategies, specifically in the area of teacher instruction.

CHAPTER 4

What Is It?

Belinda Ho

INTRODUCTION

Learning to write definitions is important to technical writing because it is characterized by specialized vocabulary (Reep, 2003). Thus, a unit on how to write definitions is included in most technical writing courses. Among the many types of definitions, such as informal, formal, expanded (Reep, 2003), and parenthetical (VanAlstyne, 1999), formal definitions are most commonly emphasized in a technical writing course.

A formal definition is written based on the formula (VanAlstyne, 1999)

Term + Class + Distinguishing Characteristics

For example,

A <u>password</u> is a [secret] **word** [that enables authorized persons to be identified.]

<u>Term</u> + **Class** + [Distinguishing Characteristics]

In writing a formal definition, the term to be defined should be placed in as specific a class or group as possible (Reep, 2003). The distinguishing characteristics cannot include every detail. The writer has to choose features that most effectively separate the term from others in the same class and will best help readers to understand it (Reep, 2003).

The game What Is It? can help students improve their ability to write definitions. It involves brainstorming the characteristics of a term and determining the most appropriate details to include in its definition. The game suits all topics in all disciplines and is a motivating activity that can be conveniently linked to the curriculum.

CONTEXT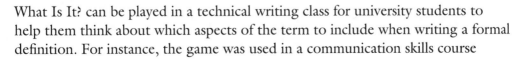

What Is It? can be played in a technical writing class for university students to help them think about which aspects of the term to include when writing a formal definition. For instance, the game was used in a communication skills course for computer studies students in a university. The game helped students define the terms for hardware and software items that were needed to write a technical proposal. It can be played in any English for specific purposes (ESP) class at the university level or can easily be adapted to suit students at the secondary level by limiting the scope of the guiding questions used to elicit the parts of the definition (see *Procedures*). The game is not culture-specific and can be played in any teaching or learning context in which writing definitions is a part of the course objectives.

CURRICULUM, TASKS, MATERIALS

Getting Started

The teacher needs to put an object (e.g., a floppy disk, disk drive cleaner, computer mouse, or other topic-relevant item) in an envelope. The teacher also needs access to a chalkboard or whiteboard for the first part of the game. A transparency or Microsoft PowerPoint slide with several formal definitions must be prepared for the second part of the game.

Overview

The game consists of two parts. In both parts, the students are divided into two teams. In the first part of the game, the teacher has each team guess the identity of an object by having them ask questions. This questioning elicits a list of aspects of the object that the students can later use as distinguishing characteristics when defining the object. In the second part of the game, formal definitions, which were prepared beforehand, are shown to the students. The two teams engage in a competition to identify the different features of the terms (e.g., class, size, color, etc.) used in the definitions. In both parts of the game, the team that gets the correct answer(s) first wins.

Procedures

1. Divide the students into two teams.

2. The teacher puts a relevant object (i.e., something the students might need to define when writing a technical paper) in an envelope. Then the teacher asks each team to take turns guessing what the object is by asking questions such as "What color is it?" (color), "What does it look like?" (shape), "What is it used for?" (function), and so on. The teacher will provide an answer to each question until the guess is correct. The team that is the first to guess correctly wins.

3. While playing the game, the teacher can make a list on the board of the aspects of the object (e.g., classification, components, shape, color, size) that have been mentioned in the game based on the questions asked. Only the categories represented by the questions, not the questions themselves, are written on the board. The following list demonstrates the different aspects of an object that can be included as distinguishing characteristics in a formal definition.

    - How is it classified? (Classification)

    - What is it made of? (Components)

    - What does it look like? (Shape)

    - What is its color? (Color)

    - How big is it? (Size)

    - How heavy is it? (Weight)

    - What are some of its most distinguishing characteristics? (Defining features)

    - What is its function? What is it for? (Function)

    - How does it operate? (Operation)

    - How long can you use it? (Duration)

    - How much does it cost? (Cost)

    - Who uses it? (User)

    - When is it used? (Time)

    - Where is it used? (Place)

    - What is it similar to? (Comparison)

    - What will be the result of using it? (Result)

4. The students will then be given some examples of formal definitions based on the formula: <u>Term</u> + *Class* + [Distinguishing Characteristics]. For example:

    > A <u>mouse</u> is a [small] [hand-held] *device* [that is moved about on a flat surface in front of a monitor screen] [to perform tasks on the screen].

    These definitions should be prepared in advance on an overhead transparency or a Microsoft PowerPoint slide. The students on each team will be asked to identify which aspects have been described in the definition that make the *term* different from the *class*. (The aspects described in this example definition are size, feature, operation, and function.) The team that identifies all of the aspects first wins.

5. The students will be asked to write their own definitions based on the formula after playing the game.

Variations

To save time, instead of writing the list of the aspects of the object on the board (see number 3 in *Procedures*), prepare a transparency with this information. Attach a paper print-out of the transparency to the left edge of the transparency with double-sided tape, making sure that each question/aspect listed on the paper (e.g., What does it look like?/Shape) covers the same question/aspect on the transparency. On the paper, use scissors to cut between each question/aspect. Cut horizontally until you reach the taped side of the paper. Flip open the slip of paper to reveal the transparency beneath when a student asks that question in the game. The students will become excited when the question on the transparency is revealed, showing that they have successfully asked a question that is on the list. If the question asked is not on the list, the teacher can write it in an empty space on the transparency.

An additional benefit of the game is that it can be an opportunity for students to practice the structures for asking questions using the words *what, who, when, where,* and *how.* Instead of having students initially ask questions about the object, teachers can write the aspects of the objects (e.g., classification, size, color, etc.) on the board, and then have students formulate questions based on the aspects using the appropriate question words. For the transparency variation, the teacher can keep the question part of the line on the transparency covered with the slips of paper, but fold back the part of the paper that covers the aspect so that the student can see only the aspect on the transparency. When a student has constructed the question, for checking purposes, the teacher can uncover the question part of the line by flipping back the entire slip of paper to let the students see the correct question on the transparency.

REFLECTIONS

I have played What Is It? with great success in different kinds of classes that involve writing a formal definition. The students enjoy the game, and those who have difficulty identifying which characteristics to include in a definition are enlightened by the activity. They became motivated to write definitions and are able to produce effective formal definitions by themselves after playing the game. What Is It? is fun, easy to manage, and effective, and it can be used in all learning contexts in which writing definitions is taught.

REFERENCES

Reep, D. C. (2003). *Technical writing: Principles, strategies and readings* (5th ed.). New York: Pearson Education.

VanAlstyne, J. S. (1999). *Professional and technical writing strategies: Communicating in technology and science* (4th ed.). Upper Saddle River, NJ: Prentice Hall.

Belinda Ho is an associate professor at City University of Hong Kong. She is experienced in teaching English as a second language and ESP. Her research interests include learning strategies, reflective teaching, reflective learning, writing, teacher education, and teaching ESP.

CHAPTER 5

Who's the Best Detective?

Nancy Ackles

INTRODUCTION

The teaching purposes of Who's the Best Detective? are:

- to help students develop their skills at presenting and supporting a thesis
- to orient students to the process of writing a research paper
- to develop listening skills
- to develop discussion and oral presentation skills (if some of the options are chosen)
- to add fun to the classroom

CONTEXT

Although originally developed for use with university students in academic preparation classes, with small adaptations this game can be used in classes of adolescent or adult learners with upper intermediate to advanced language skills. It provides rich opportunities to engage with language and develop listening skills, formal and informal speaking skills, and writing skills. This game fits into courses in which the rhetorical patterns of argument are being taught.

CURRICULUM, TASKS, MATERIALS

Playing Who's the Best Detective? requires access to an episode of *Murder, She Wrote* (available on DVD) and a way of showing it to the class. This game requires two or three class sessions but is rich with opportunities for engagement with language and allows students to practice important rhetorical forms in a fun competition. One would not want to play it every week, but several rounds could be played with the same group of students in the course of a year.

Procedures

The teacher gives the students the research question "Who committed the murder?" and a list of the characters in the *Murder, She Wrote* episode. The teacher then shows the episode up to the point at which Jessica (the fictional detective) starts to reveal the solution or trick a suspect into confessing. This plot turn usually happens after about 50 minutes. Then, for homework, students write a short paper using the rhetorical patterns of argument. Sections include: description of the problem (a plot summary), a thesis (who did it?), evidence (why should we think this person is guilty?), and refutation of counterarguments (why it could not be the other suspects). Students share their papers with classmates and reveal their theses. The teacher then plays the rest of the episode, and the winners—those who correctly identified the murderer—receive cheers from their classmates or an agreed-upon prize.

This game was originally developed as a way for students to "discover through doing" the logic behind the traditional sections of a research paper. If used for this purpose of discovery, the teacher presents the assignment without using the terms *thesis, evidence,* or *refutation of counterarguments.* Instead, the teacher asks students to summarize the story and answer the questions, "Who did it?", "Why do you think so?", and "Why couldn't it be the other suspects?" Then, when teaching the concepts *research question, thesis, evidence,* and so on, the teacher is able to refer back to the writing process students went through to help clarify the meanings of these terms. Of course, a teacher may prefer to explicitly teach these concepts before playing the game and use the game as a way for students to demonstrate their ability to understand and apply the concepts.

Quite naturally, the level and type of feedback given on the students' papers depends upon the teacher's goals for playing the game and the teacher's beliefs about effective feedback on written work. If the game is being played for the first time and as a way to provide a context for future lessons on the traditional rhetorical patterns of argument, the teacher will not expect the same type of performance as would be expected if the game is being played as a way for students to demonstrate their mastery of traditional forms.

Teacher Preparation

To prepare for the game, the teacher needs, as always, to preview the episode and assess its suitability for the particular group of students. Most episodes work well, but a few do not because there is not a clear break between the plot development and Jessica's revelation of the criminal's identity. In season one, two episodes that work well are "We're Off to Kill the Wizard" and "Death Casts a Spell."

Students need a list of characters to help them follow the action. Help preparing the list of characters can be found at *epguides.com* (http://epguides.com /MurderSheWrote/), a Web site that lists the characters and the actors who played them for each episode. The teacher may also want to prepare a list of points to be covered in the paper and a suggested order for them.

Variations

For practice with listening skills and discussion skills, divide the class into teams. The teacher stops the program at intervals so that students can confer and be sure they understand what has happened. The teams compete against each other, and each team must agree on a solution, providing opportunity for discussion and negotiation of ideas. For practice with formal presentation skills, the solutions may be presented as individual or group oral reports, using the rhetorical patterns of argument.

Culture Connections

This game is replete with opportunities to increase cultural knowledge. Murder mysteries are popular both as books and films, and *Murder, She Wrote*, providing what librarians call "cozy mysteries," is a fairly nonviolent text for becoming familiar with the genre. These stories also introduce many stock characters such as "the wealthy heiress," "the jilted lover," "the greedy business tycoon," and so on. Some of the episodes are examples of particular mystery forms as well. For example, the episode "We're Off to Kill the Wizard" is a locked-room mystery in which the body is found inside a room completely locked from the inside.

Adult students appreciate an introduction that explains that the series was very popular, ran for 12 years, and attracted many well-known and award-winning actors who appeared in single episodes. Both the series and Angela Lansbury won Golden Globe awards, and Lansbury received 12 consecutive Emmy nominations for her performances.

Resources

DVDs of the series are available for purchase or rental at all the usual sources. A Web search will quickly turn up further information on the series and its performers, writers, and directors. After the series ended, several *Murder, She Wrote* television movies were created. Also, Donald Bain, sharing credit with "Jessica Fletcher," wrote a series of *Murder, She Wrote* novels, which could provide extended reading for interested students.

REFLECTIONS

Purposes one and two are to help students develop skills at presenting a thesis and to orient students to the process of writing a research paper. Both language learners and monolingual English students often have trouble moving from narrative and report writing to thesis-driven writing. In my own classes, I define a thesis as "a sentence that answers a question and that can be argued about." The structure of the game forces students naturally, even gently, into thesis-driven writing: We have a research question (Who committed the murder?). We do research (by watching the episode). Each student develops a thesis (e.g., Character A committed the murder). If time is allowed for group or class discussion, these theses are debated (i.e., with other students who claim that Character B committed the crime). The papers or speeches that students prepare are quite naturally not narrative (although they may contain a plot summary) and not reports, like a film or book report. They are thesis-driven arguments.

Purposes three and four are to provide opportunities to develop listening and speaking skills. The game is rich in such opportunities. Although scripted, the episodes provide authentic listening material in that this is material millions of English speakers have listened to and continue to listen to in reruns. There is visual support to help make meaning clear, the actors tend to speak clearly, and the teacher can make the listening task easier by stopping the video from time to time or replaying sections when requested. Informal communicative speaking practice occurs as students discuss the video, argue for their theses, and, if required by the teacher, agree as a team on a solution. Formal speaking practice can be provided, if desired, through oral class presentations.

Purpose five is to add fun to the classroom. *Murder, She Wrote* was developed to be, and was very successful as, entertainment. The competitive element of finding out who's the best adds another opportunity for fun. Unless the listening demands are simply too high (i.e., for beginning or lower intermediate learners), students will consider this game a happy way to learn important skills.

ACKNOWLEDGMENT

This game was originally developed by Diane Clark (1951–2005), who lost her life to cancer. I present it here, with some variations, in her memory and so that one of her fine ideas will not be lost to our profession. For many of her years at the University of Washington, Diane's desk was next to mine, and I enjoyed learning from her creativity.

Nancy Ackles has taught English to speakers of other languages (ESOL) for 25 years and has taught as an adjunct professor in ESOL master's programs in the Seattle, Washington, area in the United States. Nancy holds a doctorate in theoretical linguistics.

CHAPTER 6

Pass It On! Writing Games

Robb Mark McCollum

INTRODUCTION

Pass It On! activities are collaborative, noncompetitive games that help students improve their English-language writing through group work. This set of games encourages students to work together to create meaning. Students share their work with one another and interpret their classmates' messages. These activities help students to see writing as a form of communication and not only an academic task. They also help students to practice specific vocabulary words and grammatical structures.

Additionally, Pass It On! games are based on the need for students to build their confidence as writers of public discourse. Student writers, especially second-language writers, may feel nervous or anxious about sharing their writing with anyone other than their composition instructor. Not only does this anxiety frustrate peer-review activities, it also can defeat the purpose of most writing, which is to communicate with others. Pass It On! games can help lower the affective filter (e.g., see Krashen, 2003) by exposing students to simple writing assignments that are shared freely with peers. The more frequently students share their writing with others, the more confident they may become with writing in public arenas.

CONTEXT

I have used these activities extensively in my intensive English-language program, teaching from beginning to advanced levels. These university preparation students enjoy the break from intensive academic essay writing and welcome the opportunity to share short writing samples with their classmates. These activities also are successful in our adult community English as a second language (ESL) program, where participants are excited to practice their underused writing skills in simple, yet fun, exercises. Additionally, I have used these games in English as a foreign language (EFL) contexts, where they have been enthusiastically received by students and instructors alike. Pass It On! is appropriate for low- to high-proficiency

English-language users and can even be modified for learners with emerging to experienced literacy skills.

CURRICULUM, TASKS, MATERIALS

Getting Started

The simple materials required for this activity are just one of the many benefits of Pass It On! games. The teacher requires:

- writing utensils for each student

- one strip of paper (preferably an A4 or 8½ in. x 11 in. sheet cut in half vertically) for each student

- additional sheets of paper if the game will be played more than once

- vocabulary flash cards or word strips (optional).

Pass It On! is a simple writing game similar to the popular "Telephone" sentence-sharing game common in kindergarten classrooms. Despite its simplicity, Pass It On! may be adapted for a variety of purposes wherein students must communicate and interpret meaning through writing, reading, and even drawing. In its most basic form, this game requires each student to write a sentence on a sheet of paper. Then the sentence is passed on to successive classmates who interpret and reformulate the sentence before passing it on to the next student. When students employ effective reading and writing skills, the original message will be preserved through the numerous reiterations; however, when the meaning is unclear, the result is often humorously confusing. Teachers can then use both effective and confusing examples to teach the importance of clarity in writing.

Procedures

Instructors should preface the game with a short explanation and demonstration. This brief oral presentation should focus on whatever grammar, vocabulary, or other language feature will be practiced through the game. In the explanation, teachers should inform students that they will participate in a collaborative writing activity in which they will share their writing with their classmates. It is important to preface the game in this way so that bashful students are prepared for teamwork, and so that students only write sentences (and content) that they feel comfortable sharing with their peers.

Most students benefit from a visual demonstration of the game procedure, which can be done using a sample sheet of paper or by recreating a magnified sheet of paper on a chalkboard. Create a level-appropriate and helpful demonstration that explains the basic steps of Pass It On!:

1. Place the sheet of paper such that it is vertical, or portrait, in orientation. (It is surprising how many students disregard this instruction and write on a horizontally oriented sheet that is ineffective for multiple sharing.)

2. Write a sentence at the top of the sheet, using the vocabulary words or grammatical structures assigned by the instructor.

3. Pass the sheet to the next classmate. (Instructors will want to predetermine the order of passing, whether it be to the right, to the left, or another simple-to-follow orientation.)

4. The receiving student reads the sentence and then, below the sentence, draws a simple picture that represents its meaning.

5. Upon completion of the drawing, the student folds back the sentence so that only the drawing is visible.

6. The completed drawing is now passed on to the next student, who views the picture and then writes an appropriate sentence that communicates the meaning of the picture. Students should be reminded that their new sentence should employ the assigned vocabulary words or grammatical structures. They should then fold back the picture so that only the new sentence can be seen.

7. Steps 3 through 6 can be repeated as many times as appropriate, although rounds with at least three different drawings per sheet tend to be the most enjoyable. It is also preferable to end the game with students writing a final sentence rather than a final picture, so that students can easily compare the initial and final sentences.

8. Once the round is complete, students can unfold the sheets of paper and see how the original meaning was distorted or preserved as it was passed along.

A typical round takes 10–15 minutes, depending on student writing and drawing speed. Thus, this game can be repeated for a few rounds as a major learning activity, or it can be used at the conclusion of a class period to quickly practice a language principle. I often keep a stack of paper strips in my teaching bag so that students can play this game if we have additional time at the end of a lesson.

Caution should be taken when considering content for the sentences. Although it is beneficial to recycle vocabulary and subject matter that is familiar and interesting to students, instructors should be aware that students seem to enjoy using the names of their classmates when writing the sentences and then depicting their peers in drawings. Although this can add appeal to the game, instructors should ensure that no insensitive or hurtful sentences and drawings are created.

Tomoko is learning to cook.

Tomoko is cooking vegetables.

Julia is burning the food.

The woman is burning supper.

Figure 1. Pass It On! Grammar Variation Example

Variations

Pass It On! can easily be adapted to a variety of purposes and proficiency levels. The following list includes variations with suggested student groups.

- **Grammar:** Students write sentences that employ a target grammatical structure. Depending on the complexity of the target structure, this variation is appropriate for all levels to practice grammar through writing (see Figure 1 for an example).

- **Vocabulary:** Students must use all or some of a list of required words. Instructors may randomly assign words to students using flashcards or paper

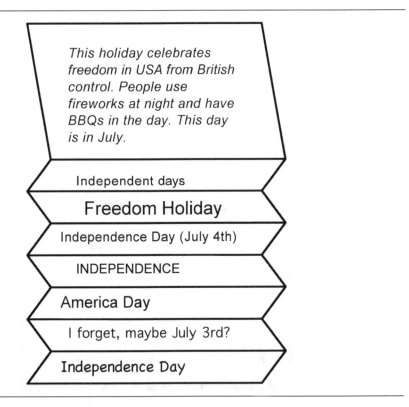

Figure 2. Pass It On! Description Variation Example

strips. Depending on the difficulty of the vocabulary, all proficiency levels can benefit from this variation to practice specific vocabulary words.

- **Description:** Students write a short descriptive paragraph about a keyword or phrase; however, they may not use the keyword or any of its roots. Classmates then attempt to guess the keyword or phrase based on the description paragraph. Rather than write their guess immediately below the paragraph, students write their guess at the bottom of the page and fold the paper over so that guesses remain hidden from peers until the round is complete. For a more competitive variation, points could be awarded to students whose descriptions garner the most correct guesses or to students who make the most correct guesses. This activity is better suited to intermediate or advanced learners (see Figure 2 for an example).

- **Paragraph Cohesion:** Students are asked to write a topic sentence at the top of the page. The next student writes a supporting sentence for that paragraph and then covers up the topic sentence. The sheet is passed to only four or five more students, with each successive sentence being folded back before passing on the new sentence to the next classmate. The final student writes a concluding sentence and then uncovers all previous sentences. If

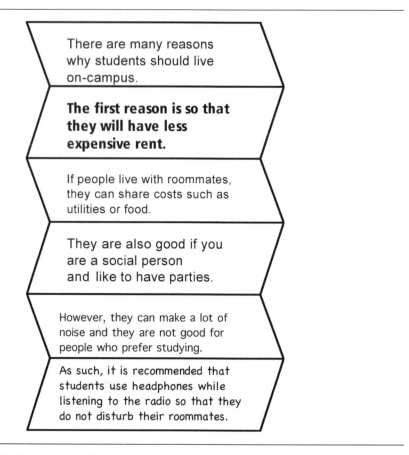

There are many reasons why students should live on-campus.

The first reason is so that they will have less expensive rent.

If people live with roommates, they can share costs such as utilities or food.

They are also good if you are a social person and like to have parties.

However, they can make a lot of noise and they are not good for people who prefer studying.

As such, it is recommended that students use headphones while listening to the radio so that they do not disturb their roommates.

Figure 3. Pass It On! Paragraph Cohesion Ineffective Example

the topic of the paragraph has changed dramatically, students should be asked to explain why it happened. It is possible for a paragraph to retain the original topic; this retention is most likely due to good cohesion practices such as repeating key words or ideas in each successive sentence before hiding the previous sentence. If such examples exist, the instructor should highlight them. Then the activity can be repeated, but this time students should be reminded to avoid ambiguous pronouns and to use key words or phrases that carry the main idea throughout the sentence. Instructors should explain that even in essay writing (and not just this game) paragraph cohesion skills will help readers better understand how sentences connect to covey meaning. This variation is most appropriate for high-intermediate or advanced learners. (Figure 3 is an example of a noncohesive collaborative paragraph. Figure 4 shows a collaborative paragraph with effective cohesion.)

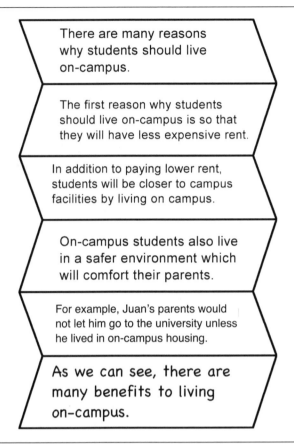

There are many reasons why students should live on-campus.

The first reason why students should live on-campus is so that they will have less expensive rent.

In addition to paying lower rent, students will be closer to campus facilities by living on campus.

On-campus students also live in a safer environment which will comfort their parents.

For example, Juan's parents would not let him go to the university unless he lived in on-campus housing.

As we can see, there are many benefits to living on-campus.

Figure 4. Pass It On! Paragraph Cohesion Effective Example

REFLECTIONS

Instructors will want to decide the degree to which students should employ error correction skills. If accuracy is a primary purpose of the game, then students should be instructed to correct any sentences that they receive before creating a drawing. Otherwise, accuracy may be important only to the degree that it interferes with meaning. Regardless of the level of formal assessment that instructors decide to use in relation to this game, students enjoy reading and sharing the completed sheets and exploring how meaning evolves during play.

This game teaches students to participate in collaborative and public writing. Pass It On! is especially helpful for students who have difficulty sharing their writing: It encourages openness with writing, and it also can help prepare for peer-review activities. Furthermore, it helps students see that the purpose of writing is to communicate. Pass It On! helps students see how meaning can change through perspective. It shows students the importance of making meaning clear and how a lack of clarity in writing can result in confusion.

REFERENCE

Krashen, S. D. (2003). *Explorations in language acquisition and use*. Portsmouth, NH: Heinemann.

Robb Mark McCollum is from British Columbia and works at the Brigham Young University (BYU) English Language Center in Provo, Utah, in the United States. In addition to ESL classes, he also teaches educational psychology to preservice teachers at BYU. His research interests are in the area of instructional psychology and technology.

PART 1: Skills Focus

B. Listening and Speaking

In the Director's Shoes: Bridging Meaning and Pleasure in an English Language Teaching Game

Vander Viana

INTRODUCTION

In 1938, Huizinga (1998) coined the term *Homo ludens* (Man the Player) to make his point that playing is part of human culture. If this point is considered, it is not surprising that young students learning English play games enthusiastically. For teachers, however, games do much more than just provide students with a relaxing atmosphere. They can be a powerful strategy for developing command of English and promoting learning at the same time. As Uberman (1998) states, "Games are not just time-filling activities but have a great educational value" (p. 20). The most important and probably the most appealing aspect of using games is that students learn English in an indirect and memorable way.

Trends, however, do not remain the same over the generations. Students' interests today have shifted toward technology, which implies computer-based tools (Murray, 2005) and requires a new kind of literacy (Leffa, 2003). Because many of today's learners are already competent with computer tools, English teachers feel compelled to update their practice by including computer games in the curriculum.

Despite their popularity, computers are not used in the same way by learners and teachers. Similarly, learners and teachers do not share the same interests when it comes to Web sites (Murray, 2005). It is teachers' responsibility to adapt their classes to students' needs and draw on new technologies with clear pedagogical aims. One possibility involves an online movie maker that allows students to design meaningful stories. Here, this activity is implemented in a game in which learners try to create the best and the most popular movie possible. In this context, learners practice their language skills in a natural way and in a different setting, while also being stimulated by the idea of the game itself.

CONTEXT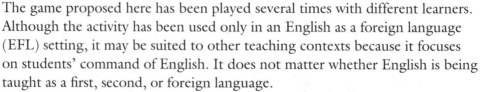

The game proposed here has been played several times with different learners. Although the activity has been used only in an English as a foreign language (EFL) setting, it may be suited to other teaching contexts because it focuses on students' command of English. It does not matter whether English is being taught as a first, second, or foreign language.

The players' ages also have varied. The game yields excellent results with teenagers, but it is probable that younger students (10–12 years old) may enjoy it. The only requirement is some command of English. The activity will produce the best results with those who have more command of the language. Because it is based on creating dialogues, the more English students know, the better their final products will be. Nevertheless, the activity has also been used with beginners taking their first semester of English, who have also been able to carry it out. In this case, lack of linguistic knowledge became a barrier, but they were able to work with the basic structures they had learned and, more important, personalize them.

Although the game has been tried in the context of private language courses, generally with a maximum of 15 students per class, it may be carried out in any school that has the necessary equipment (see *Curriculum, Tasks, Materials*) as well. If one teacher must supervise more than 15 students working on computers, however, the game may not work. It is unlikely that a teacher can monitor what each student does without assistance. This problem would be exacerbated if the school does not have control over the Web sites students access (i.e., those that are not appropriate for pedagogical purposes).

Finally, it should be pointed out that the activity has been implemented in classes in Rio de Janeiro, Brazil. Despite not having been attempted in other contexts, the game may work in other countries because it is not culture-specific.

CURRICULUM, TASKS, MATERIALS

This section offers a description of how the game may be implemented in English-language classrooms, focusing on how it was originally planned and played. The following paragraphs explain how students can create their own movies, and how teachers can carry out the election for the best movie. Some alternatives are offered so that it may be adapted to other contexts.

Initial Steps

The game enhances students' communicative abilities and encourages them to explore their creativity by means of a free online tool that allows users to make their own movies. The tool includes several preselected options for setting, plot, and characterization. Students are involved in a friendly competition in which the winner is the student who makes the best movie. Here, the word *best* is connected not only to language use, but also to the design of the movie as a whole.

The tool suggested in this chapter, Dvolver MovieMaker, is available at http://www.dfilm.com/live/mm.html. It transforms movie making into a simple activity that may be carried out in a few steps. Adding to the ease with which it can be operated, the interface will capture students' attention.

Ideally, teachers will have access to a computer lab that contains a teacher's computer with projection capability, and computers with Internet access for each pair of students. While planning the activity, teachers should also check whether the movie maker tool can be accessed without problems. If it cannot, the institution's computer support personnel should be contacted for help. Finally, teachers will need to have valid e-mail accounts to which students may send links to their movies after the films are produced. A suggestion is to create an e-mail address to be used only for this purpose.

Procedures

To guarantee students' full engagement, the activity should be explained carefully. First, learners should be informed that they are going to play the director's role; that is, they are actually going to make a digital movie. It is recommended that teachers model the activity so students understand what they are expected to do. Modeling consists of showing the learners how to use the online interface. For this reason, teachers should go through the following steps with students. Then, the students will need to choose a partner. Finally, teachers should disclose that this activity will be a contest.

As previously explained, the movie maker is simple to operate. Students will be able to create and publicize their movies in a minimum of seven steps. This number may increase if they create a longer movie with more scenes.

In the first step, two choices need to be made. Students must select both the background and the sky for the scene to contextualize where it will take place. For the former, they have 15 options. By clicking on each option, students see its enlarged version. They also have access to information about each possibility, such as its location, temperature, population, common activities, flora and fauna, and special features. It should be stressed that the type of information available is different for some backgrounds. For instance, in the case of a spaceship, learners are informed about its location, maximum speed, tour of duty, mission, and commanding officer. Students then have 12 options for the choice of sky. By clicking on the sky after having chosen the background, it is possible to see how both go together. Extra information is also offered about the different skies. Here, participants will learn about weather conditions, visibility, temperature, humidity, time, and sunset.

Next, the type of plot for the movie should be selected. Students' choices are limited because there are only four options: rendezvous, pickup, chase, and soliloquy. The first three include some interaction between two characters, and the last is based on a single character. The extra information for each plot informs participants about their possible use (see Table 1). With this information, students are more aware of the choices they can make.

After the plot has been selected, learners choose the characters. The number of characters (either one or two) is related to the plot chosen (see Table 1). Besides usual and unusual human characters, possibilities include an elf, a snowman, a pumpkin face, an alien, and Santa Claus. Additional information on the characters also is included (i.e., their names, occupations, traits, preferences, jobs, ages, styles, looks, residences, and skills).

In the fourth step, the focus changes from visual to linguistic. Now students must think of the lines that will be spoken in that specific scene. If the rendezvous, pickup, or chase plot has been chosen, three turns per character will need to be completed. In the soliloquy plot, there is only one turn for the only character in the scene. In any case, each turn may contain a maximum of 100 characters.

The fifth step concerns the choice of soundtrack. Learners may decide whether or not they want the scene to have background music. If yes, 15 music tones are available, including blues, Indian beat, and Latin beat. A single click on one of the options will play the music. The information provided includes the inspiration for the tone and what kind of movie it suits best.

At the end of the fifth step, participants must decide either to end the movie with only one scene or to add another one. After this choice is made, it is impossible for filmmakers to change their minds. It is advisable that students finish the movie at this stage. Otherwise, the activity will take much longer than expected.

After selecting to end the movie, the sixth step is final editing. Here, students will create a title and type in their names as the directors of the movie. They also will choose one title design out of the four possibilities available: classic, horror, radioactive, and 1970s.

The seventh and final step in the movie maker involves previewing the movie and e-mailing it to whomever students select. In this case, learners have to type in

Table 1. Plots and Their Possible Use

Plot	Use
Rendezvous	Romance/Drama/Comedy
Pickup	Drama/Romantic comedy
Chase	Action/Horror/Sci-fi/Romance
Soliloquy	Drama/Documentary

the receiver's name and e-mail address as well as the sender's e-mail. At this stage, it is extremely important that teachers reinforce the point that the movies must be sent to their e-mail addresses; otherwise, they will not be included in the voting. After successfully sending the movie link by e-mail, the movie maker tool provides students with a ready-made code that allows them to include the link on personal Web pages, blogs, or social network profiles.

After teachers compile a list of the links, an e-mail should be sent to a pool of other teachers—colleagues from the same institution—asking them to vote for the best one. Judges may either be given the freedom to decide on the criteria they will use to judge the movies or be asked to follow a set of predefined criteria such as coherence, consistency, creativity, and use of English, to cite a few. These invited judges should additionally be asked to justify their votes in a way that may be understood by the learners.

During the subsequent class period, teachers should show all the movies to the students so that they have a chance to see what their peers created. Then, election of the best movie takes place in the classroom when teachers read the judges' e-mails out loud. To be genuinely surprised when reading the judges' comments with the students, teachers should not read the e-mails before class. To guarantee that this happens, a new e-mail account may be opened specifically for this activity. Teachers also need to ensure that colleagues understand that their e-mails will not be screened ahead of time but will be shared directly with the students. Therefore, judges should not be critical of the students' work so that students are not offended by the comments. Judges' remarks should be written from a positive perspective. Rather than pointing out the possible flaws in the movies, they should encourage students' creativity and English development.

Variations

One possible variation to the initial steps of the game is to practice the new vocabulary students are about to be exposed to. Teachers may decide to preteach the words they anticipate as troublesome. Alternatively, teachers may have a vocabulary log on the board with words and concise definitions for vocabulary that students identify as problematic.

In relation to the equipment needed, the game could be carried out in a computer lab only. In this case, the modeling and the election, which normally occur in the classroom with one computer, would have to be adapted to fit the space available in the lab. The game may also be played in a classroom with only one computer, provided all students can see the screen or that the image can be projected. To do so, the class would have to work as a whole. Although teachers would likely be responsible for operating the computer, learners should actively take part in making choices. Because only one movie would be produced, no election of the best movie would occur. An alternative to this activity would be for another class to produce a movie, and the two classes compete against each other.

Teachers should be careful not to set up a contest between classes that differ in proficiency, though. It would be unfair for a group of beginners to compete with an intermediate class, for instance.

The number of students working together may vary according to local needs. Teachers who have larger classes may want to have trios instead of pairs. The same may hold true for those who do not have enough computers available in their labs. Teachers should be reminded that the larger the group, the higher the probability some students may not actively participate in making movies.

As far as the adoption of the movie maker suggested here is concerned, it is advisable for teachers to preview its options before using it to judge its appropriateness. In some cultures, strange or sensual characters may be considered offensive. By the same token, a romantic bubble bath may be an inappropriate setting in some cultures.

If Dvolver MovieMaker is not the best option for the sake of appropriateness, teachers may use other movie makers or online tools. One possibility is story makers, which may easily be found on the Internet. For example, Seussville Story Maker (http://www.seussville.com/games/storymaker/story_maker.html) may be of interest (i.e., see Viana, 2008), although it does not contain the same resources as Dvolver MovieMaker.

In relation to the linguistic aspect of the game, teachers may decide to control language practice. This practice may be done by asking students to use a specific function, structure, or lexical item in the dialogues they create. It is also possible to assign each pair a different task for a more comprehensive review.

Finally, the last part of the game may be completely changed if the resources are available and if teachers have the necessary skills. In the best of cases, teachers do not have to limit the election to a select group of people. The election may be open to anyone who is willing to watch the movies and vote for the best one. Voting can be done by creating an online questionnaire and inviting as many people as possible to vote for the best movie. If teachers prefer to have qualitative instead of quantitative feedback, the links may be posted in a blog so that voters may contribute comments. Alternatively, teachers may encourage students to campaign for their movies and gather as many people as they can to take part in the election.

If teachers are uncomfortable with setting up an online questionnaire or blog, if they feel it is inappropriate to open the election to virtually anyone, or if their colleagues are not interested in participating, they may develop rubrics to evaluate each movie themselves. These rubrics should take into account not only language use, but also visual, musical, and spatial choices. Additionally, some teachers who opt for the election as originally proposed may also decide to use the rubric evaluation to offer more specific feedback to students at the end of the activity.

REFLECTIONS

As with all pedagogical innovations, teachers must consider whether they have reached their objectives. This is examined from both students' and teachers' perspectives.

The Students' Perspective

This game has been carried out with different groups of students from distinct backgrounds. On two occasions, the students were asked to register their reactions by writing a short diary entry after completing the activity. To allow these students to write more freely, they were asked to do so in their mother tongue.

Regarding the affective aspect, the students pointed out that the activity raised their motivation and acted as a stimulus for them to use, practice, and recycle what they were learning. In addition, they stressed that the game was fun. The pleasant aspect of this activity was attributed to using computers and taking a break from their classes. Finally, some students focused on the activity being humorous, but this largely depends on the stories they create.

The students also mentioned a few positive cognitive aspects of the game, especially the use of creativity. They liked the possibility of developing stories based on what they had previously learned either in or outside class. Over the course of the game, they felt how important their role was in their learning process because they were responsible for creating the movie on their own. They were aware that the game was being played not only because it was fun, but because it had a pedagogical aim.

The students evaluated the movie maker itself, as well. The most captivating feature, in their opinion, was the range of characters available, making it possible to create a seemingly infinite number of movies. The choice of scenario and music also caught some students' attention. Another positive aspect of the Web site was its ease of operation; the students experienced little, if any, trouble working with it.

The evaluation did not focus solely on the advantages, however. Some students criticized the last step in the movie maker because it took more time to send the links by e-mail than they were willing to spend. This problem, which was due to the slow connection available where the activity was implemented, has not been faced in other contexts. The greatest drawback, especially to very young learners, was the fact that characters' lip movements did not correspond to what they were supposed to be uttering.

The Teacher's Perspective

All in all, the game produced successful results. First, the students were exposed to new words they had probably never heard, such as *background*, *chase*, and *character*. The descriptions provided for each character stimulated students' curiosity, and they asked what the explanatory phrases meant. When it came to the choice of music, the students learned the styles by experiencing them. Even if they had never had any contact with styles such as heavy metal or with musical instruments such as drums, they became more familiar with them through the activity.

Second, the activity provided the students with an opportunity to review what they already knew. It reinforced the work that had been carried out previously. One could suppose that the students might have been unwilling to create elaborate dialogues and would have preferred basic and simple structures. Practice showed that such unwillingness did not happen. Because the activity was a game, the students tried to do their best—in this case, create the most original, cohesive, and coherent dialogue possible—to win the competition.

Third, the activity was communicative. Students' movies were situated in a particular context, and the movies needed to make sense. Making sense was not only a matter of language use, though. All the details needed to be integrated. The dialogue had to be coherent with the choice of background, sky, plot, characters, music, and movie title. Therefore, it seemed nonsensical to choose Playa Tambor, a beach in Costa Rica, as the background with the sunny option for the sky, and the character called Glenuccio, who happened to be wearing a suit and a scarf. By the same token, it would have been somewhat illogical for students to choose a soliloquy plot and include questions and answers (unless meant as a type of interior monologue).

Fourth, the approach was student-centered. The teacher was kept in the background, acting as a facilitator who offered help only when and if necessary. This approach supports Benson's (2001) description of the role of autonomy in the language classroom: "As the theory and practice of language teaching enters a new century, the importance of helping students become more autonomous in their learning has become one of its more prominent themes" (p. 1). In this case, the approach may be described as technology-based since "it is the interaction with the technology itself that is seen to be supportive of autonomy" (Benson, 2001, p. 136). In addition to developing autonomy, if the activity is carried out in pairs as suggested, students may build stronger ties based on mutual cooperation.

Fifth, although it was a game, fierce and unfair competition was not characteristic. Students enjoyed the challenge of trying to get voters to select their movies as the best. Competition was a stimulus for students to work hard and be creative. The game showed learners that they were able to perform the tasks. Therefore, the competition involved in the game promoted self-achievement and self-development.

Finally, the students were in a relaxed atmosphere, and their motivation was increased because the activity involved using the computer. Overall, the game supported language learning objectives and also was fun.

ACKNOWLEDGMENTS

I am grateful to Sonia Zyngier, who reviewed an earlier draft of this chapter. I would also like to thank the students who so kindly agreed to write their reflections on this game, providing me with feedback for the activity.

REFERENCES

Benson, P. (2001). *Teaching and researching autonomy in language learning.* London: Longman.

Huizinga, J. (1998). *Homo ludens: A study of the play-element in culture.* London: Routledge.

Leffa, V. J. (2003). Como produzir materiais para o ensino de línguas [How to design materials to language teaching] In V. J. Leffa (Ed.), *Produção de materiais de ensino: teoria e prática* [*Producing teaching materials: Theory and practice*]. (pp. 13–38). Pelotas: Educat.

Murray, D. E. (2005). Technologies for second language literacy. *Annual Review of Applied Linguistics, 25*(1), 188–201.

Uberman, A. (1998). The use of games: For vocabulary presentation and revision. *English Teaching Forum, 36*(1), 20.

Viana, V. (2008). Seussville story maker. *Essential Teacher, 5*(1), 37.

Vander Viana has been teaching EFL for several years. His main research interests are in the fields of corpus linguistics, English language, and distance learning. He has been a representative of the Association of English Teachers in the State of Rio de Janeiro in Brazil since 2004 and a member of the Research and Development in Empirical Studies Project since 2003.

CHAPTER 8

Tabletop Role-Playing Games

Johansen Quijano

INTRODUCTION

One way to integrate the four language skills and engage students in authentic use of the target language is through tabletop role-playing games (RPGs). Some of the contemporary tabletop RPGs, such as Dungeons and Dragons 3rd Edition, include elements of board games, such as character figures and game boards. The majority of these games, including previous editions of Dungeons and Dragons and the now popular D20 Modern, however, simply require something to write with, something to write on, a guide book, and dice. This simplicity is why tabletop RPGs often are called pen-and-paper role-playing games. Regardless of the presence or absence of board game elements, when used appropriately in the English as a second language (ESL) classroom, these games provide students with an opportunity to engage in spontaneous, unrehearsed language practice. In addition to providing communicative language practice, tabletop RPGs integrate academic content such as mathematics and history into their design, thereby supporting the goals of content-based instruction. In these games, students (or players) take the role of characters in a story, and with the teacher (or game master) create a cooperative narrative while following preset rules.

The game master (GM) acts as a facilitator, and participants are required to (a) read and explore a set system of rules and conditions; (b) make annotations regarding the game in their notebooks; (c) use language in a spontaneous, unrehearsed manner; and (d) engage in weaving a collaborative narrative. These game requirements develop and reinforce a variety of language skills including reading comprehension, note-taking and listening skills, communicative ability, familiarity with discourse patterns (i.e., narratives), and writing-reflection.

CONTEXT

Tabletop RPGs are most successful with students who are at an intermediate or advanced proficiency level. For the game to be fully enjoyed, students must constantly engage in unrehearsed, authentic communication with each other and with the teacher. Students who are beginning to learn a language might feel overwhelmed by the open nature of language use required to play the game. Students who have more experience with the language, however, or at least are unafraid to speak up and feel confident in their language skills, will benefit the most from the language interaction required. At the very least, students engaged with the activity should be able to use sentences to express emotions and actions.

Through improvised, spontaneous role play, it is possible to weave a collaborative narrative between the teacher and students that touches on topics such as love, hatred, friendship, redemption, egoism, and betrayal. It may be possible that while playing the game, students find their characters in opposition to one another. Because of this possibility, tabletop RPGs are most appropriate for high school students or those who are mature enough to leave a dispute between their characters on a fictional level. Furthermore, although high school students usually are open to discussing the topics mentioned previously, younger learners may not fully understand abstract concepts such as betrayal or redemption. For these reasons, these games are most appropriate for high school or older students, although with careful supervision they can be modified for middle or elementary school learners. The ideal number of players is 5–10; however, these games can be altered to allow inclusion of up to 30 students.

For maximum comfort, these games should be played sitting around a table to allow students enough space to sort their papers and roll the dice. However, these games also can be played with students sitting at their desks if tables are not available. If this situation is the case, the desks should be arranged in a circle.

CURRICULUM, TASKS, MATERIALS

Getting Started

A few materials are required for this activity. Every student should have one set of dice, a character sheet, and a pencil. The teacher needs a notebook with detailed descriptions of the settings to be used in the story, as well as a possible outline of the story. The teacher should also have dice, a pencil, and the game's system rules. Most RPGs use several styles of dice. In addition to the traditional 6-sided die they also commonly use 4-sided, 8-sided, 10-sided, and 20-sided dice, each with its own distinct shape. These dice often are packed with the commercial games and also can be found in a variety of stores.

System rules vary depending on the type of story (i.e., fantasy, modern, historical) as well as on the publishing company of the game (e.g., Wizards of the Coast, GURPS). The most popular commercial tabletop role playing games are D20 Modern (Wizards of the Coast, 2004), Spycraft (Alderac Entertainment, 2005), Star Wars (Wizards of the Coast, 2002), WWE: Know Your Role (Comic Images, 2005), and Dungeons and Dragons (Wizards of the Coast, 1974–2003). Teachers who choose to use free RPGs, which are available online, should have one copy of the system rules per student. Commercially available RPGs usually have a GM guide book, a player's handbook, and several add-on materials such as supplementary stories and maps. Teachers who decide to use commercial RPGs should have at least one copy of the GM manual, five copies of the player's handbooks for students, and one character sheet for each student.

Before starting the game, the teacher must be familiar with the rules, including those governing dice rolls as well as allowed actions. Rules vary from version to version, so the teacher needs to read them thoroughly before starting the game. As with every game, the rules should be explained to the students before the game is played. The following guidelines provide an introduction to RPGs.

- Students will have the opportunity to use unrehearsed language to communicate with each other and the teacher by participating in a narrative. They should speak up and practice what they know.

- Each student will choose a character and, with the teacher and classmates, create or follow a story. The game is a type of role-playing activity, but students will stay seated and verbally construct the story based on the teacher's prompts. They will collaborate to accomplish a goal, but will have the chance to determine what happens in the story and what the outcome will be.

- For the students' characters to perform an action in the story, students will roll dice and the resulting score will decide the degree of success of an action.

- The characters can go anywhere in the world as long as they would be able to do so in real-life contexts. For example, a student could have his character cross a wooden bridge or swim across a river, but not swim across an entire ocean.

- When students choose a character (e.g., spy, wizard, pirate), they should play with the character's role until the end of the story.

- What happens in the game is fiction and should not reflect on real-life relationships. If two students happen to find themselves on opposing sides in the game, their rivalry should stay within the game, between their characters.

Procedures

The teacher should begin by giving some background information about the setting so that the students can begin preparing a plan of action. After all, it is not the same to play an English knight during the Crusades as it is to play a hacker for a computer company in the 21st century. The teacher should talk to the students about the chosen timeline and setting of the story and be as specific as possible with the details. Settings can range from completely historical to entirely fictional and can be in any time period. Some examples include: ancient Rome, the Vietnam War, modern-day New York, Mount Olympus, C. S. Lewis' world of Narnia, or a base in outer space. Similarly, the plot could revolve around stopping a war, returning home from an alternate world, or stopping a comet from crashing into Earth.

The next step in the game is making a character. The teacher will tell the students to fill out the character information on their character sheet (see Figure 1). Students should be as specific as possible in their descriptions and should not leave any blanks. The character's racial background and job can be chosen from among the available categories in the game's rulebook, and the character's features (i.e., hair, skin tone, height, personality) can be made up by the students. Teachers should remind students to map characters' features that are relevant to their characters. For example, a student playing the role of a soldier may want a character who is tall and of heavy build, but someone playing the role of a spy may want a character of slender build. Some of the most popular jobs are warrior and elf wizard in a fantasy setting, and spy and hacker in a modern or futuristic setting.

Player's Name: _____	
Character's name: _____	Age: _____
	Gender: _____
Character's race: _____	Height: _____
	Weight: _____
Character's job: _____	Level: _____
Attributes:	**Traits:**
Strength: ____ Bonus: ____	Skin Color:
Intelligence: ____ Bonus: ____	Hair Color:
Wisdom: ____ Bonus: ____	Eye Color:
Agility: ____ Bonus: ____	Personality:
Charisma: ____ Bonus: ____	
Items Owned:	**Information Log:**

Figure 1. Character Sheet

After filling out the character information and choosing a job, the teacher will tell the students to calculate each of the attribute scores. The most common character attributes are strength, wisdom, intelligence, agility, and charisma. To obtain the scores, the teacher will instruct the students to roll four 6-sided dice. Of the four resulting numbers, the teacher will ask the students to add the three highest numbers. For example, in a roll with resulting scores of 2, 5, 3, and 1, the student will add 5, 3, and 2, for a result of 10. The students will then write down the resulting number on a sheet of paper. Students will do this procedure five times, for a total of five scores. They will then assign each of the scores to a different attribute.

Players' characters will be more efficient at tasks involving attributes with high scores, and they will not be so efficient in tasks involving attributes with low scores. For example, a character whose job is diplomat should have high scores in intelligence, wisdom, and charisma, while scores in strength and agility can be lower. A diplomat character with intelligence and wisdom scores of, for example, 17, will learn new languages and analyze situations faster and more efficiently than, for example, a soldier character with intelligence and wisdom scores of 11. Likewise, soldier characters with strength and agility scores of 17 will be able to run faster, jump higher, and lift more weight than a diplomat character with strength and agility scores of 12.

The players (i.e., the students) roll dice to determine the success of characters' actions; high attribute scores give added bonuses to student rolls. In most table-top RPGs, attribute scores between 14 and 16 give the player a +1 bonus, scores of 17 and 18 give a +2 bonus, scores of 19 give a +3 bonus, and scores of 20 give a +4 bonus. Assume that a student has a politician character with the following attributes: agility—10, strength—11, wisdom—14, intelligence—14, and charisma—20. If a student states that he wants to perform an action that requires the strength attribute (e.g., "I want to carry the television up the stairs"), the student will have to roll a 20-sided die or five 4-sided dice to determine the success level of the action. The required score for the success of this task is 15. The student rolls the dice and gets a roll of 13. Because he has a low strength score, he will not receive any bonuses, so his attempt will fail and the television will slip from his grasp, fall down the stairs, and break. However, if the same student states that he wants to make an action involving the charisma attribute (e.g., "I want to make the people listening to my speech like me"), he has a higher chance to succeed. The required roll score to "make people like you" is 18, and the student's roll yields a 16. The student's charisma attribute, required to "make people like you," however, gives a +4 bonus to all rolls involving this attribute. These 4 points are added to the student's roll, for a total score of 20 (i.e., a natural roll of 16 + 4 bonus = a total roll of 20). The student will, therefore, succeed in his stated task.

The teacher should remind the students that those who want characters able to lift heavy objects should put the highest scores in the strength attribute, and those who want to be good at problem-solving or athletics should allocate the highest scores to the intelligence or agility attributes, respectively. Wisdom is a good ability for deciphering riddles and diplomacy, and charisma is a skill useful to students who want their characters to be politicians, bards, or artists.

The teacher will then tell the students to roll an eight-sided die and multiply the result by five. The result is their starting money. For example, a roll of 6 multiplied by 5 will result in the character starting the game with $30 or 30 gold pieces. Finally, the teacher will write a list of items available for purchase and their cost on the board so the students can "buy" them for their characters. These items will include clothing and support gear such as ropes or hooks. Students should be reminded to deduct the cost of the items from their characters' money. For example, Janice has 30 gold pieces and wants to buy a fancy dress (5 gold pieces), fancy shoes (3 gold pieces), riding boots (1 gold piece), riding uniform (3 gold pieces), gloves (1 gold piece), and a dagger (1 gold piece). Janice's character will therefore have the items and 16 gold pieces left.

After all the students have prepared their characters and purchased their items, the teacher will begin the narrative. Unless the teacher has access to one of the commercially available scenarios, this narrative must be designed beforehand. The teacher should design a setting, nonplayer characters that will take part in the narrative, and a rough outline for the plot. Major events, such as what tasks the students' characters will engage in, should also be previously designed by the teacher. Because the game allows for open exchange, however, the conversations between these characters and the players, as well as the way to accomplish the tasks given by the teacher, should be decided by the students as the narrative develops. The teacher will tell students to imagine themselves in a certain setting under certain circumstances and ask them what they would do. As the story progresses, the teacher should give students more freedom to interact and announce actions for their characters. A possible beginning to a session set in a medieval fantasy world in a 12th grade class of 10 students could have the following interaction:

> **Teacher**: Imagine yourselves as the characters you have created. All of Lemuria is in a festive mood. The uneasy truce between Lemuria, where you live, and the Highland Kingdom is finally going to become an official alliance. You are standing in a large hall. As you look around you notice the smiles of more than 100 nobles celebrating the upcoming alliance. A group of nobles wearing the emblem of the Highland Kingdom seems to stand out. The smells of burning oils and incense fill your nostrils, and the sound of the music being played makes you nervous about tomorrow's mission—to deliver a package to King Jael of the Highland Kingdom. As the King of Lemuria, Neil the Third, walks into the room, the crowd becomes silenced by the splendor of his garments.
>
> **Janice**: What is he wearing?
>
> **Teacher** (looking at the notes): He is wearing a long, red tunic, and a regal cape. The jewels in his crown shine like no other jewel you have ever seen.

> **Luis**: I look around. Are there any cute girls there?
>
> **Teacher**: You see two girls that stand out from the crowd. One has long, blonde hair; her green suit makes her seem like springtime come alive. The second girl has a dress in a shade of red that matches her hair. Both are equally beautiful.
>
> **Luis**: I approach the girl in the green suit.
>
> **Javier**: I want to talk to the girl in the red suit.
>
> **Teacher**: Very well. (To Yazmin) You see a young man approach you. He is a tall man of tanned skin and a muscular body. (To Janice) You see a short, old man with a long beard walk towards you. He seems to want to talk to you.

At this point, the students interact among themselves, asking the teacher for guidance and advice. When the students stop interacting, the teacher could help them communicate their ideas or make the story move forward by stating that the king is tired, wishes to retire for the evening, and bids that everyone else rest as well, as they will need all their energy for the upcoming day. Some students may have their characters rest, while others may decide to explore the castle. Whatever choices the students make, it is up to the teacher to guide them through the story and to their final purpose, which in the preceding example is to deliver a package to a neighboring king and return home.

Most actions performed in the game should have a check-score. For example, if a character wants to pick up and throw a boulder, the player should roll a 20-sided die for a strength check. The successful completion of this action requires a roll of 18 or more on behalf of the player. If the character has any bonus for the required attribute, in this case, strength, the bonus is added to the roll.

> **Ricardo**: I want to lift the boulder and throw it out of the way.
>
> **Teacher**: You need a strength check of 18.
>
> *Ricardo rolls the dice and gets a roll of 16. However, his character has a +3 bonus on strength, for a total of 19.*
>
> **Teacher**: You lift up the boulder with ease and cast it aside. The road is now clear.

These checks should be done for major actions only. Walking or jumping, for example, should not require dice rolls to determine success although jumping across a large gap may require an agility check.

In the end, the teacher's task is to guide the students through the story while the students' task is to actively participate in the narration. If students are hesitant to talk, the teacher should present a situation and ask the students, "What will you do?" There is no "right" or "wrong" path to take, although the teacher should attempt to keep students focused on the main goal of the quest.

Variations

Although these games are best used with small groups of students, they can be modified for larger groups. The setting and opening of the story would be the same as it would be for a small group, but instead of giving everyone a single mission, the teacher would have to give several missions to smaller groups of students, and then switch back and forth every 10–15 minutes between groups. The ideal grade level for the implementation of this game is high school, but it can also be used with middle school students who have some degree of proficiency with the language, and with university students who are already fluent and want to practice the language.

The use of computers can be integrated with this activity. Teachers could encourage students to keep Web logs (blogs) or journals about their experience after each game session. In these blogs or journal entries, students could offer narratives on how the game session went. Students also could write their opinions about the narrative itself, comment on the plot and the events experienced, and reflect on what they would have done differently. Students should also be encouraged, if possible, to keep track of their game annotations online. These can include events that took place or comments about the game itself. Besides writing about their role-play adventures, they could list their items and even plan for future sessions. To create an exchange of ideas among students, they could be asked to look at a classmate's blog and comment on it.

Topics presented in the role-play sessions also are important. Changes in theme are done through the story. It is up to the teacher to design a setting, such as fantasy, historical, modern, or futuristic, and a basic plot outline. What is important is student interaction. When designing the plot, however, the teacher should be aware of students' cultural sensibilities. It is up to the teacher to learn about the students' cultures, find what they find offensive, and exclude these elements from the game.

REFLECTIONS

Students should be evaluated on their participation and contribution to the narrative, degree of interaction, and notes on the character sheets. Teachers should develop their own rubrics in which they detail the following criteria: (a) willingness to participate; (b) effectiveness of communication; (c) performance, or how well students play their characters; and (d) cooperation with other students to accomplish a goal. Students who are willing to use language to communicate their ideas, demonstrate some degree of knowledge about the rules of the game, and try to help everyone on their team to accomplish a goal should receive a higher score than students who simply tag along. Other criteria may be added at the teacher's discretion. A student's character sheet also can be used as part of the evaluation. Students who filled out the character sheet, kept track of their items, and wrote notes regarding their scenarios should get a higher score than those who simply wrote their character's name. In the end, the real demonstration of the success of the activity is the increased willingness of students to use unrehearsed, spontaneous language in different settings.

LINKS AND RESOURCES

For a comprehensive list of free and commercial tabletop RPGs, visit John H. Kim's Web site at http://www.darkshire.net/jhkim/rpg/. The Wizards of the Coast Web site is http://www.wizards.com/. The Alderac Entertainment Group Web site is http://www.alderac.com/. The Comic Images Web site is http://www.comicimages .com/.

Butler, M. A. (1993). Communications: EFL RPG. *Games & Education, 1*(3). Retrieved July 29, 2007, from http://phillips.personal.nccu.edu.tw/rpg/ge1-3.html

Padol, L. (1996). Playing stories, telling games: Collaborative storytelling in role-playing games. Retrieved August 1, 2007, from http://www.recappub.com /games.html

Phillips, B. D. (1995). Language learning benefits of role playing games. *Gaming & Education, 2*(1). Retrieved July 29, 2007, from http://phillips.personal.nccu.edu .tw/rpg/ge2-1.html

Rieber, L. P. (1996). Seriously considering play: Designing interactive learning environments based on the blending of micro worlds, simulations, and games. *Educational Technology Research & Development, 44*(2), 43–58.

Johansen Quijano is a professor of English at the Center of Multidisciplinary Studies, Metro Campus, Puerto Rico. He holds a master's degree in Teaching English as a Second Language from the University of Puerto Rico. He enjoys working with video games and tabletop role-playing games in the ESL classroom.

CHAPTER 9

PodQuests: Language Games on the Go

Hayo Reinders and Marilyn Lewis

INTRODUCTION

This chapter introduces PodQuests, or collaborative tasks and games for out-of-class language learning, similar to WebQuests (see Reinders, 2007). PodQuests use MP3 players or other mobile devices to encourage the search for and exchange of real-world information. Directions and immediate feedback guide learners while they attempt to complete the quest. PodQuests can be used as games with different teams competing against each other. The results of the quest, including audio recordings made by students on their mobile devices, can be shared in class (or online) for discussion. PodQuests are an exciting activity that builds on work done in class, but encourages application of classroom knowledge in authentic settings. They are grounded in constructivist theory that emphasizes the importance of learning through experience. Also, they are based on the premise that successful learning is integrated into the sociocultural context of our learners' lives and encourages collaboration and lifelong learning (e.g., see Ahearn, 2001; Lamb & Reinders, 2005). The use of new technologies, in particular social software, (a loose term often used to describe applications that involve collaboration between people), allows us to bridge learning within and outside the language classroom.

What Are PodQuests?

PodQuests take their inspiration from WebQuests. These tasks generally require students to work together to explore a topic, gather and share information, and, usually, do something with that information (e.g., retell it, evaluate it, convince people of something, design something). PodQuests are similar except that they give instructions to learners on a mobile device (an Ipod in this activity) that they take with them as they interact with objects and people outside the classroom (for younger learners, a PodQuest could be organized within the school). The instructions on the device are interactive; they require students to select the appropriate answer to a series of questions (through multiple choice), with immediate feedback, to complete the quest. Students also are required to collect language samples by using the recording function of the device. PodQuests can be timed, and different teams can compete to complete the quest first.

Where Do PodQuests Fit Into the Curriculum?

PodQuests involve *interaction* and *use* of the language outside the classroom and as such are aimed at developing students' communicative competency and ability to apply new knowledge in authentic situations. Usually, preteaching and in-class preparation are required. As PodQuests involve a variety of skills (reading, listening, conversation, and discussion skills, among others), learners will need a certain level of confidence, although collaborating in small groups makes the activity less daunting, especially for less proficient students. The real-life communicative aspect of the quests and the fact that students need to actively participate in authentic situations, make them particularly suitable for use in a task-based curriculum.

CONTEXT

The PodQuest activities introduced in this chapter have been used with adult English as a second language (ESL) learners in both academic English and general English courses, and with learners of lower intermediate to advanced proficiency levels. They can be adapted for children, although in that case the activity would probably have to be limited to use within the school. Because the purpose of the PodQuest can be decided by the individual teacher, they are a highly flexible type of game. For example, teachers can decide to focus more on communication or more on formal aspects of the language, and they can choose a topic that suits work previously done in class and is appropriate for learners' level, age, and interests.

CURRICULUM, TASKS, MATERIALS

Perhaps the easiest way to demonstrate what types of activities and input Pod-Quests may involve is to describe how we have implemented them in one language center in New Zealand.

- Young tertiary students were assigned to one of three groups with the aim of gathering information about Maori (the indigenous people of New Zealand) land rights, which were hotly debated in the news media at the time, and to develop an argument in favor or against legislation proposed by the government.

- In class, students were given background reading, and some vocabulary was pretaught. They were also told about Maori culture and protocols for visiting a *marae* (a Maori sacred place).

- The PodQuest included a series of directions to explore the background and various viewpoints relating to this topic. For example, students had to visit the city council to view records, interview Maori leaders, access information on the Internet, and speak with a government representative. In each case, they were able to find and access the correct sources only by responding correctly to information on the device, which included both text and audio recordings, and providing correct answers to a series of multiple choice questions. For example, students had to ask a Maori leader about the local history of the tribe, but they were able to discover the location of the correct person to talk to only by accurately reading the text on the Ipod. They then had to use the information they had obtained from the interview to answer the questions before they could proceed.

- Students audio recorded key information they gathered using the device.

- Back in class, students assembled the information and prepared an argument to be presented to their classmates. A debate followed, with the team offering the strongest arguments (constructed with the information collected during the quest) being declared the winner (as voted by other students).

PodQuests as Games

PodQuests are extremely versatile, and the communicative element makes them suitable for use as language games. PodQuests can be timed with the first team to complete the quest (e.g., by collecting all the information or by finding the correct answers to all the questions) being the winner. Or the quest could have a fixed time limit. Any team that does not complete the quest within that time is eliminated from the race.

The teacher could give the learners a set of general knowledge questions and instruct them to find the answers to the questions in the school library, for example, or by talking to other students and teachers. The first team to find the answers wins. In a variation on this, different groups are provided with different information or instructions that they will have to share, as an information-gap activity, to solve the quest.

To focus the PodQuest more on formal aspects of the language, learners could be asked to "collect" examples of certain vocabulary (e.g., words related to a certain theme), conversational expressions, or grammar items (e.g., the use of the conditional), which they can then record onto the device. The team with the largest number of meaningful items is the winner.

In the Maori research project, we used the PodQuest so learners could practice a wide range of skills, but it would be possible to focus more on reading skills, by including more extensive notes for learners to read on the device, or more on listening skills, for example. Also, we used the results of the PodQuest for subsequent discussion, but it would be equally possible to use the information learners gathered as the starting point for a writing task with points being awarded for every item incorporated.

Finally, whereas we used audio and text as the input for students to work with, Ipods also play videos and can display photos; it would be possible to use these, or a combination of them, instead. This strategy may especially benefit lower level learners. This technology could be used to construct an "Amazing Race" (a popular reality television show in which teams of two compete against each other in a race around the world) where the teacher provides instructions and clues for learners to follow a trail. The group that reaches the finishing points first is declared the winner.

What Is New About PodQuests?

PodQuests are unique in that they combine the benefits of constructivist, Web-based approaches to learning, with the ability to extend learning to out-of-class settings and encourage authentic language use. PodQuests:

- are collaborative

- are communicative

- are guided

- include feedback

- offer mixed media input to students

- allow students to record information

- are real-life activities

- are easy to integrate into existing classes and can be used to focus more or less on any language skill, depending on the needs of the language learners

- are easy to use as the basis for language games

- from our experience, are highly motivating.

How to Create PodQuests

Creating PodQuests involves two steps: a pedagogical plan and its technical implementation. The pedagogical structure of the activity can be modeled on the example we gave earlier or adapted to suit specific needs. As previously mentioned, PodQuests can work with existing classes by focusing on certain language skills, and the results obtained can be used for subsequent practice and discussion in class. As with any lesson plan, it will probably be best to write down the aims of the activity and its links with previous and following work. One important aim of PodQuests is to encourage learners to use the language, without inhibition, by giving them a clear set of instructions that requires them to interact with their environment while benefiting from the support of their classmates. By being too strict in the implementation of the PodQuest or focusing too much on the formal aspects of the language, the teacher may limit students' interaction with the language. The idea is for the learners to have fun! If the teacher has chosen a compelling topic, the information gathered and shared during the activity may lead to significant interest and discussion, so sufficient time should be allowed.

Technically speaking, PodQuests are easy to create. In essence, the teacher creates a series of text files (called "Notes" on the Ipod) with instructions, questions, and optional accompanying multimedia files. The Notes include hyperlinks that can be used to jump to the multimedia files. They also can be used to direct learners to a new set of instructions or multimedia files, depending on their answer to the questions in the Notes. For example, if a learner has listened to an audio file and then selects the wrong multiple choice answer, that could trigger the audio file to play again. Conversely, if the learner selects the correct answer, that could start a new audio file or display a new set of instructions and questions. Figure 1 is an example of how students would use the PodQuest materials.

Creating the Notes is a simple procedure clearly outlined in the online document available at http://developer.apple.com/hardwaredrivers/ipod /iPodNoteReaderGuide.pdf. Creating the Notes takes as much time as it takes to type them. Probably the most time-consuming part is finding or creating the audio recordings to include. (An excellent source to find ESL podcasts is http:// iteslj.org/links/ESL/Listening/Podcasts/). Once the teacher has created the Notes, the files need to be transferred to the Ipod(s). Transferring the files is a simple procedure that learners will be familiar with if they have an Ipod.

REFLECTIONS

The first point we would like to make is that using the Ipod should be integrated into regular classroom teaching. It is easy to see an innovation as something separate from the rest of the curriculum. We believe that the more the PodQuest builds on whatever learning is happening in a skill area (such as listening) or in a content area (as in language across the curriculum or English for academic purposes), the more successful it will be.

A second consideration relates to the collaborative nature of the work. Although it is easy to see how collaboration is enhanced by using the Ipod, it is important to recognize that groupings for project work can exclude as well as include learners. Teachers can consider these options when assigning the pairs or groups:

- teacher decides or learners decide

- permanent grouping or changeable grouping

- equal ability grouping or gross ability grouping.

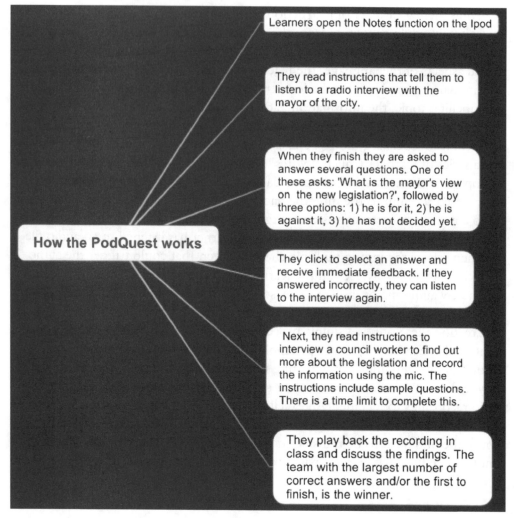

Learners open the Notes function on the Ipod

They read instructions that tell them to listen to a radio interview with the mayor of the city.

When they finish they are asked to answer several questions. One of these asks: 'What is the mayor's view on the new legislation?', followed by three options: 1) he is for it, 2) he is against it, 3) he has not decided yet.

How the PodQuest works

They click to select an answer and receive immediate feedback. If they answered incorrectly, they can listen to the interview again.

Next, they read instructions to interview a council worker to find out more about the legislation and record the information using the mic. The instructions include sample questions. There is a time limit to complete this.

They play back the recording in class and discuss the findings. The team with the largest number of correct answers and/or the first to finish, is the winner.

Figure 1. Steps for Using PodQuest Materials

Varying the composition of groups from time to time can overcome some problems.

A third consideration for teachers is determined by the local context. We have mentioned having students move around in the community. This may not be possible, but modified versions could be. For example, classes could be matched so that senior groups become informants for junior students, where *senior* refers to age or ability (either technological or language).

In addition to the pedagogical considerations above, there are also some practical limitations. One obvious point is that PodQuests require the use of expensive devices. One possible solution is to share one Ipod among several learners or to ask learners to bring their own devices (a recent survey at the University of Auckland showed that most learners had one or more MP3 players) and load the materials onto them. A related concern is that the games can become outdated as the technology evolves. We think that mobile phones will soon have the same functionality as Ipods, however, and, if anything, that PodQuests will thus become easier to implement. Also, the games' focus is on the pedagogy, and whatever technology may become available, the idea of linking classroom with out-of-class work will remain important. A final consideration is that some teachers may not be comfortable with the use of mobile technology and may need additional training and/or support from more experienced colleagues or even students (e.g., see Reinders, in press). However, if these obstacles can be overcome, PodQuests offer a fascinating and fun activity.

Although PodQuests have practical limitations, we believe that games such as this can help encourage teachers to look at ways of drawing on authentic materials and bring an element of fun into language learning.

REFERENCES

Ahearn, L. (2001). Language and agency. *Annual Reviews: Anthropology, 30,* 109–137.

Lamb, T., & Reinders, H. (2005). Learner independence in language teaching: a concept of change. In D. Cunningham & A. Hatoss (Eds.), *An international perspective on language policies, practices and proficiencies* (pp. 225–239). Belgrave: FIPLV.

Reinders, H. (2007). Podquests: Language learning on the move. *ESL Magazine, 58,* 27–28.

Reinders, H. (in press). Technology and second language teacher education. In J. Richards & A. Burns (Eds.), *The Cambridge guide to language teacher education.* Cambridge: Cambridge University Press.

Hayo Reinders (http://www.hayo.nl) is an educational consultant and editor of Innovation in Language Learning and Teaching. He helps institutions develop online language support programs and implement curriculum innovation. He was previously director of the English Language Self-Access Centre at The University of Auckland, in New Zealand, and a visiting professor at Meiji University, in Tokyo, Japan.

Marilyn Lewis is an honorary research fellow at The University of Auckland. She works in Asia with teachers of English and in New Zealand with voluntary tutors who teach English to refugees and migrants.

CHAPTER 10

The Survey Game

Kevin Cross and Patricia Pashby

INTRODUCTION

Based on the American television game show *Family Feud* (or the Spanish-language version, *Cien Mexicanos Dijeron*), The Survey Game is an engaging, interactive way for students to explore cultural differences, learn new vocabulary, and practice listening and oral fluency. Before using this activity in class, the teacher surveys a group of people about their opinions and reactions to a variety of topics and situations, and records their answers. Then, in class, students are divided into groups and asked to predict how the people surveyed answered the questions. They are rewarded for guessing the more popular answers.

One goal of language teachers is to establish in the classroom "a community of inquiry" (Lipman, 2003, p. 94), where collaboration is central. The Survey Game stimulates participation and creates a venue through which students (and teacher) can explore culture and language. For our surveys, we poll members of social groups with whom students will most likely be communicating in the target language. The Survey Game provides an excellent opportunity for students to increase their cross-cultural awareness as they discover how the target group responded and compare this to their own responses and those of their classmates.

We find The Survey Game works especially well as a schema-building activity when introducing new topics. In addition to building students' cross-cultural awareness, it introduces new vocabulary as students receive small amounts of intensive listening practice and an opportunity to interact with classmates. The game also can serve as a grammar review or prewriting activity. However it is used, our students always enjoy and value it.

CONTEXT

We have been using The Survey Game successfully in intensive program oral skills classes, adult education integrated skills classes, and culture classes in short-term special programs in the United States. Although this game is naturally suited for teen or adult English as a second language (ESL) learners at the intermediate and advanced levels, it can be adapted easily to English as a foreign language (EFL) settings, and a shortened version can be used with lower levels and younger learners to introduce vocabulary and themes at the beginning of a new unit. The Survey Game works with both small and large classes, although some variations are better for larger groups. These variations are discussed in more detail later in the chapter.

CURRICULUM, TASKS, MATERIALS

The Survey Game requires some preparation on the part of the teacher. Although the activity has many variations, each one is similar in that students try to guess the most popular answers to questions from a survey. The teacher must therefore survey a group of people (most often people who live in the area in which the activity is being done) and collect their answers. While this survey may take some time outside of class, there are ways to significantly reduce the time spent. First, lists of questions can be found in Appendices A and B. Also, results of surveys conducted by the authors, complete with descriptions of the polled groups and lists of tallied answers, can be found at http://www.ccsf.edu/esl/kcross.html. If a teacher is comfortable with using the authors' questions and results, there is almost no preparation time except for selecting appropriate questions.

Before class, the teacher must decide the purpose for the activity. If it is being used to introduce a specific topic, then the teacher must choose questions that focus on or are thematically related to that topic. For example, if the focus of the class is leisure time, then questions such as "What do you like to do in your free time?" or "How many hours of TV do you watch every day?" are appropriate. Similarly, if the focus is on work, the teacher could choose questions such as "What is a reason why people get fired?" or "What is the best way to find a new job?"

In class, but before the actual game begins, teachers must do two more things. First, they must preteach any language they want the students to use in their small-group discussions (i.e., "What do you think people said about that question?", "That sounds like a good answer," "I'm not sure a lot of people said that"). Teaching linguistic-level-appropriate language for agreeing and disagreeing often adds an extra layer of learning to this activity. Also, any new vocabulary in the survey questions should be introduced.

Second, the teacher must explain what a survey is in such a way that the students understand that they are answering the questions for the target group and not for themselves. The best way to avoid any misunderstanding is to go through a short demonstration first. To demonstrate, we usually tell our classes that we interviewed some children under the age of 5 and asked them the question, "What is your favorite thing to do?" We elicit answers from the students and write them on the blackboard. We then tell them that we interviewed some people over the age of 65. We elicit answers and again write them on the board. We then ask them to account for the differences between the answers, which shows them that the answers depend on the group of people surveyed. Finally, we ask them to answer for themselves. This demonstration clarifies for the students that their answers, while certainly correct for themselves, may not be correct in The Survey Game. We also assign "mock" points so that students get the idea that more popular answers earn more points.

At this point, the teacher can divide the students into groups. Groups of three or four work best because larger groups often allow quieter students to participate less. One member of each group is assigned the role of spokesperson (a position that can rotate from member to member throughout the game). The teacher describes the population polled and reads one question to the students. The beginning of the activity might sound like this: "I surveyed 50 people living here in San Francisco, and they wrote down their answers. I want you to tell me their most popular answers. The question was "What's a good present to give at a baby shower?" The small groups of students then discuss the answers that they think are the most popular. After the discussion, only the spokesperson may give an answer. This arrangement forces students to discuss all the answers and reach a consensus, which is part of what makes this activity so fun for the students. The groups then take turns giving what they feel are the most popular answers. The teacher gives each group the number of points corresponding to the number of people who gave that answer in the original survey. If the first group says "clothes," and 25 people in the survey said "clothes," then that group would receive 25 points. If the second group says "soap," but no one in the survey said "soap," then that group would not get any points.

The groups continue giving answers and getting points until all the answers are given or the class reaches a predetermined number of incorrect answers. Once that point has been reached, if the students have not guessed all the answers from the survey, they are allowed to brainstorm again in groups and make a final list, which they write on a piece of paper and then show to the class. Again, if their answers match the answers from the survey, they are awarded points. Depending on the amount of time allotted for the activity, the teacher may give groups an additional minute or two to generate more answers after the first round of guessing.

When playing The Survey Game in a large class, it is best to have students write down their answers so everyone gets a chance to guess. For example, the teacher might ask, "What sport do you like to watch during the Olympics?" If there are only six answers from the survey group for that question and the class has 40 students organized into 10 groups of four, it could happen that the groups called on first guess all the answers before later groups get a chance. Instead, each group can write down one answer on a piece of paper, and then they can all hold up their answers at the same time. The groups can be given points and, if all the answers still have not been revealed, they can all guess again.

Because The Survey Game involves cultural knowledge, vocabulary development, and listening and speaking skills, it can be used in a variety of learning contexts. It is an excellent starting point for exploring cross-cultural awareness. The question, "What do people often do at a party?" will most likely elicit some different answers between groups polled in the United States and those polled in a different country. Similarly, the question, "Why do supervisors sometimes get angry at their employees?" may expose students to answers that will surprise them. The teacher can then use the questions and the students' guesses (correct and incorrect) as a basis for further exploration of cultural differences. Using this activity in an EFL setting is especially fun for students because they can actually get insights into the culture whose language they are studying. And while finding native speakers of English may be a challenge for teachers working in countries where English is not spoken as a native or additional language, e-mail certainly has made completing this task possible.

The Survey Game also can be used for vocabulary review. For example, asking the question, "What is a fruit that everybody likes?" is a creative, fun way of reviewing food words for lower level students. Similarly, using questions with the verb "get" ("Why do some people get divorced?" or "What do people do when they get a cold?") can be a great way to review some different uses of this verb.

Listening to the various questions helps students develop their bottom-up skills as they listen for key words and build comprehension of natural reductions in phrases such as "what do you . . ." and "would you . . ." Also, because groups must discuss their answers before giving them to the teacher, this activity is an invaluable way for students to work on their oral fluency and on the functions of sharing ideas, agreeing and disagreeing, and asking for clarification.

Teachers also can use the survey questions to review a grammar point. For example, it is easy to design interesting questions that focus on superlative adjectives ("What's the spiciest cuisine?" or "Who was the most influential person in your life?"). Other grammar points, such as present time ("Why do most people take English classes?", "Why do people get a divorce?") or past time ("What chores did you do last weekend?"), can be elicited through various questions.

The Survey Game also is a fun way to focus on a particular theme. Questions about food ("What do people usually eat for breakfast?", "What's your least favorite vegetable?") can introduce a unit on recipes or dining out. Additionally, teachers may use a set of questions to focus on a topic for journal writing or an oral presentation. For example, the two questions, "What do most people get children for their birthdays?" and "What do guests often bring to a party?" could serve as a prewriting activity for a writing assignment about a favorite party memory.

Variations

A variation of The Survey Game can be used in all of the ways mentioned previously but with a different twist. Instead of just reading or giving students the questions, the teacher can also provide students with the list of answers (see

Appendix B). For example, after asking the question, "What chores did you do last weekend?" the teacher can then give a list of answers such as (a) clean the bathroom, (b) do the laundry, (c) do the dishes, (d) vacuum, and (e) dust. Each group of students would discuss the answers and then make a guess as to the most popular answer. As in the version previously described, teams would receive the same number of points as the number of people surveyed who gave that answer. This variation works especially well with questions that ask for numerical answers, such as the question, "How many times per month do you eat at a fast food restaurant like McDonalds?: (a) never, (b) once or twice, (c) 3–5 times, (d) more than 5 times." It is often best to limit the amount of discussion time to keep the pace quick. Thus each group might have 1 minute to discuss how they imagine the people in the target community answered the question before reporting their choice to the class.

For a greater focus on listening, the teacher can present The Survey Game questions as a dictation exercise, after which students can review pronunciation of and practice listening for natural reductions in phrases such as "what do you . . ." and "would you . . ." At very beginning levels of fluency, the questions can be given as a cloze exercise, thus providing students with most of the language in print to help their comprehension. In addition, some students benefit more if they receive questions in advance and have time to discuss the meaning of the questions in pairs, in small groups, or as a team. And if the teacher wants to use a particularly complicated question, or if the students are especially reticent to speak in class, the teacher can give the students the questions to take home and consider more carefully.

For more extensive oral skills practice, students can design their own polls and interview members of the target community. According to Hinkel (2001), interviewing native speakers is "one of the most effective activities that can be used for investigating a second culture" (p. 455). In this case, The Survey Game can be used either as a model before the students generate their own polls or as a follow-up to survey work students have already completed. Because teaching computer skills, often incorporating the use of graphs and charts, is an important component in many curricula, this activity can serve as a springboard as it focuses on various answers to one question and thus lends itself nicely to such computer applications.

The survey premise of the game can also be used without polling outside of the classroom. As an icebreaker or, even better, as an end-of-term activity, students answer a set of questions individually (giving honest responses), and submit these to the teacher or game facilitator. In groups, students work together to predict how members of the other groups answered each question.

It should be noted that creating the survey questions takes thought. We have learned that the best questions are those which elicit at least six or seven (or as many as there are groups in the class) different answers. Also, questions that elicit answers given by only one or two of the people surveyed are excellent in that students will be forced to explore the questions even more deeply and negotiate further with classmates. For example, a question such as "What did you do for fun as a kid?" usually elicits a wide range of answers among people who take the survey, and many of the answers may be given by only one survey participant. For that question, students will have to delve into culture, climate, socioeconomic class, gender, and age ranges to be able to make good guesses at a wide range of answers. There will be, in general, more discussion and more negotiation. Questions that focus on topics such as favorite fruits or useful electronic equipment, on the other hand, usually do not require the same depth of exploration by the students because the answers given in the survey usually are more standard.

REFLECTIONS

On course evaluations, students have mentioned The Survey Game as a favorite activity. We find all of our students—regardless of proficiency level and/or general motivation—strongly engaged whenever we use this activity. Brown (2001) explains that classroom activities that are "fun, interesting, useful, or challenging" are intrinsically motivating and thus "have a much greater chance for success" (p. 59). The Survey Game meets all four of these criteria and has been extremely successful with our students.

The game is fun and interesting for students because the questions relate to real-life experiences, and the answers, which are often humorous or touching, are authentic and gathered from an identified (often local) community of language users.

The game is clearly useful. Cultural knowledge of the community within which students will be communicating is central to language learning and thus should play a role in classroom instruction (Hymes, 1996; Scollon & Wong Scollon, 1995). The Survey Game provides an excellent opportunity for students to increase their cross-cultural awareness as they discover how the target group responded and compare it to their own responses and those of their classmates. At the same time, the game provides vocabulary practice as students are given opportunities for noticing, retrieving, and even generating vocabulary (Nation, 2001). During the game, teachers can explicitly teach some items while providing opportunity for students to experience implicit (or incidental) learning of other vocabulary items (DeCarrico, 2001) as groups work together to interpret the questions and produce answers. In addition, listening to the various questions helps students develop their bottom-up skills through ideal "short, focused tasks" (Helgesen, 2003, p. 32), and the small-group and whole-group discussions that ensue allow development of top-down skills (Hinkel, 2006). Oral skills are practiced in the small groups, which provide "opportunities for student initiation, for face-to-face give and take, for practice in negotiation of meaning" (Brown, 2001, p. 178).

Finally, students find The Survey Game challenging. They are inspired to go beyond simply answering information questions. They can infer and synthesize facts, ideas, experiences, and generalizations as they work with classmates to predict the most likely answers for each of the survey questions.

REFERENCES

Brown, H. D. (2001). *Teaching by principles: An interactive approach to language pedagogy* (2nd ed.). White Plains, NY: Pearson Education.

DeCarrico, J. (2001). Vocabulary learning and teaching. In M. Celce-Murcia (Ed.), *Teaching English as a second or foreign language* (3rd ed., pp. 285–300). Boston: Heinle & Heinle.

Helgesen, M. (2003). Listening. In D. Nunan (Ed.), *Practical English language teaching* (pp. 23–46). New York: McGraw-Hill.

Hinkel, E. (2001). Building awareness and practical skills to facilitate cross-cultural communication. In M. Celce-Murcia (Ed.), *Teaching English as a second or foreign language* (3rd ed., pp. 443–456). Boston: Heinle & Heinle.

Hinkel, E. (2006). Current perspectives on teaching the four skills. *TESOL Quarterly, 40*, 109–131.

Hymes, D. (1996). *Ethnography, linguistics, narrative inequality: Toward an understanding of voice*. Bristol, PA: Taylor & Francis.

Lipman, M. (2003). *Thinking in education* (2nd ed.). Cambridge: Cambridge University Press.

Nation, I. S. P. (2001). *Learning vocabulary in another language*. New York: Cambridge University Press.

Scollon, R., & Wong Scollon, S. (1995). *Intercultural communication: A discourse approach*. Cambridge, MA: Blackwell.

Kevin Cross has taught ESL throughout the San Francisco Bay Area, in the United States, as well as in Italy and Colombia. He currently teaches ESL at the Alemany/ Civic Center campus of City College of San Francisco.

Patricia Pashby, who received a master's degree from San Francisco State University and a doctorate from the University of San Francisco, has been teaching ESL–EFL in higher education for 20 years in the United States and Thailand. She is currently working in teacher training through the Department of Linguistics at the University of Oregon, in the United States.

APPENDIX A: SURVEY QUESTIONS

The following is a random collection of questions we have used over the years. We use as few as one or two questions to as many as 10 in any one class period, depending on the course, the students, and the purpose.

1. What is your favorite type of cuisine?
2. What is the best place to go for a vacation?
3. What subject do most high school students hate?
4. What do you like to eat for breakfast?
5. What kind of present do you usually get children for their birthday?
6. What do you use a computer for?
7. When you were a child, what did you do for fun?
8. What sport do you like to play?
9. What do you like to do in your free time?
10. When you go on a trip, what do you always bring with you in your carry-on luggage?
11. What are many people afraid of?
12. What's the best way to learn a foreign language?
13. What's a good job for a new immigrant who doesn't know a lot of English?
14. What do parents help their children do?
15. What do some students do that gets them in trouble?
16. What do you do at night before you go to bed?
17. What do you do in the morning before you leave the house?
18. What is something that a guest brings to a party?
19. What is a really nice holiday?
20. Who was the most influential person in your life?
21. Who is the most famous person in the United States?
22. Who is the best successful singer ever?
23. What is the most popular kind of music that people listen to at home or in their cars?
24. Why do most people study English?

25. What chores did you do last weekend?

26. What are some common physical ailments/problems for people over the age of 60?

27. Who do people often talk to when they have a problem?

28. What do you often see at a wedding?

29. What kind of food is easy to make for dinner?

30. What is a fruit that everybody likes?

31. What is an electronic gadget that is really useful?

32. What do people often do at a party?

33. What is a kind of party that people like to go to?

34. Why do supervisors sometimes get angry at their employees?

35. What do people do when they get a cold?

36. Which foreign country is the best for a vacation?

37. What's your favorite flavor of ice cream?

38. What is a famous place in this city?

39. Who is a famous person in American history?

40. How do friends sometimes help each other?

41. What's a really good job?

42. What kinds of problems do tenants have with their apartments?

43. What is something that people often lose?

44. Who do people often call on their cell phones?

45. Where do newlyweds often go on their honeymoons?

46. What's your favorite fruit?

47. What's your favorite color?

48. What's your favorite drink?

49. What do children often dress up as for Halloween?

50. Why do some people quit their jobs?

51. What sport do you like to watch during the Olympics?

52. What sport is boring to watch on TV?

APPENDIX B: SURVEY QUESTIONS WITH ANSWERS

In this version of the game, instead of just reading or giving students the questions, the teacher provides students with the list of answers. Each group of students discusses the answers and makes a guess as to the most popular answer.

1. What movie genre do you like most?

    a) comedy
    b) drama
    c) action
    d) science fiction
    e) horror

2. How would you rate pizza?
    a) I love it.
    b) I like it.
    c) It's okay.
    d) I don't like it.
    e) I hate it.

3. How many foreign countries have you visited?
    a) 0
    b) 1–2
    c) 3–5
    d) 6 or more

4. Which do you drink more often?
    a) tap water
    b) bottled water
    c) soda

5. How many hours do you usually spend online per day?
    a) less than 1
    b) 1–2
    c) 3–4
    d) 5 or more

6. Which sport do you like watching most?
    a) tennis
    b) baseball
    c) basketball
    d) American football
    e) soccer

7. Where is a good place to go on a first date?
   a) park
   b) movie theater
   c) night club/disco
   d) restaurant/café
   e) sporting event

8. What is the best pet?
   a) bird
   b) cat
   c) dog
   d) fish
   e) rodent (mouse, hamster, rat, etc.)
   f) none

9. What is a good age to get married?
   a) 18–21
   b) 22–25
   c) 26–30
   d) over 30

10. What time do you usually go to bed at night?
    a) before 10:00
    b) between 10:00 and 11:00
    c) between 11:00 and 12:00
    d) between 12:00 and 1:00
    e) after 1:00

11. What time do you usually get up on the weekend?
    a) before 7:00
    b) between 7:00 and 8:00
    c) between 8:00 and 9:00
    d) between 9:00 and 10:00
    e) after 10:00

12. How many hours of television do you usually watch each day?
    a) none
    b) around 1 hour
    c) between 1 and 2 hours
    d) between 2 and 3 hours
    e) more than 3 hours

13. What's the best thing to eat with a hamburger at a barbecue?
    a) potato chips
    b) coleslaw
    c) potato salad
    d) macaroni salad
    e) Jell-O salad

14. What's the best way to get a baby to stop crying?
    a) sing him a song
    b) bounce him up and down
    c) rock him in your arms
    d) talk to him
    e) something else

15. What's a good thing to do when you're feeling sad?
    a) talk to someone
    b) sleep
    c) have something good to eat
    d) go dancing
    e) listen to music
    f) something else

16. How many times have you moved in your lifetime?
    a) never
    b) once
    c) 2 or 3 times
    d) 4–6 times
    e) 7–10 times
    f) more than 10 times

17. How many pairs of shoes do you own?
    a) 1
    b) 2–3
    c) 4–6
    d) 7–10
    e) more than 10

PART 1: Skills Focus

C. Vocabulary

CHAPTER 11

Let's Go Shopping

Hyacinth Gaudart

INTRODUCTION

Let's Go Shopping is a multilevel card game. It enables learners to practice a number of grammatical structures and enjoy practicing them through role-playing. Each learner will play purchaser and shopkeeper at different times. The structures and situation, although controlled, are as realistic as possible for a classroom.

At the elementary and intermediate levels, the learning objectives include practicing structures to ask for something, express regret, and thank someone for something. Learners will also learn different lexical items to improve vocabulary. At the advanced level, in addition to the structures mentioned above, students will also be encouraged to negotiate.

CONTEXT

This is a multilevel game and has been used with elementary, intermediate, and advanced learners, using structures to encourage or to challenge them according to their level. The versatile game has been played by young learners as well as adults.

CURRICULUM, TASKS, MATERIALS

Getting Started

Needed resources and materials:

- Cards (about 2½ x 2 inches), cut from either manila cardstock or recycled from old name cards, name tags, etc.

- Small pictures, either drawn, cut out from magazines, or taken from stickers or computer graphics. The teacher will need four pictures for each set and 10 sets of pictures for each pack of cards. My pack of cards has the following 10 sets: sports, vegetables, animals, pets, tools, hardware, fruit (1), fruit (2), toys, and vehicles (see sample cards in Figure 1). You will need a pack of cards for each group of four, five, or six players. Five players in a group would make the game more challenging. Six players will not give some players adequate practice.

- To prepare the cards: (a) paste a picture on the left of the card, (b) write the name of the set at the top (e.g., Sports Set, Vegetable Set, etc.), (c) write down all four items in the set so the players know what they are supposed to collect, and (d) write or type the name of the item below the picture.

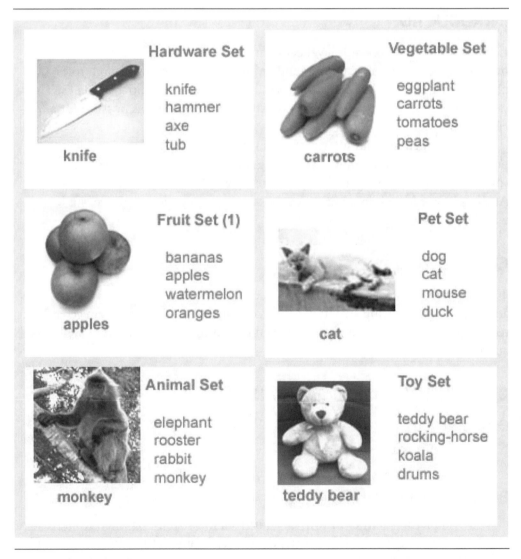

Figure 1. Examples of Cards Used in Let's Go Shopping (Teachers Need Not Use These Particular Sets and Items but Can Identify What Would Work Best for Their Students)

Overview

The idea is for the players to collect all four items in the set to get complete sets. The player with the most sets of cards wins, not the player who finishes all his cards first. A player tries to guess who has the item he needs, and then asks that person (who role-plays a shopkeeper) for the item.

To practice certain vocabulary items, paste pictures of those items on the cards. For example, you might want to introduce types of furniture (couch, armchair), or types of living quarters (apartment, hut, house, houseboat).

Procedures

Rules of the Game (Intermediate Level)

The game is intended for 4–6 intermediate-level players, sitting in a circle at a table.

1. Decide who will shuffle and distribute the cards. That person also will start the game.

2. Distribute all the cards.

3. Players arrange the cards in their hands, according to sets they may have. They do not show their cards to the other players.

4. The dealer, Player 1, acting as a purchaser, begins by asking one of the other players for an item. Player 1 can tell which items she needs by looking at the list of items on her card (see sample cards). If she already has tomatoes and peas, she will need to ask for carrots or eggplant to make a set.

5. She makes a guess about who has the vegetable she needs. A calculating player does not ask for the item right away, but asks for the category of the item—for example, for a *vehicle* or a *vegetable*, instead of *car* or *cucumber*. This tactic prevents other players from knowing exactly what she needs. For example, a player may want to collect vegetables, and the vegetable set comprises eggplant, carrots, cucumber, and lettuce. If another player knows that the first player needs cucumber, and he has lettuce, then he also knows that the player asking for the card has either carrots or eggplant. Knowing this information makes it easier for him to ask for one of these items when it is his turn.

6. Asking for a more generic category also allows more practice for the learners. For example:

    > Player 1: Excuse me, Suki. Do you have any vegetables? /
    > Do you have any vegetables, Suki? /
    > Do you sell vegetables, Suki?

Suki:	Yes, I do. What vegetable would you like?
Player 1:	Do you have carrots?
Suki:	Sorry, I don't.

Or,

Suki:	Yes, I do. (Hands over the card)
Player 1:	Thank you.

7. If the answer was *yes*, Player 1 keeps her turn. She can turn to someone else, or ask Suki for another item, such as eggplant. For example:

Player 1:	Ralf, do you have any vegetables?
Ralf:	Yes, I do. What would you like?
Player 1:	Eggplant, please.
Ralf:	Here you are. (Hands over the card)

Player 1 then has one full set, which she places face down in front of her so no one can ask for any of those cards.

8. If the answer was *no*, Player 1 loses her turn. The other player, who had played shopkeeper in the original exchange, takes over and gets the chance to try to buy an item from someone. For example:

Player 1:	Ralf, do you have any vegetables?
Ralf:	Sorry, I don't have any. Suki, do you sell vehicles?
Suki:	Sorry, I don't. Ralf, do you sell pets?

And so on.

Variations

Classroom Environments

Elementary Level

Player 1 addresses another player and asks for an item. For example:

Player 1: Mehta, may I have some carrots, please?
Mehta:	Sorry, I don't have any carrots. / Sorry, I don't have any.

Or

Mehta:	Here are some carrots. (Hands over the card)
Player 1:	Thank you.

Advanced Level

Allow learners to create their own dialogue and bargaining sessions. They will take the game to a level they are comfortable with. For example, they can ask questions without giving away what they really want. Following is an example taken from a classroom situation (the names have been changed):

Felipe: Sashi, do you have any kind of animal with fur?

Sashi: Yes, I do.

Felipe: Do you have an animal that can jump far?

Sashi: No, I don't. Are you looking for a competitor for the Olympics?

(General laughter.)

Felipe: No, I need it to jump and get an apple for me.

Sy: But you wanted an animal that can jump far, not high!

(General laughter.)

Cultural Notes

Learning styles vary according to cultural norms, personality, and situations. What is acceptable in one culture may not readily be perceived as acceptable in another culture. Situations and learner personalities also vary from class to class. The game suggested here, however, has been used with learners from different backgrounds and cultures, including Japanese engineers, Korean housewives, Islamic teachers, and Malaysian teenagers. Most learners have found the game exciting and motivating. At intermediate and advanced levels, however, there were variations in the language used and the number of turns taken, depending on the learners. One difficulty the teacher may face is stopping learners playing (i.e., at end of class or to do another activity) because they want to continue the game.

Although no cultural problems have been found when the game has been tried with learners from different backgrounds, a teacher in certain cultures might want to include some items that are popular in that culture. For example, a class in Tokyo might appreciate bionic "pets" more than real ones or small dogs rather than large ones. Some items would also be more popular with certain age groups, so the teacher can select the items accordingly.

Some learners may never have played card games before. If so, the teacher would have to give a demonstration of how this card game would be played. Use a group of students, sit down with them and play the game together, with the rest of the class looking at the teacher's cards.

Variations on a Theme

- Instead of using items, the teacher could use people so that the structure would change to "Do you know . . . ?" or "May I speak to . . . ?" or "Is . . . at home/in?"

- Instead of "buying" something, players could exchange cards, as in a barter system. For advanced learners, on the other hand, the buying and selling theme could be taken further by giving each player a sum of "money," with which they will have to buy what they need and negotiate for a good deal.

- With elementary-level learners, the teacher might want to leave the structures on an overhead projector (OHP) or on the board until the learners get more confident in interacting.

- This versatile game allows teachers to change structures and functions to supplement their curriculum materials and answer the needs of the syllabus they are using.

REFLECTIONS

Students' Reaction and Learning

When playing the game for the first time, elementary and lower intermediate students usually react quietly at first. They often glance at the OHP to look at the structures and read them out. As the game progresses and they gain confidence, they stop looking at the OHP and concentrate on playing the game and getting the cards they want. I usually turn off the OHP when they get more comfortable and use the structures naturally. Intermediate and advanced students will add to the basic structure, and the number of turns and interactions are increased.

One problem that arose with culturally mixed classes was caused by differences in pronunciation. In an advanced class I taught, a student asked for "ex." The others thought he wanted *eggs*. What he wanted was an *axe*.

How the Game Meets the Objectives

The main objective of the game is to allow practice asking for something, expressing regret that one doesn't have something, and thanking someone for something. The game allows practice every time a player asks for something. It is a drill without the tedium of simply repeating structures out of context. The game offers a context in which learners can practice with confidence. Where learning vocabulary is concerned, learners see the words and pictures constantly, allowing them to become familiar with the lexical items the teacher wants to teach.

Why the Game Is Successful

The game is carried out in a nonthreatening environment. The teacher's objectives and the students' objectives may not be the same. The teacher intends for the learners to use certain structures and learn vocabulary items. The learner wants the cards to make up a set. In doing so, the learner forgets himself and gets involved in the game, thus making the requests and replies more and more natural as the game proceeds. Guessing who has the cards also helps. It "frees" the learner to make mistakes. And wrong guesses do not make the person look foolish, just brave.

It is often the case, especially with elementary-level learners, that they translate from their own language into the forms they need in the target language. In this game, as play goes on, the translation stops and the acquisition of the forms becomes easier and is retained more successfully.

What Makes the Game Unique

The game is unique in a number of ways:

- Adults have as much fun with it as do children and teenagers. Corporate executives have enjoyed it as much as engineers and secretaries.

- It can be carried out with learners of different language levels.

- It is easy to make the cards and keep them to be played over and over again.

- It allows teachers the liberty to incorporate different vocabulary items that they need to teach.

RESOURCES

Argondizzo, C. (1992). *Children in action*. London: Prentice Hall.

Gaudart, H. (1997). *Reaching out to learners*. Shah Alam, Malaysia: Fajar Bakti.

Granger, C. (1993). *Play games with English*. (Teacher's Book and Books 1 & 2). London: Heinemann.

Hadfield, J. (1987). *Elementary communication games*. Surrey, England: Nelson.

Hadfield, J. (1990). *Intermediate communication games*. Surrey, England: Nelson.

Kealey, J., & Inness, D. (1997). *Shenanigames: Grammar-focused interactive ESL/EFL activities and games*. Brattleboro, VT: Pro Lingua Associates.

Noor, A. Y., & Gaudart, H. (1996). *Preparing and using visual aids for English language teaching*. Shah Alam: Penerbit Fajar Bakti.

Primary games. (n.d.) Retrieved September 10, 2007, from http://www.primarygames.com/games.htm

The EFL playhouse: For teachers of young English language learners (ELLs). (n.d.) Retrieved September 8, 2007, from http://www.esl4kids.net/games.html

Wright, A., Betteridge, D., & Buckby, M. (1984). *Games for language learning*. Cambridge: Cambridge University Press.

Hyacinth Gaudart is involved with training teachers of English at the University of Malaya, in Malaysia. She has written a number of books—academic as well as fiction for children and adolescents—and has developed a variety of games for learners of different ages.

CHAPTER 12

Collocations in the Foreseeable Future

Rachel Adams Goertel and Carole Adams

The single most important task facing language learners is acquiring a sufficiently large vocabulary. We now recognize that most of our vocabulary consists of prefabricated chunks of different kinds. The single most important kind of chunk is collocation. Self-evidently, then, teaching collocations should be a top priority in every language course. (Lewis, 2000, p. 8)

INTRODUCTION

Collocations are word combinations such as phrasal verbs (e.g., *take up*), adjective–noun pairs (e.g., *daily newspaper*), and lexical bundles (e.g., *I don't know if*). Corpus studies show that a large part of language in use consists of collocations, so it is important that language learning not focus just on vocabulary and grammar but also on collocations (Barlow & Burdine, 2006). In these relationships, two words or groups of words go together to form a common expression that is immediately recognizable. *Crystal + clear, lame + duck,* and *ulterior + motive* are examples of collocated pairs of words. One cannot say *crystal vivid, lame mallard,* or *ulterior reason* and be understood because there is no collocation in the pairs.

Close association of certain words prevents interchanging even synonyms such as *wide* and *broad*. For example, one would say *broad shouldered* and *wide eyed,* not *wide shouldered* and *broad eyed*. In addition, three commonly associated words in the English language are *I don't know*. This association is further linked with different completing phrases: *I don't know if, I don't know who, I don't know how,* etc. In conversation, these lexical bundles make up an important portion of discourse (Biber, Johansson, Leech, Conrad, & Finegan, 1999). Similarly, words closely associated with *do* and *make* such as *do homework* and *make a mistake,* not *make homework* and *do a mistake,* prevent interchange and present problems for English for speakers of other languages (ESOL) students. These specific variations in the occurrence of collocations in English are the basis of the three language games presented here.

Corpus linguistics has provided the classroom teacher with information about the use of spoken language. Corpus data on frequency patterns cannot be ignored. The more frequent a pattern of speech, the more important it is to introduce it to the language learner. Incorporating collocations into the classroom curriculum is essential because a student's primary goal is to understand and be understood. This goal is achieved by being familiar with high-frequency vocabulary combinations, not just singular vocabulary words.

The objective of this chapter is to present ESOL teachers with activities to help their students understand the use of frequently occurring collocations through interactive games.

CONTEXT

Regardless of their age, ESOL students who have mastered at least an intermediate level of English can enjoy these games. Teaching collocations should be implemented from elementary school through adult education. The games presented in this chapter are appropriate for pairs and small or whole groups. These student-centered games also utilize the four skill areas of reading, writing, speaking, and listening. Teaching collocations through interactive activities provides students with an alternate and fresh approach to language learning.

Two reference books about collocations ESOL teachers will find helpful are *Teaching Collocation: Further Development in the Lexical Approach* (Lewis, 2000), and *LTP Dictionary of Selected Collocations* (Hill & Lewis, 1997). Both texts discuss the frequency patterns of collocations and provide further insight to the importance of teaching them to the language student. In addition, one of the most comprehensive lists of collocations can be found in the *Longman Grammar of Spoken and Written English* (Biber et al., 1999). This book enables ESOL teachers to choose groups of collocations quickly and easily for particular lesson plans.

CURRICULUM, TASKS, MATERIALS

Games and student-centered activities such as those described next will help foster understanding and use of collocations.

Collocation Cross

- **Objective:** Students understand the meaning of the collocations.

- **Materials:** Pencil, paper, online crossword puzzle generation tool (Puzzlemaker, 2007).

- **Directions:** Go to http://puzzlemaker.discoveryeducation.com and select *Criss-Cross.* Follow the steps, including typing in the collocations (words) and the appropriate meaning of each (clues). Select *Create My Puzzle!* Cut the crossword puzzle and paste it on a blank page. Provide a word bank for students who may need extra help. (Figure 1 is an example of a puzzle made with an online crossword puzzle generation tool.)

- **Assessment:** The teacher should check the puzzle for accuracy. Students can write sentences using the newly learned collocations.

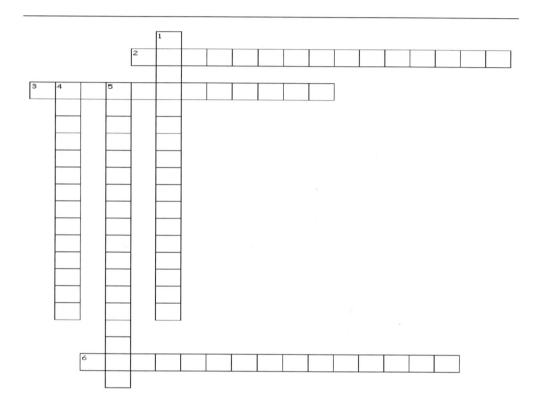

Across

  2. medical procedure to look better

  3. an agreement relating to business

  6. become friendly with someone

Down

  1. very soon

  4. having another reason

  5. a place to get much information

Word Bank

business deal

ulterior motive

foreseeable future

make friends with

information highway

cosmetic surgery

Figure 1. An Example of a Puzzle Made with an Online Crossword Puzzle Generation Tool (Puzzlemaker, 2007)

Concentration With Lexical Bundles

- **Objective:** Students understand the word associations of lexical bundles.

- **Materials:** Flashcards and a lexical bundle wordlist.

- **Directions:** Write an incomplete lexical bundle on a flashcard. On another flashcard, write a word that would possibly complete the lexical bundle. Make at least five possible pairs. (Figure 2 shows an example of possible pairs.) Next, add a few cards that would not complete a lexical bundle. (Figure 3 shows examples of cards that would not complete a lexical bundle.) Place all cards upside down on a table. One student must choose two cards, and if they create a possible lexical bundle, the student keeps them and chooses again. If the cards do not make a correct lexical bundle, they are returned and the next student chooses. Students must try to remember where the cards are. The game ends when all possible matches are made.

- **Assessment:** The teacher should observe the game and ensure accurate matches. Students can write sentences using the newly learned lexical bundles.

3-D Tic-Tac-Toe With *Do* & *Make*

- **Objective:** Students understand the use of *do* and *make* in sentences.

- **Materials:** Blank white paper, a black marker, string, and a list of correct and incorrect teacher-generated statements using *do* and *make*. Correct example: *Joe **makes** a mistake. We **do** our chores.* Incorrect example: *I need to **do** an appointment for the dentist. She **makes** her homework.*

I don't know	if
I don't know	when
I don't know	how
I don't know	why
I don't know	who

Figure 2. Examples of Possible Lexical Bundles

Must
Can
Is

Figure 3. Examples of Cards that Do Not Complete Lexical Bundles

- **Directions:** Three students sit on the floor, three students sit in chairs behind them, and three students stand behind the chairs to create a 3-D grid of nine students. These students are called grid students (GS). Each grid student has a piece of paper with a black **X** on one side and a black **O** on the other side. The grid students hold the sheets of paper on their laps. Figure 4 shows the arrangement of people.

  Two other students are chosen to be contestants (**Cx** and **Co**). Each contestant has a piece of paper attached to string around his or her neck. One is the **X** contestant and the other is the **O** contestant. The contestants take turns fielding questions from the teacher. Once a question is asked, the contestant chooses one of the grid students to answer the question.

Teacher:	We need to *make* an appointment for the dentist.
GS:	Correct.

  The contestant says either "I agree" or "I disagree" with the grid student. Additional students in the classroom hold up an **Agree** or **Disagree** card to help the contestant decide.

Cx:	I agree.
Teacher:	Correct. A person *makes* an appointment, not *does* an appointment.

  When the contestant answers correctly, he gets his **X** on the 3-D grid on the GS who answered the question. If he answers incorrectly, his opponent gets an **O**. Whichever contestant gets three in a row first, wins the competition.

- **Assessment:** The teacher should observe and note the accuracy of the students' responses.

Assessment

These games provide a means for students to have fun practicing collocations in a fresh and nonthreatening medium, and they also provide teachers with rich,

GS	GS	GS
GS	GS	GS
GS	GS	GS

Cx   Co   Teacher

AS   AS   AS   AS   AS   AS

Figure 4. Arrangement of Grid Students, Contestants, Additional Students (AS), and Teacher

authentic student-generated material from which to assess each student's grasp of collocations. With innovative ways available to assess language performance, especially through electronic media such as digital recordings, video recordings, and Web cams, teachers must not overlook the value of self-assessment. Students often provide the best measure of their own grasp of a particular lesson. One way students can self-assess is to keep a daily log recording collocations they hear used and use themselves. Further, they could give themselves a point for each log entry, striving for 5 or 10 points a day as a measure of their success recognizing and using collocations. Additional daily self-assessment can be incorporated by having students rate their own success and articulate a justification. For more thorough self-assessments, students can videotape themselves. When they watch their own videotape, they can objectively see their verbal communication skills and their nonverbal communication skills as well.

Throughout each of these games—Collocation Cross, Concentration with Lexical Bundles, and 3-D Tic-Tac-Toe—the ESOL teacher should observe and record each student's grasp of the material. Reteaching and further practice may be needed to sharpen student proficiency recognizing and using these multiword structures. Extending these games by using the structures in written sentences and employing them in skits that students write and perform will display mastery of the collocation and can be maintained in a portfolio.

REFLECTIONS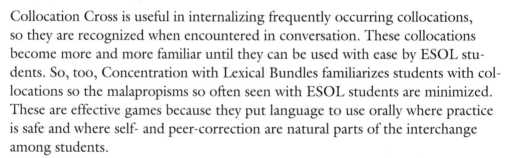

Collocation Cross is useful in internalizing frequently occurring collocations, so they are recognized when encountered in conversation. These collocations become more and more familiar until they can be used with ease by ESOL students. So, too, Concentration with Lexical Bundles familiarizes students with collocations so the malapropisms so often seen with ESOL students are minimized. These are effective games because they put language to use orally where practice is safe and where self- and peer-correction are natural parts of the interchange among students.

These games would present a challenge to the instructor were it not for the extensive body of corpus linguistics available in print and online that provides the raw material, examples, and frequency data to assist the teacher in deciding which collocations to use in the games. By examining the research at hand, which is so readily available, it is easy to see that word combinations with a high-frequency use record might be more useful for students to learn than rarely occurring combinations.

REFERENCES

Barlow, M., & Burdine, S. (2006). *Phrasal verbs: American English*. Houston, TX: Athelstan Publications.

Biber, D., Johansson, S., Leech, G., Conrad, S., & Finegan, E. (1999). *Longman grammar of spoken and written English*. Harlow, England: Pearson Education.

Hill, M., & Lewis, J. M. (1997). *LTP dictionary of selected collocations*. Hove, England: Language Teaching Publications.

Lewis, M. (2000). *Teaching collocations: Further development in the lexical approach*. Hove, England: Language Teaching Publications.

Puzzlemaker. (2007). Retrieved June 23, 2008, from http://puzzlemaker .discoveryeducation.com

---

Rachel Adams Goertel earned her master's degree in ESOL from the School for International Training. She teaches English and English as a second language (ESL) for the Elmira City School District and Mansfield University in Pennsylvania in the United States.

Carole Adams has taught ESL in the Rochester, New York, City School District, in the United States, for 20 years and has been an online instructor with Columbia University's Business English for Employees of Companies Abroad.

CHAPTER 13

Urban Myths: Fact or Fiction?

Timothy Doe

INTRODUCTION

High-frequency word lists (Coxhead, 2000; West, 1953) give teachers a wealth of resources for designing language activities specific to their students' vocabulary learning needs. Teaching vocabulary is not simply a matter of presenting a list of words with corresponding meanings, however, because students need to notice, retrieve, and creatively generate target vocabulary to have a word available for both receptive and productive use (Nation, 2001). Students can benefit from exposure to target vocabulary in both decontextualized and meaning-based activities, and these activities should be seen as complementary, not oppositional (Hunt & Beglar, 2005). I have used the concept of urban myths, unusual modern stories of reputable origin, to recycle target vocabulary to students in a communicative game where they must focus on language meaning rather than form. This game uses *read and retell* tasks that make the classroom a space in which students can encounter and use target vocabulary in a variety of different contexts. The overall objective is for students to guess which stories are true and which are urban myths through a process of reading, speaking, listening, and writing.

CONTEXT

I have used this game extensively with English as a foreign language (EFL) students in a vocabulary–reading fluency course, which is part of an intensive English program at the Tokyo campus of Temple University. The students, mostly young adults, have scores on the paper Test of English as a Foreign Language (TOEFL) ranging from 400 to 500, and many find that a lack of vocabulary knowledge is one of their biggest problems when confronted with academic text. This game can be a fun way to review and consolidate items from the sublists of Coxhead's (2000) Academic Word List (AWL). With a few modifications, I have also successfully used this game with Japanese high school students; providing the instructor selects appropriate texts, the game can be adapted for students at many levels of language proficiency.

CURRICULUM, TASKS, MATERIALS

First, the teacher needs to select the news items, which can be found at various Web sites. Stories need not be thematically linked; however, they need to contain the vocabulary items the teacher wishes to recycle (the teacher may also adapt the story and insert the desired vocabulary items, though). One particularly useful site is http://www.snopes.com, where one can find a selection of real and fabricated urban myths ideal for the game. The teacher will then need to simplify the text to an appropriate number of words and level of vocabulary. A helpful resource for controlling the text's level of difficulty in terms of coverage of high-frequency vocabulary is the Web site http://www.lextutor.ca, where texts can be cut and pasted into a vocabulary profiler. This site is particularly useful for ensuring that texts are not too difficult, given that unassisted learners need to know 98% of a text in order to gain comprehension (Hu & Nation, 2000). Although students are encouraged to negotiate the meaning of unknown words during the game, even two or three difficult items can noticeably slow down lower level groups. After selecting the texts and adjusting the vocabulary level, teachers should think of three or four open-ended discussion, or *signpost*, questions (i.e., see Nuttall, 1996) and insert them below the story. These questions will allow students to check whether they have noticed the most important events in the text. Once a set of suitable texts has been prepared, the game can be played. Briefly, the objectives of the game are for students to (a) read and summarize a short news item in groups, (b) exchange these items with other groups, (c) rewrite an urban myth that they have listened to, and (d) decide which items are factual and which are fictitious.

Procedures

I divide a class of 12–20 students into four groups (A, B, C, and D), ideally with 4 students in each group. For clarity purposes, these original groupings shall be referred to as *home groups*. Each group receives a different story, two of them being factual and two of them being fictitious. The game has four main steps:

1. (10–15 minutes) Each group receives its urban myth, and the students get small cards for writing their retell notes. Students read their story at least two times; individually and together as a group. Groups then go through the open-ended discussion questions. As students discuss these, the teacher moves from group to group, giving assistance where necessary. Each group decides on a title for its story and makes a list of keywords on the retell note card, allowing the members to convey the story without access to it.

2. (10–15 minutes) The teacher collects the stories and makes new groups. Half of the members of each group exchange places with half from another group. For example, half of group A moves to group B's area,

being replaced by half of group B. The newly formed groups begin to exchange their stories using their retell cards as needed. Students may take notes on the reverse side of their retell note card while they listen, and should be encouraged to ask questions for clarification and check their understanding by retelling the story they are listening to.

3. (10–15 minutes) The home groups reconvene and take a short amount of time to rewrite on the whiteboard the urban myths they have heard. Once the texts have been reconstructed, the groups evaluate their approximation to the originals on a scale of 1–4. They must tell the writers what major points were missed and whether any other errors were made.

4. Finally, home groups decide which stories are factual and which are mythical, and the teacher reveals the true nature of each story. Each home group receives 1 point for a correct answer, and the team with the most points wins. With such a narrow range of possible scores (0–4), there is often a tie, and students do not tend to pay much attention to who has won or lost. A good way to end the game is to have groups discuss the factors that led to their conclusions about each story.

Variations

Generally, I have found that my higher level students (with TOEFL scores just under 500), can deal with a 200–300-word text and complete the game within 1 hour, while 100-word texts are more suitable for lower-level students. Although the objective of the game is for students to focus on target vocabulary, it also can be adapted to develop language fluency. Nation (2001) describes fluency activities as those that contain language well within students' abilities. Shorter texts may be more suitable for these activities because learners will not have as much unfamiliar content to process. This lack of unfamiliar content allows students to attempt to increase the speed with which they complete the game's various steps, potentially developing their language fluency.

For more advanced classes, a variation I have used is limiting the retelling groups to pairs in step 2. Students then rewrite their stories individually on paper, rather than in groups on the board. Each group compares its four versions of the story and gives a "best reteller" award to the student who has provided the clearest and most detailed information.

A point to consider carefully when selecting or editing the texts is the amount of cultural knowledge readers must have. Texts can be greatly simplified by replacing terms specific to one culture with more general ones. For example *important politician* is much less demanding than *senator* in the EFL classes I teach in Japan.

In terms of vocabulary language learning, this game works well when the texts cover items that have been studied previously in decontextualized activities. Most students already have a sense of the words' general meanings. Both language-focused and fluency-based activities are very easy to include as follow-up tasks after the game is completed (see sample activities in Appendix A and Appendix B).

REFLECTIONS

Because urban myths are offbeat and unusual, they present a motivating and enjoyable way for students to review previously learned vocabulary. During the game, it is common to see students negotiating the meaning of target words, paying attention to previously learned items, and trying to see how these words fit in different contexts. Students also focus attention on understanding the causes of the events in the text. Negotiation of meaning is one of the optimal conditions for acquisition to take place in the language classroom (Lee, 2000) and this game gives students ample opportunities for doing so, making it particularly useful for groups of mixed levels. The game is also beneficial because students must integrate the four main language skills to complete the tasks, which resembles authentic language interaction and also can be highly motivating (Oxford, 2001).

REFERENCES

Coxhead, A. (2000). A new academic word list. *TESOL Quarterly, 34*, 213–238.

Hu, M., & Nation, P. (2000). Unknown vocabulary density and reading comprehension. *Reading in a Foreign Language, 13*(1), 403–430.

Hunt, A., & Beglar, P. (2005). A framework for developing EFL reading vocabulary. *Reading in a Foreign Language, 17*(1), 23–59.

Lee, J. (2000). *Tasks and communicating in language classrooms.* Boston: McGraw Hill.

Nation, I. S. P. (2001). *Learning vocabulary in another language.* Cambridge: Cambridge University Press.

Nuttall, C. (1996). *Teaching reading skills in a foreign language* (3rd ed.). Oxford, England: Heinemann.

Oxford, R. (2001). Integrated skills in the ESL/EFL classroom. *ESL Magazine, 6*(1), 18–20.

West, M. (1953). *A general service list of English words.* London: Longman Green.

Timothy Doe, from New Zealand, has a master's degree in teaching English to speakers of other languages (TESOL) from Temple University Japan, where he teaches. His main interests include content-based instruction and metaphor instruction for second-language learners.

APPENDIX A: SAMPLE URBAN MYTHS

Target vocabulary is bold in these texts.

(a) An American man recently lost $6,000. Police **authorities** said he was in a parking lot **area** of a **department** store when he was **approached** by a woman, who told him that she had $8,000 in cash, but did not like the numbers on the money because she thought that they were unlucky. She asked the man to go to his bank with her, take out $6,000, and give it to her, and then she would give him $8,000. The man went to the bank, took out $6,000, and gave it to the woman, but she quickly ran away without giving him anything. The man was not hurt, but he was angry about being "**treated** like a fool." The police gave the man some advice: "Ask yourself, why would someone give you money for nothing?" (Fictitious)

Discussion Questions:

1. Do you think the woman really thought her money was unlucky?

2. Why do you think the man agreed to exchange the money with the woman?

(b) Many people **treat** their pets like children, but a woman from a suburban **area** of Houston is in trouble after calling 911 and saying that her "baby," which was really a cat named Baby, was trapped in a sewer. The woman called the Houston Fire **Department** three times saying that her cat was stuck in the sewer, said police **authorities**. On the fourth call, the woman said her 2-year-old baby was trapped in the sewer. The firefighters thought they were going to find a child but **rescued** the cat from the sewer anyway. **Authorities** gave the woman a $500 fine for making a false report. Members of the woman's family had tried to **approach** the cat themselves before calling for help, but the sewer proved too dangerous, they reported. (Factual)

Discussion Questions:

1. Why do you think the woman had to call the fire department four times?

2. Do you think the woman intended for the firefighters to believe there was a human baby in the sewer?

APPENDIX B: FOLLOW-UP ACTIVITIES

(a) Vocabulary categorization activity

Today's texts contain the following six high-frequency words:

authorities   department   treat   rescue   approach   area

With your partners, group the words into the two boxes below. You can group the words in any way you can think of (e.g., the meanings of the words, the parts of speech to which they belong, or any other connection that you can explain). Create a title that explains the connections you found between each group of words. Finally, compare your work with another group.

1	2

(b) Vocabulary connection activity

With a partner, use the remaining high-frequency words from the categorization activity to make a story. You can use the words in any order you choose. Once you have made your story, change partners and exchange ideas.

Start: Authority

_____

_____

_____

_____

Finish: Treat

(c) Fluency activity

Choose one topic from today's texts and write as much as you can.

1. You are the woman in the parking lot. Why did you steal $6,000 from the man? What are you going to do with the money?

2. You are Baby's owner who called the fire department. You do not have the $500 to pay the fine. Write a letter explaining your mistake and why you think you should not have to pay.

CHAPTER 14

Speaking Through Art

Barnaby Ralph

Our interpretation is more important than what we are looking at. Just because the painting looks like something does not mean that it is successful. (Lynch, 2000, p.17)

INTRODUCTION

When teaching English to speakers of other languages, visual aids are an important part of the process. The association of ideas with pictures is a long-standing and reliable technique to aid vocabulary retention (O'Brien, 1989). This association is generally, however, based on the primary or literal level of perception. To give a simple example, the student is shown a picture of a dog and associates it with the word *dog*. To engage the secondary or interpretive level, something more than basic visual aids is required.

In essence, the aim of the activities described here is to give English as a second language (ESL) students an opportunity to use words that they already know to express complex ideas, as well as to build a methodology for the intellectual examination of a topic to approach subject analysis within a clearly structured framework. Imagery, to paraphrase Fleckenstein (1996), is thus able to compensate for the limitations of language. In addition, students will have an opportunity to learn and practice some new topic-based vocabulary and, at the same time, they are likely to learn something new about art by using terms they already know in English, their target language. This, in turn, is an aid in the ongoing process of cultural contextualization that is a useful, if often neglected, aspect of effective language acquisition and usage (Muldoon, 1994).

Finally, the interpretive aspect of these activities allows students to engage with art emotionally. There are no right or wrong answers to the questions posed, which places greater value on students' opinions and can help build confidence and encourage lively debate, especially if the teacher is careful not to be overtly partisan. It has been noted that speakers of conversational English can feel intimidated by the language of art (Murry, 2006); thus, the methods here are designed to introduce vocabulary and content in as nonjudgmental a way possible.

CONTEXT

The activities presented here were designed for 1st- and 2nd-year Japanese university students, usually between 18 and 20 years old, and have proven successful in that context. In addition, the activities have been employed with adult English as a foreign language (EFL) students as part of an ongoing 2-month course of integrated, intensive study. As well as proving entertaining, they demonstrated to the students that learning new ways to express ideas with familiar vocabulary is just as useful as learning new words. The former aids in an understanding of nuance and idiom, two difficult areas for nonnative speakers of any language.

Exploring Western painting within Japanese institutions was one concern when initially setting up the activity. This concern proved to be a nonissue. Students were, for the most part, familiar with well-known works such as Van Gogh's *Sunflowers*. In addition, in the larger classes, usually three or four students had a more advanced knowledge of art, including some familiarity with major artistic movements and artists. Interpretive aspects of the discussion are not culturally specific, and teachers can base activities on works of art from any culture. It often is useful to choose works created within the cultural heritage of the students in class. Applying a target language to these works can challenge learners to think in new ways, different from their responses in their native language.

In general, students of different levels all were able to find something useful in this activity. Learners included low-intermediate-level English speakers to fairly advanced college-level students. I have not tried this activity with senior high school students, but I see no reason why it could not be successful in that context.

CURRICULUM, TASKS, MATERIALS

Getting Started

To prepare for this activity, teachers need the following materials:

- handouts (see Appendix), including reproductions of several paintings (10 has proven to be an effective number) for the ranking activity (see *Procedures* section), and lists of appropriate adjectives

- a way to display paintings for the whole class to see, such as slides, overheads, or Microsoft PowerPoint

Teacher Preparation

Handouts containing around 10 thumbnail reproductions of paintings for student reference should be prepared. Each painting should have a space next to it for a ranking number and an adjective. The paintings also can be displayed on an overhead projector or Microsoft PowerPoint slide in full color, so students can see the details more clearly.

Any painting can be chosen, but the teacher should be aware of the background and interpretive context for each, and also should choose from a broad range of styles. In the original version of this activity, paintings were selected for variety in genre, period, and narrative elements. Some were well known to students, but many were not. I used the following 10 works of art for the ranking activity:

- Kasimir Malevich: *Black Square* (1913)

- Eugene Delacroix: *Liberty Guiding the People* (1830)

- Edward Munch: *The Scream* (1893)

- Pablo Picasso: *Still Life With Guitar* (1922)

- Vincent Van Gogh: *Sunflowers* (1888)

- Pierre August Renoir: *Luncheon of the Boating Party* (1881)

- Rene Magritte: *Son of Man* (1964)

- Giuseppe Archimboldo: *Spring* (1573)

- Jean-Antoine Watteau: *Le Faux Pas* (c. 1717)

- Jan Vermeer: *Girl with a Pearl Earring* (1665–1666)

Follow-up materials may include a list of Web sites that display chosen paintings with historical backgrounds and interpretive notes, such as http://www.abcgallery.com, http://www.ibiblio.org/wm/paint, and http://www.artcyclopedia.com. In addition, for homework students can answer questions about a painting or an artist using only English Web resources, such as Wikipedia, http://en.wikipedia.org/wiki/Main_Page.

The session can take between 60 and 120 minutes, depending on the extent and scope of discussion allowed and the activities chosen or omitted. Originally, it was designed as a 90-minute class. It can be broken down into the following broad sections:

1. Ranking Activity and Discussion

2. Emotions

3. Visual Elements

4. Styles

5. Guess the Story

6. Descriptive Writing Task and Discussion

7. Final Discussion

Procedures

The stages have been designed to build upon each other, leading toward an independent interpretive writing activity and discussion. In general, students tend to engage with this material because one of the teacher's primary tasks throughout is to reiterate the point that there are no right or wrong answers and that everybody's opinion is equally valid. This tends to give students more confidence in expressing their opinions.

Working in pairs is effective for smaller classes (containing up to 10 or so students), and small groups are more useful for larger classes. For instance, in a class of 30 students, 6 groups of 5 students works well. An odd number of participants also means that it is more difficult for each small group to split down the middle.

Section 1: Ranking Activity and Discussion

After distributing the handouts, draw students' attention to the small reproductions of the paintings. Students have 5 minutes to complete the first task. They must first rank the paintings from 1–10, with 1 being their favorite and 10 their least favorite. Ranking enforces the importance of their opinion at the outset. Then, they must choose one adjective from the descriptive words list for each painting. If they are not sure of the meaning of a word, they can ask their group members or the teacher, or consult a dictionary. At this time, the teacher will display the large, full-color versions of the paintings using Microsoft PowerPoint or some other method.

The teacher next tallies up the numbers from each group and assigns each painting a class ranking accordingly. Thus, in a class of 20 students, the best possible mark a painting could receive would be 20 (where everyone agreed that it is number 1) and the worst would be 200. Then each painting is discussed. Groups can elect a spokesperson to engage in dialogue with the teacher as to how they feel about each one. This is a good opportunity to explain briefly the stories, motivation, or history of each painting, along with some introductory ideas about art interpretation. Obviously, this background information should be pitched at the appropriate level for the students and should not take up too much class time.

After the discussion, students are asked to rank the paintings again, based on their new perceptions. Results are compared again and are generally very different from the first set, especially regarding modern art. For example, the handout used in initial versions of this activity starts with Kazimir Malevich's *Black Square* as the first painting. This work usually is ranked last initially, but it tends to move up to second or third position after discussion in class, perhaps because students are, at first, unfamiliar with the rationale behind works of this type. Similarly, Antoine Watteau's *Le Faux Pas* tends to rank poorly at first because it is confusing and the characters' actions somewhat obscure. Once the teacher explains the story behind this work, however, it usually moves to a higher spot. Table 1 is based on data gathered from five different classes of varying size. Definite trends were noticeable in both initial preference and perception, as well as similar changes in each sample group.

I often use this data at the end of this activity, comparing class results to the mean. It can be interesting for students to see their personal tastes and trends within the class in the context of a wider sample group. It should be stressed again here to the students that, just because the information comes from many people, answers are not better or worse if they are more or less common in the wider sample. Discussing this data can be a starting point for further discussions on culture, aesthetics, and popular perceptions.

Sections 2–4: Emotions, Visual Elements, and Styles

The next three vocabulary-building exercises work in the same way as each other, and are competitive. Using overhead transparencies or Microsoft PowerPoint slides, the groups view a series of paintings, sketches, and sculptures (different from those used in the initial ranking activity) that represent different emotions, visual elements, and styles. The vocabulary lists on the handout—titled "Emotions," "Visual Elements," and "Styles"—should correspond to the first few works of art in each group. The teacher can choose words to suit the works but should reflect the level of the class. Corpus lists can be useful for deciding on

Table 1. Before and After Rankings

Painting Title	Overall Rank	
	Before	After
Black Square	10	2
Liberty Guiding the People	2	5
The Scream	6	7
Still Life With Guitar	5	6
Sunflowers	3	9
Luncheon of the Boating Party	1	1
Son of Man	9	8
Spring	8	10
Le Faux Pas	7	3
Girl With a Pearl Earring	4	4

the suitability of a word. Then the students have to use their own language to describe the relevant elements. Scoring is set up in the following way:

- a single word (e.g., *passionate*) = 0 points

- a list word in a sentence that matches the painting (e.g., *She looks passionate.*) = 1 point

- a nonlist word in a sentence that matches the painting (e.g., *She looks desirous.*) = 2 points

- giving an appropriate reason why the adjective applies (e.g., *He is scared because the other man is going to hit him.*) = +1 point

Because it is more difficult for students to make sentences about styles and visual elements, the section on emotion is also a warm-up activity.

A Microsoft PowerPoint presentation I used in previous versions of this activity showed pictures associated first with listed words and then moved to nonlisted words to help students in the transition from substitution of handout vocabulary to the employment of a wider variety of terms. It is best to ask groups to rotate the role of spokesperson, so everybody has opportunities to speak in class.

Section 5: Guess the Story

In the next component of the activity, a new series of paintings is shown on the screen. Groups are given 5 minutes to guess what is happening and make a story to match, as well as to brainstorm as much as they can about the painting. Then, a spokesperson stands up and offers the group's ideas to the class. The teacher finishes by explaining the context and the artist's idea in the painting. There is, again, a competitive element here, as the teacher chooses the best group answer and awards points for creativity (0–5), use of the new vocabulary choices from the list (1 point for each new vocabulary word used correctly), and clarity (0–5). Points are not awarded for guessing the story correctly, however, because of the underlying principle that individual perceptions of art all are equally valid.

At the end, overall points are tallied, and a winning group is selected. Prizes can be awarded if appropriate, although this practice depends on the class dynamics and the teacher's preference.

Section 6: Descriptive Writing Task and Discussion

After the Guess the Story activity, the teacher displays a painting that matches the description in the handouts. An example of such a description, aimed at a low to midlevel group of students, is in the handout template (see Appendix). Note that this description relies on simple connecting phrases and vocabulary drawn primarily from the adjective banks on the handout. With more advanced groups, the sample should be altered appropriately. This should be an opportunity for students to use the new vocabulary and ideas explored in the session. They look at the painting, read the sample description, and use it as a basis for their own interpretation of another work, which is displayed immediately afterward. It is best if this subsequent painting is a work of a different era and style from that used as an example. These descriptions can be collected by the teacher at the end of the session and used as an assessment tool, if desired.

As a guide, following are two examples of painting analyses from actual classes. The first is by a low-intermediate-level English student and the second is by a high-intermediate-level English student.

> **Example One:** Caravaggio's *Judith Beheading Holofernes*
>
> This painting is scary because the characters are very violence [*sic*]. There is a lot of darkness and the faces show many details. It is historical and shows a man's head being cut off.

> **Example Two:** Dali's *Sleep*
>
> In this painting, the main character is 'Sleep.' The artist has painted him as a large, soft figure who is held up by sticks. This makes him look heavier than if he was painted resting on the ground. Because a sleeping figure does not use his body, the artist made this very small and made the head very large. It is a surrealist painting and makes good use of color and light. There are not many details apart from the central figure, which makes it stronger.

Note that, in the first example, the student follows the format of the handout example almost exactly, but the second student departs from the formula and expands on some points.

Section 7: Final Discussion

Finally, there is a group discussion on a question related to art. In the past, this discussion has been based on reactions to the statement, "Modern art is all rubbish. Only old paintings are any good," but it could be anything that the teacher finds relevant to the topic at hand. The teacher can move between groups, listening and commenting. As mentioned, the Descriptive Writing Task can be collected and assessed by the teacher at the end of class. It could also be assigned as homework if there are time constraints.

Caveats

It is important to consider the age and cultural background of students when selecting works. Many paintings contain nudity, sexuality, and violence, which may or may not be appropriate for a given situation or group of students. Generally speaking, teachers are advised to use their own judgment on this point, but it is better to err on the side of caution.

Any paintings can be used, providing that there is a sufficient variety of styles and thematic material. They should be works with which the teacher is familiar, and it is important to be aware of dates, styles, and the major elements of the work. The teacher should be able to interpret based on both opinion and contextual knowledge.

Assessment

During small-group discussion times, the teacher's role is to circulate, listen to different opinions, facilitate conversation by adding suggestions or comments, and evaluate the contribution of each student to the group. Requiring small groups to rotate their spokespeople ensures that every student has a chance to speak in front of the class and also allows the teacher to assess fluency and the ability to offer an effective précis of a group consensus—or lack thereof.

As mentioned previously, the Descriptive Writing Task can be collected and assessed. It is important to base assessment of this activity on the student's use of English, not the opinions expressed, although it can be good to offer positive comments on the latter if a point is made particularly well. The teacher should avoid telling any student that an opinion or interpretation is wrong.

Depending on students' Internet access, additional homework or follow-up activities can be assigned using, for example, the Web sites mentioned in the *Getting Started* section. Alternatively, the teacher could create a short reading list of books about art from the university library (or similar resource) and assign a homework activity based on this list. I often assign a question or series of questions about either specific works of art or general periods and ask students to write responses of appropriate length. For example, a recent homework assignment given to high-intermediate students asked for a response of 150–200 words to each of the following two questions:

Homework Assignment

1. Please choose one of the periods or styles discussed today and explain what you think are its main characteristics.

2. Who is an important artist from this period or working in this style? How do you feel about his work?

REFLECTIONS

These activities have proven successful in the classroom for several reasons. First, students seem to enjoy the fact that their opinions all carry equal weight, regardless of background or relative English ability. Second, students can choose to use as much or as little new vocabulary as they wish. The general vocabulary of the average 1st-year university student is more than equal to the task of offering an opinion on a work of art. Students often are surprised to find that this is the case and, rather than this leading to them simply taking the easy option, such encouragement actually serves to make them more interested in trying to use new, related language.

Third, understanding both nuance and idiom is built through these activities. By using language to express nonliteral ideas, students connect with subtext and have to deal with metaphor in a practical, visual way. They discover that they are able to express complex ideas through simple language, which, in turn, makes them more able to understand how a technical terminological set can be derived and employed effectively.

Finally, these activities allow students to relate to aesthetics. The ideas expressed through art often transcend cultural boundaries, which can help build confidence in speakers for whom English is not their first language (Brew, 2004). The unique aspect of these activities is in the layered use of language and meaning and in the employment of visual aids as nonliteral, rather than purely literal, educative devices.

REFERENCES

Brew, C.A. (2004). Art breaks the language barrier. *Arts and Activities, 134*(5), 22.

Fleckenstein, K. S. (1996). Images, words, and narrative epistemology. *College English, 58*(8), 914–934.

Hausman, C. R. (1989). *Metaphor and art: Interactionism and reference in the verbal and nonverbal arts.* Cambridge: Cambridge University Press.

Lynch, T. (2000). *Tom Lynch's watercolor secrets: A master painter reveals his strategies for success.* Cincinnati, OH: North Light Books.

Muldoon, T. M. (1994). *Language acquisition of ESL students in a discipline-based art education classroom using collaborative learning and whole language.* (Master's thesis, University of North Texas, 1994). UMI No. AAT 1357160

Murry, K. (2006). Senior visual art students' experiences of appraising. *Queensland Art Teachers Association Journal, 1*(1), 28–29.

O'Brien, L. (1989). Learning styles: Make the student aware. *NASSP Bulletin, 73*(519), 85–89.

Additional Resources

Berger, J. (1972). *Ways of seeing.* Harmondsworth, England: Penguin.

Carr-Gomm, S. (1995). *The dictionary of symbols in art.* Carlton, Australia: CIS Cardigan Street Publishers.

Duro, P., & Greenhalgh, M. P. (1992). *Essential art history.* London: Bloomsbury.

Barnaby Ralph is a graduate of the University of Adelaide and the Queensland Conservatorium of Music, both in Australia. He lectures at Aoyama Gakuin University in Tokyo, Japan, and also is active as a writer and professional classical musician. His recordings have been released worldwide by Naxos. Most recently, he completed his Doctor of Philosophy through the University of Queensland.

APPENDIX: TALKING ABOUT ART HANDOUT TEMPLATE

Warm-Up Activity: Please rank the following paintings from 1–10 (1=best, 10=worst). Then, choose a word from list 1 (descriptive words) that you think describes each painting. You may choose a word more than once. There is no correct answer, just your opinion!

List 1: Descriptive Words	Adjective Bank: Emotions	Adjective Bank: Visual Elements	Adjective Bank: Styles
beautiful	loving	colorful	Modern
clever	hateful	monochrome	Baroque
complex	confused	light	Classical
good	lucid	dark	Allegorical
funny	fearful or frightened	cluttered or crowded	Surrealist
structured	joyful	sparse	Cubist
abstract	passionate	detailed	Art Deco
powerful	thoughtful	unfocussed	Pre-Raphaelite
dramatic	happy	bold	Realistic
evocative	sad	gentle	Abstract
ugly	hopeful	beautiful	Historical
stupid	despairing	ugly	Still-life
simple	excited		
bad	bored		
boring	angry		
thoughtless	amused		
realistic			
meaningless			
dull			
passionless			

Descriptive Activity

Example: *This painting is <u>interesting</u> because the <u>colors</u> are very <u>beautiful</u>. There is a lot of <u>contrast between light and dark</u> and the <u>people in the painting show different emotions</u>. It is <u>historical</u> and shows <u>some sort of battle</u>.*

This painting is _____ (good/bad/interesting/dull/own choice) because . . .

CHAPTER 15

Define Your Terms

Michael Shehane and Michael Moraga

INTRODUCTION

Define Your Terms provides students with the opportunity to practice phrases—
or chunks of language—commonly used when uttering definitions (i.e., *It's a
kind of . . . It's when . . . It's a place where you . . .*), not only to define concrete
terms such as *pineapple*, *lecture*, and *classroom*, but also to express their personal
understandings of abstract words such as *marriage*, *culture*, and *education*. The
game also helps build student awareness of the academic responsibility to explicitly define one's terms when reasoning. Academic writing courses train students
to pay special attention to word choice and not assume that readers will share the
same word definitions. Therefore, Define Your Terms brings to light this point in
an authentic, lively, and interactive manner.

In the context of academic instruction, this game should be introduced early
in the semester to acquaint the students with the phrases needed to define terms.
Playing the game in the first month of the course also allows the instructor to
recycle the phrases throughout the rest of the semester. Define Your Terms can
be incorporated easily into a reading unit that encourages students to use the
phrases to guess unfamiliar words from context and talk about their guesses
with classmates: "I think *rush* is when you walk really fast." "What do you think
rush means?" In a writing unit, Define Your Terms encourages students to use
the phrases when defining terms they feel might be unfamiliar to their readers
and, in doing so, they make their ideas clearer. For example, one student of ours
wrote, "I don't like *daikon*. Do you know *daikon*? *Daikon* is a kind of radish from
Japan."

CONTEXT

Although it is specifically designed for use in English for academic purposes
(EAP) courses, Define Your Terms is suitable for any teaching context and is
recommend for intermediate levels and up. The game is valuable for students who
need practical phrases for defining concrete and abstract ideas in English. In our

125

experience, the students who perceive the game as especially helpful in their language development have been in English as a second language (ESL) and English as a foreign language (EFL) contexts at preuniversity and university levels. Outside the EAP context, we believe this game would benefit students such as those in adult community ESL, workplace ESL–EFL, and EFL conversation classes.

Define Your Terms assumes students can categorize, an academic skill for characterizing, labeling, and classifying ideas. For example, "It's an *animal* from Antarctica." Or, "It's a way to move inside a pool." Therefore, we recommend that teachers address this skill before playing the game.

Students who already have a good command of the language might find Define Your Terms a fun and active way to expand their vocabulary. For lower level students, this game might provide a spirited way to introduce, practice, and reinforce categorization skills.

CURRICULUM, TASKS, MATERIALS

The following is a 90-minute lesson planned around the Define Your Terms game. Before the lesson begins, the teacher should prepare the following items:

- a list of about 10 words photocopied onto a piece of paper (see Appendix for possible choices)

- 40–50 slips of blank paper

- a watch to keep time

- a bag or hat to collect the slips of paper

First, inductively introduce the phrases commonly used to give a definition either orally or written through question and answer. For example, give students the sentence, *It's a fruit from Hawaii.* Students try to guess the answer (*pineapple*). Next, explicitly draw students' attention to similar phrases used to give a definition (see Appendix). We recommend putting these phrases up on the blackboard to showcase them as the focus of the game. Then, build the rationale for learning and practicing the phrases.

One way to build rationale for the phrases is to elicit from students the purpose for learning the phrases. First, start by asking a question like "Where can a person hear the phrases *It's a kind of . . .* and *It's a place where . . .* ?" Look for the responses "in school" or "in the classroom." Then follow up with questions such as "Who typically uses these phrases?" and "Why do people use these phrases?" Look for responses that explain how teachers and students might use these phrases in their speech because articulating ideas as clearly as possible is conducive to successful learning. These questions build rationale that language learners should learn and incorporate the phrases into their everyday speech because these phrases will help them express their ideas more clearly and, therefore, maximize their learning potential at school.

After building the rationale, we suggest that pairs of students practice the phrases in an information-gap activity. This practice is done by giving each student the same list of terms, (e.g., *nap, doctor, rose, syllabus, lecture*). These words should be terms the students are familiar with. They should not be too difficult; otherwise, the vocabulary will distract the students from learning the phrases. Student A chooses a term from the list and then defines it using the appropriate phrase from the blackboard. Student B guesses the term from the list. For example, Student A says, "It's a kind of flower," and Student B looks at the list of possible answers, and says, "It's a rose."

With this initial practice, the students are now ready to play Define Your Terms as an entire class. The concept of the game is similar to *Taboo*, a board game in which team members guess terms from players' extemporaneously generated definitions. Follow these steps to play the game:

1. The teacher divides the class into teams of three to four students. Just for fun, each team can decide on a team name.

2. The teacher passes out 8–10 slips of paper to each team.

3. Together, the team writes one term on each slip of paper. (They can choose these terms at random, or they can be connected to the current curriculum or from a vocabulary list.) If the teacher wishes to make the game less challenging, he can request that the teams also write their words on the board.

4. All the slips of paper are then collected by the teacher in a bag or hat.

5. After the order of teams is determined, the teacher briefly reminds the students of the phrases written on the blackboard and that they can refer back to them throughout the game. This reminder will not only help the students' possible stage fright but also reinforce accurate use of the phrases.

6. In front of the class, a person from the first team pulls a single term out of the bag or hat. He has 20 seconds to decide how to best define the term and then speaks.

7. The student's teammates attempt to guess the word within a 1-minute time limit. If they guess the term successfully, the team scores a point. If the team does not guess the word, then opposing teams have a chance to guess the term within 30 seconds and win an extra point.

8. The team that acquires the most points wins. We do not recommend the use of gestures and drawings because these compensation strategies might obscure the objective of the game: the use of the phrases.

REFLECTIONS

We find that the game is most successful when we have given due attention to the rationale for the game. Nevertheless, we find that students frequently drop the phrases or chunks of language and try to communicate their meaning without the use of the complete phrase. For example, instead of saying, "It's a fruit from Hawaii," the student will say, "Fruit! Hawaii!" or "It fruit from Hawaii." The phrases are taught as chunks of language rather than from the bottom up; that is, instead of breaking them down into smaller grammatical parts, they are introduced as fixed expressions, or sentence frames (Nattinger, 1980). For example, "It's a . . ." is usually followed by an entity or thing while "It's a way to . . ." is followed by an action. In some cases, students may become hazy about the purpose of the phrases and, consequently, omit the chunks of language from their utterances. Moreover, students may simply get caught up in the moment of the game and lose focus on the objective of the game, to practice using the phrases. In either case, we have found that repetition of the rationale and focused practice of the phrases yield the most success.

The instructor may choose to explicitly address the grammar in follow-up activities. To do this, the teacher can note the students' grammar mistakes during the game. Then, if a common grammar mistake presents itself, the teacher can elicit the correction from the students. If there is a common error, potentially the students will need to review the grammar point and then revisit the grammar point in the context of the phrases used to give definitions.

Because the game merely introduces the phrases, we recommend that teachers continue to recycle these phrases and reinforce their use throughout the rest of the semester by writing them on the board when appropriate and incorporating them into new contexts. In addition, teachers can use the game to recycle previously taught vocabulary. The more opportunities the students have to hear and use the vocabulary through receptive and/or productive retrieval, the more likely they will learn the vocabulary (Joe, Nation, & Newton, 1996; Nagy, 1988).

For more information on explicitly teaching the predictable chunks of language often heard during classroom events, we recommend reading Sherak and Sarosy's 2002 article "Empowering Students by Teaching the Language of the Classroom." In this article, the authors provide reasons that teaching "classroom language" can facilitate classroom learning tasks and encourage critical thinking.

By playing Define Your Terms and then recycling the phrases in postlessons, we have observed students incorporating the phrases into their everyday language and written work. This usage demonstrates that our learning objectives have been met. The students appreciate how the phrases ensure clearer and more effective communication. As a final point, we recommend using a time clock with an alarm to keep the game moving and add extra excitement.

ACKNOWLEDGMENT

We would like to thank Kathy Sherak and Peg Sarosy at the American Language Institute, San Francisco, for their training and inspiration for writing this article.

REFERENCES

Joe, A., Nation, P., & Newton, J. (1996). Vocabulary learning and speaking activities. *English Teaching Forum, 34*(1), 2–7. Retrieved November 1, 2007, from http://exchanges.state.gov/forum/vols/vol34/no1/p2.htm

Nagy, W. E. (1988). *Teaching vocabulary to improve reading comprehension.* Newark, DE: International Reading Association.

Nattinger, J. (1980). A lexical phrase grammar for ESL. *TESOL Quarterly, 14,* 337–344.

Sarosy, P., & Sherak, K. (2002). Empowering students by teaching the language of the classroom. *CATESOL Journal, 14*(1), 271–281.

Michael Shehane graduated with a master's degree from the TESOL Program at San Francisco State University (SFSU), in the United States. He is a former teacher at SFSU's American Language Institute and a professor at Kansai Gaidai University in Osaka, Japan.

Michael Moraga, a graduate of San Francisco State University, has taught ESL and English as an international language for a variety of purposes in Japan, Spain, and San Francisco. From 2003 to 2005, he served as an English Language Fellow at Anadolu University in Turkey and Ateneo de Manila University in the Philippines.

APPENDIX: PHRASES AND WORDS

Phrases	Example Sentence
1. It means _____.	It means a long, instructive talk.
2. It's a _____.	It's an animal from Antarctica.
3. It's a kind of _____.	It's a kind of flower.
4. It's a kind of _____ that _____.	It's a kind of computer that talks.
5. It's the same as _____.	It's the same as small.
6. It's kind of like _____.	It's kind of like running.
7. It's like when _____.	It's like when two people talk to each other.
8. It's a person who _____.	It's a person who lives in Hollywood.
9. It's a place where you _____.	It's a place where you rent DVDs.
10. It's a way to _____.	It's a way to walk.
11. It's when you _____.	It's when you go somewhere very fast.

Answers: **1.** lecture **2.** a penguin **3.** a rose **4.** a robot **5.** tiny, little **6.** jogging **7.** a conversation **8.** a movie star **9.** a store/a shop **10.** slowly, quickly **11.** rush

PART 1: Skills Focus

D. Grammar

CHAPTER 16

Treasure Hunting With Grammar

Xiao Lan Curdt-Christiansen

INTRODUCTION

When Ms. Lee announces, at the beginning of her English class, that today is treasure hunt day, everyone is thrilled and excited, and many children clap their hands. Ms. Lee hands out the clues after the children in the class have been divided into four color-coded groups—red, green, yellow, and blue. Twenty minutes later, when the treasures have been found, a child from each group writes the clues on the blackboard and Ms. Lee begins an analysis of the grammatical features of each clue.

In *Mind in Society*, Vygotsky (1978) remarks that "play contains all the developmental tendencies in a condensed form and is itself a major source of development" (p. 102). This remark reflects the common experience that when something is fun, it is easy to learn, and emphasizes that there are enjoyable and affective ways of introducing children to reading and writing. Children's games can be designed and adjusted to facilitate learning as well as their inherent benefits of vigor, intensity, concentration, and problem solving. But how can the dramatic and social aspects of games and play contribute to learning? How does learning take place under such playful conditions? How can children's pleasure be harnessed to benefit their understanding of grammatical rules?

This chapter explores the role of play in language development in a group of Singaporean English as a second language (ESL) third-grade students. Specifically, it looks at how the game Treasure Hunting With Grammar can be used to teach children grammatical items such as prepositions, passive voice, past tense, and comparative and superlative of adjectives. Viewing languages and literacies as intertwined, mediated, sociocultural phenomena, this chapter shows how games can be used to help children discover that reading and writing can be useful and functional, and that the grammatical rules are meaningful in authentic situations. The chapter further describes how children become language researchers when they are given the opportunity to enjoy the process of understanding how language works in the world.

Rationale

Games play an important role in children's language development with regard to both their first and second languages (Pelligrini & Galda, 2000; Wright, Betteridge, & Buckby, 2006). Games as language learning activities can be entertaining and engaging as well as challenging. The functions of games in language development are affective, cognitive, and social because children focus on solving problems, negotiating meanings, constructing products, and building arguments (Roskos & Christie, 2000).

Games as Entertainment

Games as engaging learning tools are strongly connected to motivation and interest (Guthrie & Knowles, 2001). Motivation refers to the desire to be engaged in a task and is driven by curiosity or interest. When children are curious about and interested in something, they respond willingly with prolonged engagement, focused attention, and increased knowledge recall. Games provide a playful mode of learning and a setting where language learners can exercise creativity and use imagination in problem solving, enjoy competition, and find satisfaction.

Games as Tools for Cognitive Development

Playing games involves cognitive skills that facilitate the acquisition of second-language literacy. When games involve thinking, problem solving, and rule negotiation, language learners are required to make an effort to understand others and make themselves understood in authentic situations. The creative, thought-provoking, and interest-stimulating aspects of games enhance children's cognitive thinking abilities, promote the use of various language features and accurate language forms, and are a source of motivation. Simultaneously, when this developmental function of games and play increases the opportunities for exploration of different language features and forms, it helps clarify the children's thoughts and encourages a higher level of playing.

Games as Social Interaction

Games as learning tools also provide opportunities for social interactions. In the process of playing games, group members are encouraged to share ideas, challenge each other's thinking, and work collaboratively. Interactivity, problem solving, reflection, and analysis are promoted. Negotiations among group players about rules and roles provide them with authentic and meaningful learning opportunities for using language to express themselves clearly with focus on language forms. Although treasure hunting in the classroom setting is teacher initiated, it is directed by the children themselves when it comes to the actual plan for hiding the treasure and writing the clues. Therefore, it promotes a social negotiation about where to hide the treasure, what language forms to use in clues, and how to use those clues, and it creates opportunities for using language in an authentic and meaningful way. In the Vygotskian perspective, treasure hunting provides scaffolding for language development.

Entertainment, cognitive development, and social interaction are best understood through Halliday's Model of Language Learning (1980). In this model, learning activities are designed to engage students in authentic and meaningful language learning. There are three aspects of language learning: learning language, learning about language, and learning through language. Learning language refers to using language as a meaning-making system; learning about language refers to understanding how texts operate and how they are coded through rules and grammar; learning about language refers to using reading and writing as tools for learning about the world. When these three aspects operate together within a meaningful context, learning is likely to take place. With this understanding and by engaging students in use and analysis of various language functions, educators will have an opportunity to further gain knowledge of how their students learn language, learn about language, learn through language, and learn to use language.

CONTEXT

Children in Singaporean schools are from different ethnic and language backgrounds. There are four major ethnic groups in Singapore: The majority is Chinese with minorities of Indians, Malays, and Eurasians. There are, however, more than four languages spoken in this island nation. Chinese speakers comprise various dialectal groups, including Hokkien, Teochew, Cantonese, and Hakka, although most of the younger generation speak Mandarin. In the Indian group, there are speakers of Punjabi from northern India and speakers of Tamil from southern India. The Malays can be divided into Malay, Bahasa Minangkabau, and Bugis. Regardless of the languages used by Singaporeans at home, the medium of instruction in all schools and at all levels is English. This unique landscape of languages and cultures not only implies a degree of difficulty in defining Singaporean children as ESL or English as a foreign language (EFL) learners, but also points to the possibility that some of the children may encounter difficulties in learning English in school.

The treasure hunting game has been used with good results in a typical Singapore primary school with boys and girls ranging in age from 6 to 12 years. The school is well-equipped with modern facilities and special classrooms, and offers education in three mother-tongue languages: Chinese, Malay, and Tamil. The student population comprises 47% Chinese, 42% Malay, 7% Indian, and 4% other ethnic groups.

The following example is typical of the linguistic backgrounds of a class in this school: In Ms. Lee's class, twenty-five 8- and 9-year-old students of different ethnic groups at the third-grade level are taught English grammar by the treasure hunt method. Most of the children speak two languages at home, either their mother tongue or English, depending on their interlocutors. Although they tend to use more mother tongue with their parents, they use more English with their siblings. About half of the students in the class knew little English before they started school. The other half of the students started their formal English education in kindergarten and speak English well. All of the children, however, speak Singlish, a local vernacular of English that borrows expressions and vocabularies from the many different languages spoken in Singapore. Like many other classes and schools in the world, this class is a mixed-ability class where some children read more English and are more capable of solving problems in English and others are more proficient in their mother tongues. Therefore, the level of their English abilities and the level of using English for reasoning are also different.

CURRICULUM, TASKS, MATERIALS

As described in the beginning of the chapter, the teacher needs to demonstrate how to play treasure hunt games where target grammar items are used in the clues. In doing so, the teacher needs to:

1. Design the game and phrase the clues to include specific grammar items. (A minimum of four clues is required, and all clues must include the grammatical features to be learned.)

2. Deliver the first clue to the class, which may have to be divided into groups if it is a large class.

3. Introduce the target grammar items and analyze the clues after the children have found the treasure(s).

4. Set up rules for students to play the game by themselves, using the target grammar items.

The following is an illustration of the game with clues. After dividing the class into two or four groups (in the latter case, the groups will have to be paired because each group writes its clues for an opponent group and vice versa), the teacher may give these instructions for a treasure hunt where prepositions are the grammatical feature of focus:

1. Each group decides on suitable locations for the treasure and the clues that will lead the hunters of their opponent group to the treasure.

2. Each group phrases its four clues, using prepositions in any way the members wish.

3. A representative from each group hides the group's treasure and clues somewhere in the school building. (This could be limited to the classroom, to the same floor, or to some part of the school.)

4. The group gives the first clue to its opponent group.

Clue #1 (to be handed out to the opponent group):

> Llah eth ni erotskoob eht ta draob eciton
> eht no dnuof eb nac deen uoy noitamrofni eht

The opponent group now will have to figure out that this text has to be read backwards:

> "The information you need can be found **on** the notice board **at** the bookstore **in** the hall."

*The prepositions used are **on**, **at**, and **in**.*

Clue #2 (located on the notice board at the bookstore):

> Now go up and down as you please,
> but make sure you look before hot and after cold.

The opponent group will need to relate "up and down" to an elevator and figure out that the clue is located between the two drink dispensers (with hot and cold drinks) next to the elevator.

*The prepositions used are **up**, **down**, **before**, and **after**.*

Clue #3 (located next to the elevator and between the hot and cold drink dispensers in the school snack bar):

Congratulations! You are smarter than we thought. But now try this one: Behind the *Fairy Tales of Hans Christian Andersen*, you'll find the next clue.

The opponent group must identify this as a book that can found in the school library. Library books are kept in alphabetical order according to the author's name, so the group must realize that the author's name is Andersen and the book can be found under "A."

*Prepositions used are **behind**, **of**, and **for**.*

Clue #4 (behind a book on a shelf in the library):

> On your way back to the classroom, against the wall,
> under Italy, you'll find what you have been looking for for so long.

*This final clue should lead the opponent group to look under the map of Italy hanging on the wall in the corridor. The treasure has been attached to the wall with tape. Prepositions used are **on**, **to**, **against**, and **under**.*

The winning group could be the group that found their treasure first, the group that used the highest number of prepositions, or some other variation. This particular treasure hunt would be suitable for fourth- and fifth-grade students. Materials needed are: pencils and paper, tape, and a treasure (e.g., candy, a chocolate bar, or cookies).

Variations

Treasure hunt games are suitable for teaching school children at any age; the complexity of the clues, however, must correspond to their general knowledge and language skills. If it were a group of alphabet learners, the teacher could hide various letters in places with which the children are familiar. Clues could be given orally. If the students have acquired a more advanced level of literacy, (e.g., fifth-grade students), the complexity level of the clues, linguistically and otherwise, can be more challenging.

The following is an example of a treasure hunt with adjectives. The teacher may give these instructions for a treasure hunt where adjectives are the grammatical feature of focus:

1. Each group decides on suitable locations for the treasure and the clues that will lead the hunters in their opponent group to the treasure.

2. Each group phrases its four clues, using adjectives in any way they wish.

3. A representative from each group hides the group's treasure and clues somewhere in the school building. (This could be limited to the classroom as in this example, to the same floor, or to some part of the school.)

Clue #1 (to be handed out to the opponent group):

TH FRST CL S N TH BL BK N TH MDDL SHLF

*The opponent group will now have to insert the missing vowels so that the full text reads: "The first clue is in the blue book on the middle shelf." The adjectives used are **first**, **blue**, and **middle**.*

Clue #2 (located in a book with a blue cover on the middle shelf of the bookcase):

In white on black, the next clue is at the right edge.

*The opponent group will need to relate "white on black" to the blackboard and figure out that the clue is located at the right edge of the blackboard. Adjectives used are **white**, **black**, **next**, and **right**.*

Clue #3 (located at the right edge of the blackboard):

This important clue is very small but big enough to cover Rome.

*The opponent group must realize that this is a small piece of paper that covers Rome on the map of Italy hanging on the wall in the classroom. Adjectives used are **important**, **small**, and **big**.*

Clue #4 (attached to the map of Italy, covering Rome):

The last and final clue:
Where you rest your tired feet,
you'll find something sweet.

*This final clue should lead the opponent group members to look under their own desks where the treasure, in this case a candy bar, is attached with tape to the foot rest. Adjectives used are **last**, **final**, **tired**, and **sweet**.*

The winning group could be the group that found its treasure first or the group that used the highest number of adjectives, etc. This particular treasure hunt would be suitable for third- and fourth-grade students. Materials needed are: pencils and paper, tape, and a treasure (e.g., candy, a chocolate bar, a book, a magazine, or pens and pencils in different colors).

REFLECTIONS

The treasure hunting game focuses on the role of engagement and enjoyment of learning. From a sociocultural perspective, this game acknowledges that language development is not only a social activity and a cognitive endeavor, but also an affective undertaking.

Because of the entertainment value of the treasure hunt method, students apply all their energy to the task at hand and focus their undivided attention on the topic to be studied. Because the game involves authentic problem-solving situations, students do their best to use the various grammar items accurately, efficiently, and properly. Because the game method entails increased knowledge recall, students can consolidate the acquired knowledge without difficulty in their compositions or sentence constructions. Whereas the conventional drill exercises in grammar lack communicative purpose and are dreary and insufficient when it comes to the actual functions of the language features in real situations, the game provides authentic and meaningful contexts for using the particular language forms. Students do not study the language anymore; they experience the language (Wright et al., 2006).

There are different ways in which a classroom teacher can create and engage students in language learning. Treasure Hunting With Grammar can provide ESL and EFL learners with a nonthreatening environment that encourages students to take risks while using the various functions of language to reach their full potential as language learners. Creating a map and writing a clue for treasure hunting not only provides students with opportunities for using language, it also motivates and enriches their learning experiences as language learners.

This game is developed within a social constructivist perspective with the understanding that it is children's nature to try to make sense of the world in which they find themselves; therefore, the game meets the needs of children from all language and social backgrounds.

REFERENCES

Guthrie, J. T., & Knowles, K. (2001). Promoting reading motivation. In L. Verhoever & C. Snow (Eds.), *Literacy and motivation* (pp. 159–176). Mahwah, NJ: Lawrence Erlbaum.

Halliday, M. (1980). Three aspects of children's language development: Learning language, learning through language, learning about language. In Y. Goodman, M. H. Haussler, & D. Strickland (Eds.), *Oral and written language development research* (pp. 7–19). Urbana, IL: National Council of Teachers of English.

Pelligrini, A. D., & Galda, L. (2000). Cognitive development, play, and literacy: Issues of definition and developmental function. In K. Roskos & J. Christie (Eds.), *Play and literacy in early childhood* (pp. 63–74). Mahwah, NJ: Lawrence Erlbaum.

Roskos, K., & Christie, J. (Eds.). (2000). *Play and literacy in early childhood.* Mahwah, NJ: Lawrence Erlbaum.

Vygotsky, L. S. (1978). *Mind in society: The development of higher psychological processes.* Cambridge, MA: Harvard University Press.

Wright, A., Betteridge, D., & Buckby, M. (2006). *Games for language learning.* Cambridge: Cambridge University Press.

Additional Resource

Halliday, M. H. K. (1994). *Introduction to functional grammar* (2nd ed.). London: Edward Arnold.

Xiao Lan Curdt-Christiansen is an assistant professor at the National Institute of Education, Nanyang Technological University, in Singapore. She teaches undergraduate and graduate courses in language and literacy education. Her publications have appeared in International Journal of Language, Cultural and Curriculum; Language and Education; Sociolinguistics; and International Handbook of Student Experience.

CHAPTER 17

Nice Tower, But It May Fall Down: A Game for Teaching Modals of Probability

Mark Wolfersberger

INTRODUCTION

One of the main challenges of teaching modals is helping students understand their meaning. Modals have multiple meanings that are often ambiguous and overlap with other modals. This complexity can make it difficult for students to understand them and recognize appropriate situations in which to use them. The purpose of this game is to help students better understand the meaning of modals that express probability and practice using them within a communicative context. The goal is to build the tallest tower out of plastic, paper, or disposable cups while the onlooking students give commentary on the likelihood that the tower will fall down.

CONTEXT

This game can be successful with students of all ages and in both English as a foreign language (EFL) and English as a second language (ESL) contexts. It is best suited for intermediate students who have some ability with participating in uncontrolled conversations. Nevertheless, both beginning and advanced students also may benefit from participating in this activity. Beginning students who are building an understanding of English modals may benefit from using prepared phrases containing modals of probability within the context of this game. Advanced students may further refine their understanding of the modals of probability while enjoying the open interaction this game provides.

CURRICULUM, TASKS, MATERIALS

Materials

The only materials needed for this game are plastic, paper, or disposable cups for building a tower. The number of cups necessary will vary depending on the size of the cups and the number of towers students will build. If just one tower is being built with medium-sized cups, 15–20 cups should be enough.

Before class, the teacher can build a tower to check whether there are enough cups. If the teacher can stack all of the available cups into a tower without the tower falling down, more cups are necessary. The teacher should have more cups than can be stacked into a standing tower.

Preparing to Play

Before playing this tower-building game, students must learn the various modal verbs they will need to express a range of probabilities that the cup tower will fall down. Table 1 contains the modal verbs that I suggest teaching for this particular game.

The three important elements of grammatical knowledge are form, meaning, and use (Larsen-Freeman, 2001). Teaching the grammatical form of modals is relatively simple because modal verbs are always followed by the dictionary form of a verb. Thus, in Table 1, the verb *fall* is always used in its dictionary form, as any other verb used after these modals would be. Meanings for modals are more difficult because modals have multiple meanings that can be ambiguous and overlap with other modals. For this activity, however, Table 1 attempts to define the level of probability each modal expresses. Because probability is the focus of this game, the other meanings of the modals can be set aside for now. Practicing these modals within the context of a game allows students to build pragmatic competence and better understand the situations in which they can appropriately select and use these grammatical forms. After students understand the grammatical form

Table 1. Suggested Modal Verbs for Tower Falling

Modal Verbs	Probability Expressed
Won't fall Can't fall	0% chance of falling
Could fall May fall Might fall	30–40% chance of falling
Should fall	80–90% chance of falling
Will fall (am/is/are) Going to fall	100% chance of falling

and general meaning of these words, it is time to help them better understand their meaning in relation to each other through using the modals while building a cup tower.

To build a cup tower, the builder places the first cup upright on a table just as if he were going to pour something into it. Then he turns the second cup upside down and places it on top of the first cup so that the cups are positioned mouth-to-mouth. Then he turns the third cup upright and places it bottom-to-bottom on top of the second cup. Next, he places the fourth cup mouth-to-mouth on top of the third cup. The builder continues placing cups in this manner until the tower falls.

To practice using the modals and understanding their meaning, one student stands in front of the class and builds a cup tower while the other students give an oral commentary, using the probability modals, on the likelihood that the cup tower will fall down. Typically, the following happens: In the beginning when only one or two cups are in the tower, students use the modals expressing 0% chance. As the cup tower gets a bit taller, the students will begin using the modals expressing 30–40% chance. As the tower grows to exceptional heights or begins to wobble a bit, students begin using the 80–90% chance modal. And as the students watch the tower builder stretch to uneasily perch a final cup on the top of the tower, they use the 100% modals. The combination of the visual stimulus from the cup tower and the running commentary gives students a stronger sense of the relationships between these modal verbs for expressing probability.

Playing Games With Cup Towers

Once students understand how to create a probability commentary for the cup towers through doing a practice run with one student building the tower as described previously, teachers can have students practice in many game-like situations.

The simplest game is a competition to see which student can build the tallest cup tower by counting the number of cups stacked up before the tower falls. This activity can be done as a whole class with each student coming to the front to take turns building a tower. Or, if multiple cup sets are available, teachers can divide the class into groups, give each group a set of cups, and have the students compete within their groups to see who can build the tallest tower. Teachers should remember that each time a student builds a tower, the students watching should give an oral commentary about the likelihood that the tower will fall.

Adding the element of time also can change the game. Imposing a time limit on the tower-building can cause students to become hurried and more careless with their cup placements, resulting in crooked towers that lean and tumble more quickly. When adding the element of time, teachers can have students individually build towers and keep track of who builds the tallest tower within the time limit. Alternatively, they can have two students simultaneously build towers within a particular time limit to see whose tower is the tallest when the time limit expires.

Having two students build at the same time gives observing students the chance to give probability commentary on two different aspects of what they are observing. First, they can comment on the cup towers and the probability of either of the two towers falling down. Second, they can comment on the contestants and the probability that one of the contestants will build the tallest tower and win.

Another variation of this game is to put students in groups of four. Two students are the tower builders while two students are the "radio announcers." The radio announcers give a commentary of the tower competition as if they were broadcasting the event over the radio to people who cannot see the towers.

An additional caveat is to add more options for expressing probability once students have mastered some of the basic modal verbs. For example, by adding the word *stand* into Table 1, a whole new range of probabilities emerges. Now students can discuss the probability that the towers will either stand or fall. Because these words are opposites, the probability modals work in the opposite direction (as shown in Table 2).

Variations

Building cup towers can work with modals of ability also. This particular variation works well after students have practiced with modals of probability. First, the teacher should teach students about using modals of ability to describe past, present, and future abilities. Table 3 may be helpful.

Table 2. Suggested Modal Verbs for Tower Falling or Standing

Modal Verbs	Probability Expressed
Won't fall Can't fall Will stand Going to stand	0% chance of falling
Should stand	10–20% chance of falling
Could fall May fall Might fall	30–40% chance of falling
Couldn't stand May not stand Might not stand	60–70% chance of falling
Should fall	80–90% chance of falling
Will fall Going to fall Won't stand Can't stand	100% chance of falling

Table 3. Modals of Ability in Past, Present, and Future

Modal Verbs	Time Frame
Will be able to	Future
Can Be able to	Present
Could Was/were able to	Past

After teaching these modals, the teacher should have a team of students come to the front of the class to build a tower. Before building the tower, students should describe the team's ability to construct a tower that is 20 cups tall (or whatever height the teacher decides) within a particular period of time. This discussion gives the students practice describing ability in the present and future. After the time has expired, the students use the outcome of the tower construction to describe ability in the past.

During the conversation before building the tower, students might say things such as: "I think the team has a long time, so they will be able to build the tower." "There are a lot of cups to stack, so I don't think they can do it." "I don't know. Those students are good at building towers, but the time is short. Maybe they will be able to do it." And in the conversation after building, students might say things such as the following: "It was easy. They could do it without any problems." "They almost did it, but they couldn't get the last cup to stay on top." "They were able to finish the tower just before the time finished." After building, the teacher can encourage mixing past and future ability by encouraging students to try phrases such as: "That last tower was a bit too difficult and they couldn't do it, but if we give them more time, I think next time they will be able to do it."

Assessment

Because this game generates much vocal activity in the classroom, determining the accuracy of individual students' modal use amidst the storm of speaking can seem challenging. Nevertheless, the key to assessing students' understanding is extracting reasons and evidence from them for their predictions. In other words, the teacher should ask students what they see about the tower or what they know about the builder that supports their predictions. The evidence they provide will allow the teacher to determine whether or not the modals they are using reflect the likelihood that they intended.

Following are two ways the teacher can go about extracting this evidence from the students: First, the teacher should become part of the class and interact with the students during the game. As the teacher watches the tower being constructed and creates predictions with probability modals, he should interact with the students and challenge predictions he thinks are inaccurate. Second, occasionally the teacher should slow down the game. The teacher should prompt the builder to place one cup at a time onto the cup tower and pause between each placement. During the pause, the teacher should ask students what their predictions are and the reasons for their predictions. This method creates a more controlled environment through the slower pace of the game, and it also can help struggling students better understand how to connect the evidence they are seeing with the modals they are using.

REFLECTIONS

After building towers and practicing with the probability modals, it is important to help students apply their understanding to new contexts beyond the game. There are several possible ways to do this.

One way is to discuss current events and the probability of various outcomes for those current events. For example, if a political election is to be held in the near future, what is the probability of each candidate being elected? How likely is a music artist to produce a new CD or perform locally on a concert tour? What are the chances that the school will invest in the latest technology for students to use?

Another possible extension activity is to discuss the weather and the likelihood of various meteorological patterns affecting the area. Teachers can discuss the possibility of sunshine, clouds, wind, rain, snow, frost, hail, thunderstorms, or anything else affecting the local area in the near and distant future.

To assess the accuracy of students' use of probability modals during these extension activities, teachers should use the question word *why* as a follow-up to a prediction. *Why* questions elicit reasons and support for the prediction and provide evidence to both the teacher and other listening students to support the strength of the prediction modal used. For example, in response to the question about the school adopting a particular technology, if a student says that the school might buy MP3 players for students to use in the computer lab, the teacher (or another student) could ask the reason for that prediction with a *why* question. If the student explains that several students have recently made formal requests for MP3 players, there is support for the weak probability modal. If, however, the student reveals that he overheard the computer lab supervisor finalizing a purchase over the phone, this is evidence that the student needed to use a stronger probability modal.

REFERENCE

Larsen-Freeman, D. (2001). Teaching grammar. In M. Celce-Murcia (Ed.), *Teaching English as a second or foreign language* (3rd ed., pp. 251–266). Boston, MA: Heinle & Heinle.

Mark Wolfersberger has a doctorate in second-language teaching and learning from the University of Auckland, New Zealand. He works at Brigham Young University Hawaii, in the United States, as a teacher trainer and language teacher. His main teaching and research interest is in the area of second-language writing.

CHAPTER 18

The Teacher's Choice Game

Karen Hilgeman

INTRODUCTION

The Teacher's Choice Game allows students to increase their fluency, practice mastery of a grammatical structure, and, best of all, take turns being the "teacher." On the surface, the Teacher's Choice Game is a fun, intriguing activity. English as a second language (ESL) teachers will know, however, that it is actually a practice activity in disguise. When ESL students learn new vocabulary or new structures, they need a great deal of practice before they can use the new material on their own. This game provides practice using participial adjectives, something that many ESL students have problems using correctly. The game allows students to review the adjectives, discuss the nuances of what words such as *interesting*, *tiring*, and *comforting* mean, and apply those adjectives in new contexts. Furthermore, the Teacher's Choice Game allows students to increase their fluency with English by discussing the rules and procedures of the game. As an added benefit, because the students themselves are the ones who create the playing cards, this game uses the level of English at which the students are most comfortable and proficient.

CONTEXT

This game is suitable for intermediate and advanced students in high school, adult education, and higher education in an ESL or English as a foreign language (EFL) setting. Variations that make the game easier or more complex are included later in the chapter.

This game is to be used as an additional practice or review activity after a lesson on using participial adjectives, which ESL students often use incorrectly. For example, they may say "Teacher, I'm boring" when they mean that they are bored, or they may say "The movie was interested" when they are the interested party. The Teacher's Choice Game provides a fun opportunity to practice those adjectives in a new way (see Appendix B for the participial adjectives used in the game).

CURRICULUM, TASKS, MATERIALS

In this game, students practice their fluency in English by brainstorming words and phrases to make the playing cards. After making the playing cards, cutting them out, and shuffling them, students are ready to play. In each round of the game, one student acts as the "teacher." The teacher selects which of the playing cards that the other students submit is the best match for the participial adjective on the adjective card. Throughout the game, each student gets several chances to be the teacher. When not taking their turn as the teacher, students earn a point every time the playing card they submit is chosen. Throughout the game, students use their language skills to negotiate meaning, explain their choices, and keep the game running smoothly.

Configuration of the Game

The game works best with groups of four to six students. For larger classes, several groups of students can play separate games at the same time. Teachers should calculate how many groups they will have so they can prepare the materials properly.

Teacher Preparation

In addition to teaching students how to use participial adjectives, teachers must collect the following items before the class period in which the game is to be played:

- copies of the playing cards (see Appendix A) on blue paper (one page per student)

- copies of the adjective cards (see Appendix B) on yellow paper, preferably cardstock or construction paper. Adjective cards must be cut out (one set of cards per group of students)

- scissors (one or two pairs per group).

How to Prepare

1. Review participial adjectives with students (the use of participial adjectives and the specific adjectives used in the game must have been studied previously.) The words listed in Appendix B are *comforting, exciting, worrying, amusing, depressing, confusing, boring, amazing, interesting, frightening, tiring*, and *annoying*.

2. Divide the class into groups of four to six students each. Give each group one set of yellow adjective cards, one blue playing card page per student, and scissors.

3. Model on the board or overhead how students are to fill out the squares on the blue playing card page (see Figure 1). Each square instructs students to write a person, place, thing, or activity. Brainstorm some creative answers with students before having them fill out their own pages.

4. As students finish, instruct them to cut out the blue playing cards. All the blue cards from the group should be shuffled together and placed in a pile.

5. Together as a whole class or in groups, have students look at the yellow adjective cards (see Appendix B). Have them review the meanings of those words and ask each other or consult a dictionary if they have forgotten the meaning.

6. Finally, have one student shuffle the blue playing cards and then deal six to each member of the group. Students can look at their playing cards but should not show them to anyone else. The remaining blue playing cards should be kept in a pile.

How to Play

1. Assign a student to be the teacher for the first round of play. The teacher's blue cards should be put aside for the round.

2. The teacher in each group picks one yellow adjective card and reads it aloud.

3. All of the other students in the group must pick which of their blue playing cards best fits that adjective and then lay the card face down in front of the teacher.

4. The teacher then turns the blue playing cards over and reads them aloud. Then the teacher picks which of the cards best fits the adjective. Finally the teacher must explain the reason that card was picked (see Figure 2).

mailman	doctor's office	hammer	dancing
(person)	(place)	(thing)	(activity)
Tom Hanks			
(person)	(place)	(thing)	(activity)

Figure 1. Playing Cards on Blue Paper

5. The student who submitted the blue playing card that is picked gets a point. Students should choose one player to keep track of the score on a piece of paper.

6. All of the students except the teacher should then take a new blue card from the pile. Each student should always have six blue playing cards.

7. For the next round, the student on the right becomes the new teacher, and the play continues.

How to Win

1. The game can end in several ways:

    - It could end after students have gone through all 12 adjective cards.

    - Alternately, the game could go on for a set period for time. If a longer game is desired, halfway through the game, take the discarded blue cards from one group and add them to the new blue card pile of another group, continuing around the room until each group has a "new" set of blue playing cards. Then students could go through the yellow adjective cards a second time.

2. The winner is the student with the most points at the end of the game.

Variations

For Lower Level Students

Teachers can change the adjective cards to simpler words such as *big, small, fun,* and *scary* (see Appendix B for a suggested list of 12 easier adjectives).

Comforting		
	the Principal (person)	playing piano (activity)
	coffee shop (place)	reading (activity)

Figure 2. How to Play

For Higher Level Students

If desired, teachers can add a reading element to this game by giving students written instructions to follow (see Appendix C). Tell students that they are going to play a fun game only if they can figure out the instructions and preparation. Assure students that they will enjoy the game and that they will be able to figure it out if they read carefully, discuss the directions, and work together. In this case, teachers should give each group of students all the necessary materials, but leave it up to the students to read, discuss, and figure out the preparation and procedures for the game. Give each group of students the following materials:

- student instruction page (one copy per student)
- playing cards page (one copy per student)
- scissors (several per group)
- adjective cards (one set per group, already cut apart).

REFLECTIONS

Students often are noticeably pleased with themselves after playing this game. They feel proud that they know enough English to create the playing cards and select which ones to use for each adjective. They especially enjoy taking their turn as teacher. As teacher, their decision about which word best fits the participial adjective is final—a unique experience for second-language learners who are far more used to being told what is correct.

Teachers like this game because students practice discussing the nuances of the adjectives when they select which playing card is most suitable and explain why. The negotiation skills the students use when discussing how the game should be played, whose turn it is, and what happens next are valuable skills for future collaborative activities.

Karen Hilgeman is a professional development specialist at the Adult Learning Resource Center in Arlington Heights, Illinois, in the United States. She teaches ESL and citizenship preparation classes to adult students, presents regularly at TESOL conventions and other forums, and has conducted teacher training in the United States, Japan, and China.

APPENDIX A: PLAYING CARDS

Preparation: The following chart should be copied onto blue paper. Each student needs one. If desired, the chart may be enlarged before copying to make the cards bigger.

Procedure: To form the playing cards for the game, the students write one item per square and then cut the squares apart.

(person)	(place)	(thing)	(activity)
(person)	(place)	(thing)	(activity)
(person)	(place)	(thing)	(activity)

APPENDIX B: ADJECTIVE CARDS

Preparation: The following chart should be copied onto yellow paper, preferably card stock. Each group of four to six students needs one. If desired, the chart may be enlarged before copying to make the cards bigger. The cards should be cut apart and kept together with a rubber band, paper clip, or envelope.

comforting	exciting	worrying
amusing	depressing	confusing
boring	amazing	interesting
frightening	tiring	annoying

Note: For lower level students, use these adjectives instead:

big	small	beautiful	ugly	soft	hard
loud	quiet	fun	fast	slow	scary

APPENDIX C: STUDENT INSTRUCTIONS

How to Prepare

1. Each student takes a blue sheet of paper.

2. Each student fills out the squares on the blue paper. Here are some examples of the kind of things students can write:

    Person: *a firefighter, Brad Pitt, a vampire, George Washington*

    Place: *New York, a gas station, jail, a restroom*

    Thing: *a frying pan, a pencil sharpener, a truck*

    Activities: *doing the dishes, playing soccer, driving a car, robbing a bank*

    Everyone should try to think of interesting, unusual words or phrases to write down. Do not use only good words. For example, words such as *cockroach* for a thing or *thief* for person can be used. Students should use words for both good and bad people, places, things, and activities.

3. Students cut the squares apart to make 12 playing cards each.

4. One student collects all the cards, shuffles them together, and puts them in a pile.

5. Together, students look at the 12 yellow adjective cards and talk about what each adjective means. Each group makes sure that every person in the group understands. Students can ask the teacher or use the dictionary if they have forgotten one of the words.

6. One student shuffles the yellow adjective cards and puts them in a pile face down in the middle of the table. Students can look at their blue playing cards but should not show them to anyone else.

How to Play

1. Students decide who will go first. That person gets to be the teacher. The blue cards of the teacher are not needed at this time and should be put aside until the next turn.

2. The teacher picks a yellow adjective card and reads it aloud.

3. Everyone else decides which of his blue playing cards is best for the adjective that the teacher says. For example, if the teacher says "boring," all of the other players need to choose one of their blue playing cards that is the most boring. Even if students do not have a card that is truly boring, they have to pick one.

4. All of the other students put their blue cards face down in front of the teacher.

5. The teacher turns the blue playing cards over and reads them aloud.

6. Then, the teacher picks the playing card that best fits the adjective. The teacher explains the reason for picking that card.

7. The student whose card the teacher picks gets a point. One student should keep track of the points on a piece of paper.

8. The blue playing cards that were used go into a discard pile. Then each student except the teacher takes a new blue card. Players should always have six blue playing cards.

9. The next student to the right becomes the new teacher and picks a new adjective card.

10. The student who has the most points at the end of the game is the winner.

CHAPTER 19

What's the Problem?

Leong Ping Alvin

INTRODUCTION

This chapter outlines a proposal to use problem-based games to complement grammar lessons for students at the primary and secondary levels. Problem-based games focus on specific grammar items (e.g., definite articles, prepositions, plurals) and are worded as problems requiring students to come up with observations or principles about usage. The approach is an adaptation of problem-based learning (PBL), a more widely known pedagogical strategy first used extensively in the medical faculty of McMaster University (Ontario, Canada) in the 1970s (Barrows & Tamblyn, 1980). PBL uses contextualized, real-world situations (often with complex solutions) to develop content knowledge and problem-solving skills in learners. Over the years, PBL has been extended to a wide range of other disciplines, notably business and the sciences (e.g., see Boud & Feletti, 1997; Duch, Groh, & Allen, 2001). Its applicability in language education and the humanities, however, has remained modest, possibly because such disciplines, as some claim, are not quite suited to solving the real-world problems that PBL activities pose.

This lack of PBL in the humanities is ironic because we use language every day and the real-world problems themselves need to be worded in language. Indeed, the very structure of language can be viewed as a puzzle to be sorted out. This is where problem-based games come in. As the focus is on grammar, the tasks will need to be considerably more constrained than true PBL activities. The main thrust of PBL, nevertheless, is retained: Students are led in such activities to examine relevant data carefully and work out solutions for themselves. The benefits, too, are likely to be equally significant (e.g., see Barron et al., 1998): The games serve as a means to guide students to become problem-solvers and more critical thinkers, and, hence, to understand abstract concepts better.

CONTEXT

The education system in Singapore poses an interesting challenge, underscoring the need for innovative approaches to the teaching of English grammar. All mainstream Singaporean schools use English as the medium of instruction. Many local families, however, use a variety of other languages as their home language (e.g., Mandarin Chinese, Malay, Tamil, various Chinese dialects). Therefore, even though English is the dominant language in education, not all Singaporean children may use it at home or with their friends (Dixon, 2005).

This discrepancy naturally raises the worry that Singaporean children may be confused by the grammatical systems of the different languages that they use or encounter. The present English Language Syllabus (2001), which is followed by all mainstream schools in Singapore, addresses this problem by placing "clear emphasis not just on fluency but also on accuracy" (Chew, 2005, p. 13). It focuses on grammar in relation to different text types (or genres):

> Knowledge of grammar and how it functions contributes to effective language use. The study of grammatical features and lexis is closely related to the study of text types. Grammar and lexis contribute to the meaning of the text. (English Language Syllabus, 2001, p. 6)

It is hoped that grammar teaching can be contextualized in a print-rich environment. This emphasis on grammar (and text types) goes some way to help students grapple with the structure of the language.

In practice, though, it is not uncommon for grammar lessons to revert to the form of explicit statements about various rules and principles, followed by practice questions. The convenience of this deductive approach, unfortunately, comes at a cost. Teachers run the risk of producing passive learners, students who are mere appliers of rules and principles. Such students become followers, not discoverers.

We can reverse this tendency by introducing an inductive component in grammar teaching. This component can be achieved through the use of problem-based games as part of the grammar class. Through these games, students discover the rules and principles for themselves, and so take ownership of that discovery.

CURRICULUM, TASKS, MATERIALS

In this section, I illustrate two problem-based games. One is more suited to children at midprimary level, and the other to children at lower secondary level. The teacher has full control over the design of each activity: He or she decides on the complexity of the task and customizes it so that it is both level- and age-appropriate. The teacher can also choose to use authentic texts to contextualize the problem or ask students to gather evidence on their own.

Ideally, problem-based games should be attempted as a group activity, with three or four students in each group. The learning is facilitated not only through the individual struggle to solve the puzzle but also through the collective discussion and sharing of ideas. Because this is a discovery process for students, it goes without saying that all their contributions should be treated with respect and given the attention they deserve. Some of their answers may be markedly different from the teacher's, but if they are just as insightful, the teacher should accept them and warmly congratulate the students for the effort.

Problem-Based Game #1: The Problem With The

- **Suitability level:** Midprimary level (9–10 years of age).

- **Grammar focus:** The use of the definite article with names of bodies of water.

- **Puzzle:** How should the word the be used with names of oceans, seas, rivers, and lakes?

- **Preparation:** Because this is an activity for midprimary students, the teacher should be careful to select a text that is easy to read and contains a representative sample of names of bodies of water. The following text serves as a guide:

> Lake Baikal is the world's deepest lake and is located in Siberia, Russia, north of the Mongolian border. It is 5,369 ft (1,637 m) deep—more than 1 mile straight down. The Pacific Ocean takes the award for being the largest ocean in the world. It covers almost a third of the Earth's surface and goes from the Bering Sea in the Arctic north to the icy waters of the Ross Sea in the Antarctic south. The smallest ocean is the Arctic Ocean, which is about 10 times smaller than the Pacific Ocean. The Nile River in Egypt is the longest river. It's 4,145 miles (6,671 km) long and flows into the Mediterranean Sea. The world's shortest river, according to the *Guinness Book of World Records*, is the Roe River. It is only 200 ft (61 m) long and flows between Giant Springs and the Missouri River near Great Falls, Montana. There has been debate, though, about which river is really the shortest. The D River in Oregon has been measured as being only 120 ft (37 m) long. It connects Devil's Lake directly to the Pacific Ocean near Lincoln City. Because the D River flows into the ocean though, its length changes according to the tide. Therefore, it has been measured at several different lengths. (adapted from *World Geography Facts—Water*, n.d.)

- **Procedure:** The teacher divides the class into groups comprising two or three children apiece and gives each group the prepared text. Then the teacher introduces the puzzle and gives all of the groups a time limit to work on the problem (e.g., 15 minutes). The teacher may want to set aside an additional 5 minutes for each group to write a brief but specific statement about how the definite article is used. At the end of the activity, the teacher discusses these statements and reinforces the grammar focus. He may also want to award prizes to deserving groups (e.g., for writing the clearest statement, for putting in the best effort, or for just trying their hardest).

- **Solution:** From the text, students should be able to see quite clearly that while names of oceans, seas, and rivers take the definite article, names of lakes do not.

Similar activities can also be introduced to heighten the students' awareness of using the definite article with names of mountain groups (e.g., *the Himalayas*, but not *the Everest*) and names of countries bearing common nouns (e.g., *the People's Republic of China*, but not *the China*). This general approach can be extended further to other grammar items as well, such as the appropriate use of prepositions with general and specific addresses (e.g., *on Meadow Road*, but *at 24 Meadow Road*), and modes of transport (e.g., *on the bus*, but *in the car*).

Problem-Based Game #2: Why Not Chineses?

- **Suitability level:** Lower to midsecondary level (14–16 years of age).

- **Grammar focus:** Singular and plural nouns of nationalities.

- **Puzzle:** Why can we say "The Malays are kind," but not "The Chineses are kind?"

- **Preparation:** The teacher has the option of either preparing a list of nouns or asking the students to come up with a list on their own. The teacher may wish to use the following frame for consistency:

  He is a/an _____./They are _____.
  (e.g., He is an American./They are Americans.)

  The following list is offered as a suggestion:

He is a *Spaniard*.	They are *Spaniards*.
He is a *Portuguese*.	They are *Portuguese*.
He is an *Indian*.	They are *Indians*.
He is a *Vietnamese*.	They are *Vietnamese*.
He is a *Pakistani*.	They are *Pakistanis*.
He is a *Malaysian*.	They are *Malaysians*.
He is a *Swiss*.	They are Swiss.
He is a *Pole*.	They are *Poles*.
He is a *Taiwanese*.	They are *Taiwanese*.

- **Procedure:** The teacher first divides the class into groups comprising two or three children each. If a prepared list of nouns is to be used, the teacher gives that list to each group at the start of the activity.

If the teacher prefers instead for the students to come up with their own lists, he will first need to set this as a preliminary task, say, a day or two before the main activity. Students creating their own lists should be told explicitly to select only singular and plural nouns (e.g., *Frenchman*, *Frenchmen*), not adjectives (e.g., *French*). This is an important point to note as many (singular) nouns and adjectives of nationalities have identical forms (e.g., *Indian*, *Singaporean*, *American*), which may mislead students into thinking that words such as *English*, *Dutch*, *Scottish*, etc. are also nouns, when they are actually adjectives.

At the start of the activity, the teacher presents the puzzle to the class. He should also mention that it may have more than one solution. The time limit for the activity is variable, depending on the general abilities of the students in the class. The time needed may range from 20 minutes to 45 minutes. Groups should present their solutions in the form of a clear statement.

At the end of the activity, the teacher discusses the various solutions. The teacher may also wish to set aside time to review and comment on the lists of nouns compiled by the groups themselves. Prizes can be awarded to groups for writing the best statement, for cooperating well as a group, and for coming up with the best list of nouns (if this was required of the students).

- **Solutions:** There are at least two solutions to the puzzle. The first, perhaps more obvious one, is that singular nouns ending in the /s/ sound (technically, *sibilant* sound) have identical plural forms (see Figure 1).

  The second solution, which some discerning students might notice, is that in all cases, the singular and plural nouns of nationalities have the same number of syllables (see Figure 2).

Singular	Plural
Portuguese	Portuguese
Vietnamese	Vietnamese
Swiss	Swiss
Taiwanese	Taiwanese

Figure 1. First Solution

Singular	Plural	Syllables
Portuguese	Portuguese	3 syllables each
Indian	Indians	3 syllables each
Malaysian	Malaysians	3 syllables each
Swiss	Swiss	1 syllable each

Figure 2. Second Solution

A possible reason why the singular and plural forms of some nouns are identical now becomes clear. If the addition of the plural marker adds another syllable to the plural noun (e.g., *Swiss, Swiss+es*), the plural marker is dropped to ensure that the singular and plural forms have the same number of syllables. Hence, the plural form of *Chinese* is still *Chinese* because the addition of the plural marker will result in a word (i.e., *Chineses*) with one more syllable than the singular form, which is not permitted. This solution can be particularly exciting to students because such a "rule" cannot be found in textbooks or even grammar reference books. Yet, it can be teased out through a problem-solving activity.

A variant of this activity involves compound pronouns (e.g., *everyone, nothing, anybody*). Many students often are bewildered as to why such pronouns can take only the singular verb (e.g., *everyone is here*, not *everyone are here*). Taking the singular verb is especially puzzling in the case of *everyone* and *everybody* because they refer to more than one person, although, rightfully, it is the entire group that is being referred to, rather than the individual members within the group.

By focusing on the component morphemes of the pronouns (i.e., *someone = some + one; everything = every + thing; anybody = any + body*), however, students can quite easily see that the second morpheme is always singular in form (i.e., *–one, –thing, –body*):

Everyone (= *Every + one*) is here.

Nothing (= *No + thing*) is here.

Everybody (= *Every + body*) has gone home.

Because the second morpheme is closest to the verb, it is possibly for this grammatical reason that all compound pronouns take only singular verbs.

REFLECTIONS

Children are by nature inquisitive; they are keen to know more and learn new things. Traditionally, teachers have been the ones to impart knowledge. This is perhaps still necessary in many situations, but there are other situations involving specific grammar items where it may be more beneficial for students to discover rules and principles for themselves. Problem-solving games offer learners the chance to study a language puzzle and work out a solution by and for themselves.

Through the process of discussing and examining the evidence, students are led to think about the structure of the language more deeply and make sense of various norms of usage. It is in this struggle to arrive at an answer that they become acutely aware of the systemic nature of language and how it influences language use. The emphasis of such activities is on discovery: Students discover something about language (use) in a fun, yet challenging, way. The activities are tremendously valuable in exposing students to norms of usage that may not be covered in traditional grammar lessons or textbooks. They show students the precise contexts in which certain words are used and the preferred norms in those environments.

More importantly, perhaps, through such activities we move away from a teacher-centered paradigm to a student-centered one, heightening students' awareness of how language is naturally used in context. The grammar lesson, as it were, becomes real and relevant to them.

REFERENCES

Barron, B. J., Schwartz, D. L., Vye, N. J., Moore, A., Petrosino, A., Zech, L., et al. (1998). Doing with understanding: Lessons from research on problem- and project-based learning. *Journal of the Learning Sciences, 7,* 271–311.

Barrows, H. S., & Tamblyn, R. M. (1980). *Problem-based learning: An approach to medical education.* New York: Springer.

Boud, D., & Feletti, G. (Eds.). (1997). *The challenge of problem-based learning* (2nd ed.). London: Routledge.

Chew, G. L. P. (2005). Change and continuity: English language teaching in Singapore. *Asian EFL Journal, 7*(1), 1–21.

Dixon, L. Q. (2005). Bilingual education policy in Singapore: An analysis of its sociohistorical roots and current academic outcomes. *International Journal of Bilingual Education and Bilingualism, 8*(1), 25–47.

Duch, B. J., Groh, S. E., & Allen, D. E. (Eds.). (2001). *The power of problem-based learning.* Sterling, VA: Stylus Publishing.

English language syllabus for primary and secondary schools. (2001). (Available from Curriculum Planning and Development Division, Ministry of Education, Singapore, 1 North Buona Vista Drive, Singapore 138675, http://www.moe.edu.sg /education/syllabuses/languages-and-literature/files/english-primary-secondary .pdf)

World geography facts—water. (n.d.). Retrieved June 20, 2007, from http://www .kidzworld.com/article/1751-world-geography-facts-water

Additional Resource

Dods, R. F. (1997). An action research study of the effectiveness of problem-based learning in promoting the acquisition and retention of knowledge. *Journal for the Education of the Gifted, 20,* 423–437.

Leong Ping Alvin works at the National Institute of Education, Singapore. His research interests are in systemic-functional grammar, writing, and text analysis. His recent book publications are English Grammar FAQs (McGraw-Hill, 2008), Free and Situational Writing (Learners Publishing, 2006), and Theme and Rheme (Peter Lang, 2004).

PART 2: Beyond Skills

A. Game Templates

CHAPTER 20

Pass the Clothespin: Cleaning Up in the ESL Classroom

Amanda A. B. Wallace

INTRODUCTION

I began using the game Pass the Clothespin while teaching high school in New Zealand a few years ago. Generally, I use this game to activate students' knowledge and review lessons as they relate to course objectives. Sometimes I use it as a review to help students prepare for a quiz or test. I have also used Pass the Clothespin to help students remember and use vocabulary and skill strategies in all four of the language-learning curriculum areas of reading, writing, listening, and speaking.

CONTEXT

I have found that Pass the Clothespin continues to work its way successfully across curriculum levels, age groups, multicultural environments, and in a variety of learning contexts. It is a very effective activity in the English as a foreign language (EFL) or English as a second language (ESL) classroom. I currently teach ESL in a fully matriculated American university program for international students preparing to enter their general education and major university courses. Pass the Clothespin has engaged my ESL university students at all levels of English language proficiency as they perform a variety of academic tasks. It is adaptable to the needs of the classroom learner and teacher and activates learning in a lively and fun way. It also develops a sense of teamwork and collaboration among the learners.

CURRICULUM, TASKS, MATERIALS

Playing the game requires a large enough space to allow two rows of chairs to be set up facing each other. The following materials are required to play: three clothespins (or other items, such as whiteboard markers, that can be used as game tokens), chairs for each student playing (desk chairs will work), and a set of questions with answers to be used as the content for the game. If the teacher wishes to begin the game with a coin toss, then a large coin with a "heads" and "tails" stamp on either side, such as a U.S. quarter, is needed.

To set up, students are divided into two teams and lined up in chairs with the two teams facing each other. The chairs in each row should be placed close enough next to each other so that a student can pass the token to the next student on a team. An extra chair or small table should be placed at one end of this configuration in the middle of the two rows so that the students at the ends of the rows have access to it. A clothespin or token is set in the middle of this table or chair (see Figure 1).

Each student at the head of each row is given the team's token before the game begins. The game can start with a coin toss or with a verbal "Go!" from the teacher or the person directing the game (a student can also direct the game). If a coin toss is used, it may require a quick cultural explanation of what is meant by heads and tails. For example, if a U.S. quarter is used, the students will need to know that the stamp of President George Washington on one side of the coin is called heads and that the eagle on the other side is designated tails. In a coin toss, the game begins if the coin lands on heads. Students will need to be taught to watch for this and move quickly if they see the coin land heads-up at the starting end of their rows.

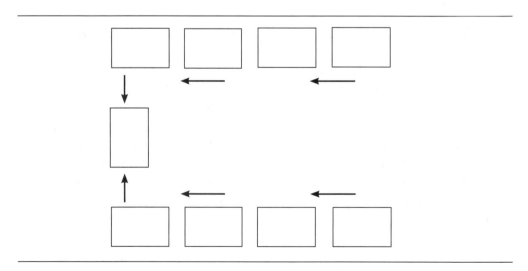

Figure 1. The Game Setup and Team Passing of the Clothespin

Once the game starts, each student passes the clothespin token hand-to-hand to the next student on the team until the token reaches the end of the row. Students may not throw the clothespin; it has to be handed carefully and quickly into the hand of the next person. The last member of the first team to complete passing its token grabs the token off of the table in the middle at the end of the row.

The student who grabs the center token is then asked a question from the list of prepared questions. If he does not know the answer to the question, the student may ask one team member for help. If neither knows the answer, the question is given to the last person on the opposite team. The team that successfully answers the question receives a point, and the winning team for that question rotates so that the last person goes to the head of the line. The game is repeated until all the questions are used or the time designated for the activity is up.

As the game progresses, it usually increases in speed and movement, encouraging fluency among team members as they work to move quickly and answer the questions correctly. Increased fluency in answering can be encouraged if answers are timed. Students also appreciate the competitiveness of the activity as their teams work to earn the most points.

Variations

As a variation, I sometimes have the teams switch sides to sit in the opposite row, so those who are right- or left-handed do not have an unfair advantage or disadvantage passing the clothespin. Another variation of the game is to ask the students to prepare the questions and answers for the game content. This activity adds an additional learning element to the game. For example, in a recent writing class activity, I asked students to each write down three questions with answers from a chapter in our writing text that reviewed aspects of sentence structure. The students' questions included, *Name the type of sentence that contains one independent clause and at least one dependent clause* and *What is the difference between a clause and a phrase?* These questions became the content of the game and turned the class period into an energetic and fun way to review the chapter content and prepare the students for a quick quiz following the game. The students were able to better remember the structure points from the lesson and did well on the quiz.

Pass the Clothespin has also helped my listening-speaking course students at the beginning level remember terms and phrases used in basic conversation as well as basic academic vocabulary. I might, for example, ask students at this level to demonstrate an appropriate way to formally introduce themselves when meeting someone else for the first time. In upper level listening-speaking courses, I have used the game in academic word list vocabulary review and to promote vocabulary retention: "How would you use the word *hypothesis* in a sentence?" "Give a synonym for the word *investigate*." In my ESL reading classes, the game has helped students remember literary terms and identify literary features in readings done in class: *What is the setting for this chapter of the novel? Describe an example of irony in this story.* It is an extremely versatile game that can assist teachers and students at all levels and in a variety of course activities to develop language skills.

REFLECTIONS

Students tend to better remember what they review or learn by playing this game because of the movement, fun, and focus it generates. I have had continual success with Pass the Clothespin because it promotes language learning in a lively setting: Class members are fully engaged in the activity and in the learning that takes place within the context of the game. It also gives students a chance to compete in a friendly way. The teacher wins, too, with a successful educational activity that adds variety to classroom lessons.

ACKNOWLEDGMENT

My thanks to Michelle Campbell, secretary of the English Language Teaching and Learning Department at Brigham Young University Hawaii, who assisted with the graphic design for this chapter, and to James Ah Mu, a teacher in New Zealand, who first introduced this game to me.

Amanda A. B. Wallace has a bachelor's degree in teaching English to speakers of other languages from Brigham Young University Hawaii and a master's degree in teaching English as a second language (TESL) from Hawaii Pacific University, both in the United States. She is a lecturer and listening–speaking curriculum specialist in the English as an International Language Program at BYUH and book review editor for the TESL Reporter.

CHAPTER 21

On-the-Spot Games From Student Content

Kevin McCaughey

INTRODUCTION

Guessing games do not require much material or planning. In fact, they can be created right in the classroom—with students themselves supplying the content—and played during the very same lesson. When designed well, these games can target specific grammar structures or vocabulary. When implemented well, they provide sustained speaking practice.

Ten years ago, as a teacher at a language school in Chisinau, Moldova, I discovered—as all teachers do—little scraps of paper and how they can be used in making guessing games. Distribute them, ask students to write down, for instance, the name of a famous person, have one student describe that person, and let the rest of the class guess the name.

Guessing games offer many opportunities for speaking. The problem is, in the classroom they do not translate well into optimal language practice because teachers often arrange such games as if they were playing at home with family or friends, with only one person speaking at a time. There is little of what Penny Ur calls *volume*, "the sheer amount of . . . [comprehensible] language that is spoken, heard, or written in the course of an activity," or *repetition*, the recurring "reception and production . . . of different examples of the form's structure and meaning" (1985, p. 12).

My first games in Moldova were not arranged so that many students could do the describing task simultaneously (volume), or so that every student had many chances to describe (repetition). Over the next 5 years or so, I traveled as a teacher trainer in Russia, Ukraine, Tajikistan, and Turkmenistan. Teachers desperately wanted activities that did not require materials or much planning, so I offered workshops covering on-the-spot games, endeavoring to increase volume and repetition and work out the kinks inherent to the process.

In this chapter, I will show the basic guidelines for making games on the spot.

Using one game (Secret Creatures) as a paradigm and following the principles outlined, the teacher can guide students through an unlimited number of similar games, even board games, as I will illustrate.

CONTEXT

Basic guessing games are suitable for young and beginning learners (e.g., I Spy With My Little Eye, in which children, perhaps on a car trip, describe something they see while fellow passengers guess). Games that demand student-created content, on the other hand, work best with intermediate- or advanced-level groups. The complexity of the game is commensurate with the complexity of the student content, so the content of Secret Creatures requires less time invested than the game to follow, Guessing Cards, which in turn, requires less than the creation of board games. In general, though, the strategy of creating games from student content works because students naturally and inevitably tend to choose content at their current proficiency level.

These games will work regardless of the makeup of the classroom. As both creators and players of the game, students are assured an active and central role. Learners who share a common first language (L1), however, have the advantage of using their native tongue, not only English, during the creation period.

CURRICULUM, TASKS, MATERIALS

Getting Started

Scratch paper and a pair of scissors are the key tools. A blackboard is useful for writing the language models or paradigms upon which the students will base their descriptions. This particular version of Secret Creatures is for students of intermediate to advanced level, although it can easily be modified for beginners.

How to Play

1. **Use a model.** The teacher writes this model on the board:

   If I were this creature,

   I would eat . . . .

   I would live . . . .

   I would . . . . (do what?)

   I would be afraid of . . . .

   My colors would be . . . .

2. **Discover, as a class, what a *secret creature* is.** Ask students to think of unusual creatures: grasshopper, woodpecker, eel, mosquito, lizard, sea anemone, etc. A sampling from different habitats is useful. This exercise gets students on track. It keeps them away from cat, dog, lion, and other

common animals. (The teacher might even outlaw cats and dogs, saying that they are not "secret" enough.)

3. **Demonstrate the model on the board.** Describe one or two creatures without saying their names. The model on the board is a guideline, not a requirement, and demonstrations should reflect that. Students guess the creatures described by the teacher. Next, the teacher asks a volunteer to do what the teacher has done, describe a secret creature for the whole class.

    When students actually play the game, they will encounter the same creatures more than once and likely will skip the description. Therefore, it is useful to include among the demonstrations a description of a creature that has already been chosen, describing it in a new way and letting students know they should do the same.

4. **Generate the student content.** Now students know what to expect in terms of how the game is played and what kind of creatures are involved. Their next task is to write the names of five secret creatures on a scrap of paper. The number of creatures selected can be adjusted according to level; however, the more content the students produce, the longer the game will last, and a greater amount of descriptive speaking will be generated. Besides, among the student-contributed content, there will be duplicate, illegible, or unknown creatures. Asking the students to contribute the names of more, rather than fewer, creatures makes up for deficiencies and keeps the game from falling flat in the early stages. Thus, during this stage, students should not be rushed. This can be a contemplative period (5–10 minutes) where students can consult their dictionaries, consider, prepare, and perhaps practice describing in their heads. Remind students that their creatures are secret. They should not show them to anyone.

    If the class shares a native tongue, instruct the students to write the name of the creature in their L1. The game will become slow if a student does not recognize the name of the creature written on the piece of paper. The point is to practice speaking and describing in English, not to learn the English words for various creatures. The guessers, too, are allowed to guess the creature in the native language if they do not know the English word. When the game is finished, the class may brainstorm the English names of the creatures they did not know.

    In a class that features a mix of tongues, students will need to write the content in English. They may be encouraged to draw a picture of the creature or provide a brief definition. Encourage the use of dictionaries during both the preparation and playing stages.

5. **Divide the students into small groups of three or four.** Each student will choose a Creature Card, (i.e., the small pieces of paper on which

the students have written the creatures' names), and describe his five creatures. The other group members listen and guess. When that card is finished, the next student describes the five creatures on his card. Students are encouraged to use the model written on the board if needed.

6. **Redistribute the content.** During the speaking part of the game, the teacher helps and encourages students, and manages the student-created content. To begin, students describe the creatures on their own cards to the members of this group. After that initial stage, the teacher will rotate the content, which means keeping an eye on all the groups, noting when someone finishes a card, and passing that card along, in a systematic way, to the next group. The goal is to keep the game and the speaking practice going.

Variations

The primary objective of Secret Creatures is to provide sustained low-anxiety speaking practice. It is easy to see in this case a target grammar structure, that of the conditional aspect ("If I were this creature, I would . . . ."). By adjusting the game design to focus on particular structures, teachers can incorporate these games into the curriculum at almost any stage, supplementing textbook grammar drills with energizing games that allow students to explore the structure through unscripted speech.

Figures 1–4 demonstrate several ways to revise the model of Secret Creatures to produce high-repetition practice of different forms. The method of generating student content remains the same.

More Student-Made Guessing Cards

The next step toward more involved guessing games is prompting students to create more involved content. Any subject is possible, such as *Excuses You Make for Being Late to School, Your Favorite Foods and Drinks, Action Verbs, Things to Do with Travel, Household Items, Adjectives to Describe People*, or even, for instance, *Parts of an Airplane* for aviation students of English.

The models-paradigms in this case are in the form of cards. The first thing to do is explore topics like those listed above. The teacher may solicit 10 or 20 topics from the class and write them on the board. Students may then choose from the topics on the board or create their own, writing them across the top of 3 x 5 cards or on slips of paper. Figure 5 illustrates the cards with topics.

Next, students list 3, 5, or 7 items under the topic. Figure 6 illustrates the cards with item lists.

Now the class has content. Each group of students has created a number of cards, each with a topic heading and items listed below. A demonstration is again in order. The teacher or a student takes one card, reads the topic to the class, and then describes each item until it has been guessed.

Once students understand the nature of this game, they will choose fascinating

I am this secret creature.	I live . . . .
	I eat . . . .
	I like . . . .
	I don't like . . . .
	My colors are . . . .

Figure 1. Basic Level: First Person

This creature . . .	lives . . . .
	eats . . . .
	looks like . . . .
	doesn't like . . . .
	has these colors . . . .

Figure 2. Basic Level: Third-Person "s"

Before I was a person, I was this creature. I used to . . .	live . . . .
	eat . . . .
	go . . . .
	like to . . . .
	be . . . .
	have . . . .

Figure 3. Intermediate Level: Used to

If I had been this creature in a previous life . . .	I would have lived . . . .
	I would have eaten . . . .
	I would have . . . . (done what?)
	I would have been afraid of . . . .
	My colors would have been . . . .

Figure 4. Higher Levels: Unreal Conditionals in the Past

Things That Have to Do With Valentines Day	Things in Paris	Adjectives That Describe People

Figure 5. Cards With Topics

Things That Have to Do With Valentines Day	Things in Paris	Adjectives That Describe People
1. candy	1. French people	1. stubborn
2. love	2. Eiffel Tower	2. sly
3. kisses	3. wine	3. generous
4. cards	4. the Seine (river)	4. talented
5. pink	5. good food	5. wild
6. flowers	6. cheese	6. stupid
7. romance	7. shopping	7. nice

Figure 6. Cards With Item Lists

topics and enjoy creating guessing cards. In 10 minutes or so, a class as a whole can generate 25 or 50 cards, which will translate into a large amount of speaking practice.

Each group's guessing cards will be shifted to a neighboring group, so that they begin playing with fresh and unknown content. When they have finished with the cards at hand, the teacher will rotate new cards from another group, thus sustaining the game and speaking practice.

Student-Made Board Games

The two board game templates included in Appendixes A and B, Board Games 1 and 2, are based on the model of Name Three Things. That is, students roll a die, land on a square, and respond orally to the cue written there. For instance, the square may read, . . . *you like to eat in winter*, and the student will name three things accordingly. Naming three or more things instead of just one increases the volume and repetition of student responses.

The direction of the content is established by the teacher because he will have completed the first several squares of the board, offering students patterns on which to base the remaining content. Students in groups will then complete the game boards themselves. In this way, the creation of the game—not just the playing of it—is an effective language activity.

Board Game 1 offers no theme or grammar; its objective is speaking practice. Games can be simply designed to practice or explore vocabulary themes or grammar structures.

Board Game 2 offers advanced learners a way to explore the differences between *should* and *to be supposed to*—no easy task as the terms are on occasion interchangeable. Accordingly, students should be allowed sufficient time to complete the board game with accurate and applicable examples of the target vocabulary.

If the teacher cannot supply a board game template, one copy per group, students can draw the board, which has a simple layout, on a blank piece of paper or a cardboard sheet. One class can then create half a dozen related but different games to be played by groups that same day, or even some time in the future.

REFLECTIONS

Classroom games in general can appear untidy, which is one reason teachers may relegate them to the unswept corners of the classroom hour. Players become "so engrossed . . . that they forget to act in the classic classroom patterns" (Rixon, 1981, p. 5). The games discussed here, with student-derived content, may appear messier still because none of the content has been field-tested. That untidiness is, for the most part, only appearance. True, there are always hurdles, such as enigmatic content, groups working at different speeds, and bottlenecks in the redistribution process. Still, all considered, even a messy game session is never a disappointment. For one thing, learners tend to be highly motivated and invested. After all, they themselves have contributed to the game's creation, and their contributions help ensure that the content is appropriate to their level and interests. They also are pleased to hear themselves speaking so much English and glad to know that each time someone guesses whatever they have described, they have communicated a successful English-language message. Additionally, games driven by student content require little to no time, preparation, or financial investment from the teacher.

REFERENCES

Rixon, S. (1981). *How to use games in language teaching*. London: MacMillan.

Ur, P. (1987). *Grammar practice activities*. Cambridge: Cambridge University Press.

Additional Resources

Lee, W. R. (1979). *Language teaching games and contests*. Oxford: Oxford University Press.

Wright, A., Betteridge, D., & Buckby, M. (1983). *Games for language learning*. Cambridge: Cambridge University Press.

Kevin McCaughey has worked as a teaching English as a foreign language consultant throughout the former Soviet republics, in Saudi Arabia, and in the United States. His experience includes being a Fulbright lecturer in Minsk, Belarus. Kevin's Web site, English Teachers Everywhere (http://www.etseverywhere.com), offers a wide range of original ESL audio.

APPENDIX A: BOARD GAME TEMPLATE 1 FOR NAME THREE THINGS—GENERAL THEMES (PRE-INTERMEDIATE AND UP)

Name Three Things You Should and Shouldn't Do

Finishing the Game Board	Playing
1. Follow the examples in the first five squares. Players who land on that square will have to list the three things requested in that square. 2. Work together as a group to complete all the squares on the board. Take your time thinking of interesting situations and write them in the squares.	1. Role the die and move your token to the appropriate square. 2. Name the three things requested on that square. 3. Take turns. 4. Everyone should make it to the finish!

FINISH (YOU SHOULD BE PROUD) 25	24	23	22	21
20	19	18	17	16
11	12	13	14	15
10	9	8	7	6 ↑
START 1	. . . you shouldn't say to your wife/ husband/love 2	. . . you shouldn't do in a library 3	. . . you should do if you visit Paris 4	. . .you shouldn't do when it's raining 5

APPENDIX B: BOARD GAME TEMPLATE 2 FOR NAME THREE THINGS—*SHOULD & BE SUPPOSED TO* (ADVANCED)

Name Three Things—*Should & Be Supposed To*

Finishing the Game Board		Playing	
1. Follow the examples in the first five squares. Players who land on that square will have to list the three things requested in that square. 2. Work together as a group to complete all the squares on the board. Take your time thinking of interesting situations and write them in the squares.		1. Role the die and move your token to the appropriate square. 2. Name the three things requested on that square. 3. Take turns. 4. Everyone should make it to the finish!	

FINISH (YOU SHOULD BE PROUD)				
25	24	23	22	21
20	19	18	17	16
11	12	13	14	15
. . . you shouldn't do when it's raining	. . . you're not supposed to do late at night	. . . you should do with your dog	. . . you shouldn't say when someone gives you a gift	. . . you're supposed to do to be a good citizen of your country
10	9	8	7	6 ↑
START	. . . you shouldn't say to your wife/husband/love	. . . you're not supposed to do in a library	. . . you should do if you visit Paris	. . . you're supposed to do to be healthy
1	2	3	4	5

CHAPTER 22

Energize and Educate!

Karen Hilgeman

INTRODUCTION

Suffering from sluggish, sleepy students? Energize them! Give them chances to move around and have fun while they learn. They will become enthusiastic, stay on task, and be focused on learning much longer than in a regular practice session. Energizing games are the way to go!

In the course of a lesson, teachers present new material and then arrange a series of practice activities to help students understand, use, and master the new information, structures, or vocabulary. There are many kinds of practice activities, some involving listening and speaking, some involving reading and writing. They can be done individually or collaboratively. Students need practice, so teachers must have a repertoire of activities. Games are an essential part of that repertoire because they are so fun that students do not even realize that they are learning. Instead, they concentrate on having fun, cooperating, or competing. In doing so, they practice and use the target material in new ways.

The following eight games are energizing options for practice or review activities. None of them are for teaching new content—they are all for practicing and reviewing in novel ways what has already been taught. Each of them shows a way to practice the target content in a way that is fun, exciting, and often competitive, thereby causing students to try harder and longer. Best of all, these games involve the students moving while learning. Movement, excitement, competition, and interest all add up to energy.

The presentation of each game includes example content such as job vocabulary or prepositions. But the content listed should be used only if it is the content teachers are currently teaching their students. Otherwise, teachers should adapt these games to reflect and practice the content they have recently taught their class. That is the purpose of these eight activities; they are highly adaptable and can be remade to match the exact content that students need. In the *Variations* section after each game, ways and examples for how to alter the content to fit students' needs are given.

CONTEXT

In addition to adaptable content, the eight games can be adjusted to accommodate students with lower or higher levels of English proficiency. Therefore, these games work in nearly any English as a second language (ESL) or English as a foreign language (EFL) setting, including elementary and secondary school, adult education, and higher education. Most of these games are suitable for both children and adults, but teachers should determine whether each game is appropriate for their classes.

CURRICULUM, TASKS, MATERIALS

DRAWING RELAY RACE

Overview

Relay races are fun ways to get classes to practice because they force students to move quickly. Because they are contests, students often jump right in to the activity rather than hesitating and overthinking as they sometimes do when there is no time factor. A drawing relay race provides extra fun because of the often hilarious results of hastily drawn figures.

Materials

- a board with the alphabet written out for each team (Figure 1) or, if no board is available, poster board or newsprint taped to the wall

- several markers or chalk, depending on the board or paper used

- copies of the alphabet drawing list cut into strips (one set per team; see Figure 2).

a	b	c	d	e	
f	g	h	i	j	
k	l	m	n	o	
p	q	r	s	t	
u	v	w	x	y	z

Figure 1. Alphabet Grid on Board

Make the "t" into a person.

Make the "n" into an umbrella.

Make the "o" into a face.

Make the "b" into a bicycle.

Make the "v" into an ice cream cone

Make the "p" into something.

Make the "m" into a bird.

Make the "e" into a person.

Make the "l" into a house.

Make the "k" into something.

Make the "j" into a shoe.

Make the "x" into a fish.

Figure 2. Alphabet Drawing List

Content: Names of Letters

Students often have trouble saying the names of the letters, but being able to do so is an essential compensation skill when someone does not understand their pronunciation. For instance, students might have to spell out their last names, street names, or countries to be understood. Before being able to do that, students must be able to correctly pronounce the names of the letters in the English alphabet. The Drawing Relay Race is a fun, fast-paced review for students who have mastered or nearly mastered the letter names.

Procedures

1. Write the lowercase alphabet in a grid at the board or on poster board on the wall. Put the letters in a square with five or six letters per row (see Figure 1). Make the letters about 5 inches high. Make one copy of the alphabet for each team.

   Cut up a copy of the drawing list for each group (see Figure 2). Put a complete set (with each strip of paper folded in half once) in a bowl or on a paper plate.

2. Divide the class into teams of five to six students. Give each team a few minutes to review the names of the letters. Tell them that it is a contest, so they should work together to review.

3. Have each team form a line. Make sure that each team's line begins a short distance away from the board so that students can move to and from the board in a relay style.

4. Give the first student in each line a marker or chalk as appropriate, and explain that that student will be running to the board.

5. Place a bowl with the instructions next to the second student in each line. Explain that this student will be reading the instruction to the first student.

6. Explain the game to the students. When the game begins, the second student will read the instruction to the first student, who will rush to the board, quickly complete the drawing task, rush back to the line, and give the marker or chalk to the second student, who then becomes the new first student in line. The student who just drew should go to the end of the line after returning the marker or chalk. Then all the students should move up one step.

7. The new second person in line picks another instruction from the bowl and reads it to the first person in line, who rushes to the board.

8. Then the reader says the next instruction to the next student in line.

9. The game is over once a team has finished drawing all of the items in the instructions.

Note: If students are hesitant to start drawing, remind them that this is a race!

Variations

Uppercase activity: The instructions on the alphabet drawing list are designed to be used with the lowercase alphabet. If practice of the uppercase alphabet is desired, change the items on the list to ones that can be easily drawn out of capital letters.

Vocabulary activity: This relay race also could be used to practice vocabulary. In this case, put words on the board in front of each team of students. Have the reader give definitions to teammates who then race to the board and circle the vocabulary word that fits the definition.

WORD RANK LINE-UP

Overview

ESL students often are confused by words with similar meanings. Even if they can identify the basic meaning of the word, they do not know the nuances, such as how a fine work of art is called *beautiful*, not *cute*. Line-up activities allow students to rank words in order of their intensity. These activities ask students to establish, evaluate, and redo a ranking of similar vocabulary words. The fact that the students themselves are physically moving around allows them to try out several ways to rank the words until they settle on an order they like.

Materials

- thick markers and large pieces of paper (preferably cardstock)
- one prewritten sign that says *good* and one that says *bad*.

Content: Small Talk—Answering "How Are You?"

"How are you?" is a question that may pop up at least half a dozen times a day, yet ESL students often only know a few ways to respond to it. Additionally, they may not be able to distinguish that a response like "Great" or "Fantastic" is stronger and more positive than "OK" or "Pretty good." This activity will help them learn when to use common answers to this question.

Procedures

1. At the beginning of class, ask students how they are.

2. Write their answers on the board.

3. Facilitate a discussion about whether any of the answers basically mean the same thing as *good*. Do any mean *bad*?

4. Encourage students to think of some more answers to "How are you?" that mean either *good* or *bad* to some degree and list them in a chart (see Figure 3). Do this by asking questions such as "What if you just broke your leg? How would you answer then?" or "What if you just got a raise at your job?" Also discuss whether there are any answers that are in the middle between *good* and *bad*. The word list generated by the class might look like Figure 3.

5. Assign each word to a student who should use a thick marker to copy the word onto a full sheet of cardstock (one word per page.) Encourage students to write as neatly and as largely as possible.

6. Choose an area of the room, preferably along a wall, for the line-up activity.

Bad	Middle	Good
Terrible	OK	Great
Pretty bad	So-so	Fantastic
Horrible		Fine
Bad		Pretty good
		Not bad

Figure 3. Example Chart of Answers to "How Are You?"

7. Hang the premade sign that says *good* at one side of the space and the one that says *bad* at the other.

8. Collect the words, shuffle them, and hand them out to students. If there are enough, give each student one. If there are not, the students who did not get words will help direct the activity.

9. Have the students stand in random order with their backs to the wall between the *good* and *bad* signs. They should hold their word card facing away from them so that everyone can see, and then begin to line themselves up according to the intensity of the words (see Figure 4).

10. Encourage any students who do not have words to stand back, view the big picture, decide where the words should be, and direct students to move accordingly.

Facilitate by asking questions such as "Think about it . . . if Maria says she's *fine*, but Yvonna says she is *great*, who do you think is happier?" to help lead students toward a logical ranking.

Variations

For higher level students: Have students rank other groups of similar adjectives. For example, advanced students could rank *uneasy, apprehensive, anxious, ill at ease,* and *worried*. In this case, the signs at either end of the line-up should read *stronger* and *weaker*. Students could use dictionaries to see sample sentences using these words before deciding how to rank them.

Extension activity: In subsequent lessons, students can also practice asking follow-up questions to ascertain why someone is doing *great* or *terrible*. This could also lead into a discussion and some practices on what to say upon hearing good or bad news.

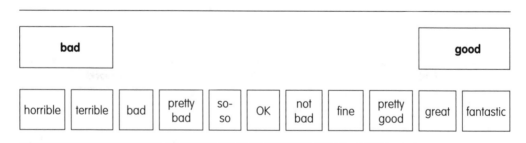

Note: Ranking words like this is a subjective activity. Not all English speakers would rank these words in exactly this order, but proficient English speakers would likely choose a similar order. The purpose of this activity is to raise students' awareness of the nuances and usages of similar words.

Figure 4. Example of Line-up of Word Order from Figure 3

SPORTSCASTING GAME

Overview

The Sportscasting Game is a fun and interactive way for students to practice the present progressive tense. It allows a student to perform actions while another student tells what is happening using sportscaster-style speech. The fact that the sportscaster does not know what the student will do next allows students to produce present progressive sentences in an authentic, nonscripted way. The silly yet fun use of an ordinary marker as a "microphone" often amuses the students and makes them more eager to keep playing the game.

Materials

- a thick marker or similar object to be used as the "microphone" (one per group)
- sportscaster game role cards, cut apart (one set per group; see Figure 5).

Content: Present Progressive Actions

Teaching about the present progressive can be tricky because of the nature of the verb tense. It is mostly used for actions happening at the current time, so it is difficult to say, "Chen is riding a bicycle," when Chen and all the other students are sitting in the classroom. This activity involves students taking turns performing actions and reporting on what others are doing.

Procedures

1. Divide students into groups of three or four.

2. Pass out role cards A, B, C, and D so that each student in the group has a different letter role card (see Figure 5). If the cards contain an action that is not possible given the constraints of the classroom, rewrite the card before copying it and giving it to students.

Role Card A	Role Card B	Role Card C	Role Card D
1. Walk to the door	1. Stand up	1. Open your book	1. Stand up
2. Open the door	2. Sit down	2. Close your book	2. Turn around
3. Close the door	3. Smile	3. Pick up your pencil	3. Walk to a wall
4. Knock on the door two times	4. Stand up	4. Put your pencil in your book	4. Knock on the wall
5. Walk to the board	5. Turn around	5. Stand up	5. Walk to your desk
6. Draw a rabbit	6. Walk to the board	6. Walk to the teacher's desk	6. Move your chair
7. _____	7. _____	7. _____	7. _____
8. _____	8. _____	8. _____	8. _____

Figure 5. Sportscaster Game Role Cards

3. Instruct students to read their card and add two more steps in the spaces at the end.

4. Assign which role card—A, B, C, or D—each group will start with so that not all groups are performing the same task (such as *walk to the door* on role card A) at the same time.

5. While the first student is performing the actions on the role card, the student to the right is the first sportscaster. The sportscaster holds the marker as if it is a microphone and tells what the first student is doing much as a sportscaster commentates on a game. The sportscaster should keep up a running commentary using the present progressive, such as "Niki is standing up. She is walking to the board. She is picking up the chalk."

6. Encourage the other students in the group to help the sportscaster with any unknown vocabulary.

7. After one round is finished, the person to the right performs the role card actions while the student who just performed the last set of actions becomes the new sportscaster.

Variations

For lower level students: Lower level students may benefit from an additional step before playing the game. Students can be grouped according to the letter of the card they have. Then they can discuss what each action means and work together to create the last two steps in the process. After that, they can be divided into groups in which each group has a student with role cards A, B, C, and D.

With other verb tenses: This activity also could be adapted to other verb tenses. For example, each role card could be shortened to just four activities. Then a student could act out the four steps, after which the other students write what the student did using simple past tense.

FLASHCARD BOARD GAME

Overview

Flashcards, although sometimes overlooked, can be a fun and effective classroom tool. After the new vocabulary has been taught, countless flashcard games and activities can be used to practice and master new vocabulary. This activity is an easy way to turn flashcards into a game that students love. The example below shows flashcards with pictures on them, but any flashcards could work.

Materials

- flashcards with a picture of one clothing item on each (one set per group)
- cardstock copies of the flashcard board game pieces cut out (one set per group; see Figure 6)
- dice (one die per group)
- something to use as tokens to move across the game board after students roll the die, such as the game pieces from a commercial board game, different colored paper disks, or different coins
- space to set up the board games. (This activity works best if there are tables in the classroom. With children, the board games could be set up on the floor.)

Content: Clothing Items—Vocabulary

The names of clothing items are usually taught to ESL beginners, so they are used here as an example of how flashcards with pictures on them can be made into a game. Nearly any kind of flashcard can be used in this game, however, as shown in the *Variations* section.

Procedures

1. Divide students into groups of three to five.

2. Give each group a set of flash cards, a set of board game pieces (see Figure 6), and playing tokens. Alternately, if appropriate, ask groups to furnish their own change so that each student uses a different coin as a playing token during the board game.

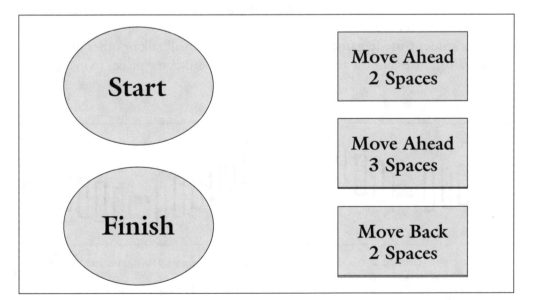

Figure 6. Flashcard Board Game Pieces

3. Instruct groups to create their own board games by setting the Start piece at one end of the table and the Finish piece at the other. Have them set the flashcards and the other board game pieces on a path in between. Encourage them to have fun discussing where the Move Ahead and Go Back cards should be placed (see Figure 7).

4. Have students put their tokens or coins at *Start*.

5. Choose or allow students to choose who goes first.

6. The first person should roll the die and move the appropriate number of spaces. For very beginners, the first person can just name the item of clothing landed on, such as *hat*. For students who are more advanced, the first person can create a sentence that names the item and tells where it is worn (e.g., "I wear a hat on my head").

7. The next student to the right then rolls the die and takes a turn.

8. The game ends either when one or all students have reached *Finish*.

9. Encourage students to help each other when one cannot remember the name of the vocabulary on the flashcard.

Variations

For flashcards with English words on them: Have students use the word in a sentence or give a definition.

For flashcards with foreign words on them: Have students give the equivalent English word.

For flashcards with questions on them: Have students read the question aloud and answer it. Alternately, the student who lands on the question can ask it to the person to the right.

For a student-made game: Have students write small talk or other questions on blank flashcards and use these along with the board game pieces to make the game.

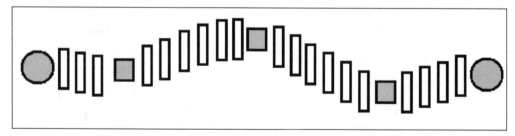

Note: The circles represent the Start and Finish pieces, the squares represent the Move Ahead and Move Back pieces, and the thin rectangles represent ordinary flashcards.

Figure 7. Example Setup of a Flashcard Board Game

FLIP A COIN

Overview

At the end of a unit on a particular topic, such as making requests, it is both rewarding and beneficial to have a comprehensive activity that draws upon everything that students have learned. Think of it as a fun final exam in a game format. The Making Requests game shows specifically how to set up such an activity featuring making and answering requests. The added element of flipping coins lends a fun element of chance as to whether or not the request will be honored. In addition, students are often shocked and amused to find that not every culture flips coins in the same manner.

Materials

- copies of the Making Requests game cards (see Figure 8), cut up (approximately one page for every other student)

- enough quarters (or similar coins) for every other student to have one (supplied by the teacher or students as appropriate).

Content: Making Requests

Making requests is often difficult for ESL students. In addition to finding the proper wording for the request, there is also a question of levels of formality. Even answering requests can prove difficult: There are often issues about how to say *no* politely. This game is to be used as a final review after extensive study and practice of how to make and answer requests.

Procedures

1. Divide the class into two halves.

2. Explain that in the first part of the game, half the class will be making requests and the other half will be answering them.

3. Start with one half of the class. Hand out "Game One: Make the Requests" (see Figure 8). Have the students work together to fill in the beginning of the requests. If there are too many students to work all together, divide them into several smaller groups.

4. While the first half is working on the previous step, tell the second half that they will be answering requests. Together, brainstorm a list of ways to say *yes* (e.g., "Sure," "Of course," or "Here you are") and *no* (e.g., "I'm sorry," "I can't help you," or "I don't have one"). Hand out "Game One: Answer the Request" (see Figure 8) and have the students fill out one *yes* answer and one *no* answer for each request. This activity could also be done in pairs.

Game One: Make the Request	Game One: Answer the Request	
1. _____ borrow a pen?	1. . . . . borrow a pen? (yes)	(no)
2. _____ use your dictionary?	2. . . . use your dictionary? (yes)	(no)
3. _____ ask you a question?	3. . . . ask you a question? (yes)	(no)
4. _____ have a tissue?	4. . . . have a tissue? (yes)	(no)
5. _____ borrow $5?	5. . . . borrow $5? (yes)	(no)

Figure 8. Making Requests Game Cards

5. After the second half has finished, pass out a coin or ask them to produce their own. Each student in this half of the class will need one.

6. On the board, draw a rough sketch showing that the head of the coin equals *yes* and the tail of the coin equals *no*. Let them practice flipping the coins a few times. Explain to them that for this game, when a student makes a request of them, they will flip the coin to determine which answer to give. Have them practice flipping the coins a few times.

7. When both halves of the class are ready, send the students who will be answering the requests to different parts of the room. Have them spread out and then sit down. They will not move; the students making the requests will be coming to them. All students should have their "Game One" paper with them.

8. Explain to the students making the requests that they will stand up and walk to the seated students. They will make a request and wait for an answer. If they get a *yes* answer, they can mark that request off of their list. If they get a *no* answer, they cannot. In either case, after making one request of a seated student, they must move to another student.

9. To make sure that everyone understands what will happen, before beginning, ask a few students from each half what they will be doing.

10. Begin the game and let students make and answer requests. Stop the game once one of the students making requests has received a *yes* answer to all of the requests.

11. After this round, have the students reassemble into the original two halves. Repeat steps 3 through 10 with "Game Two" (see Figure 9), so that the students who made the requests before will now be answering and students who answered before will be making the requests.

Variations

Added step for formal versus informal feature: If desired, have the students answering requests wear name tags that have different members of society on them such as *brother, stranger, roommate, teacher, grandfather,* and *best friend.* Then the students making the requests will have to use an appropriate formal or informal language based on to whom they are speaking

Other games with flipping coins: Coins can be used in place of dice in board games. Heads would mean moving one space and tails would mean moving two. Students could also flip coins to practice vocabulary words in small groups. For each vocabulary word, students could flip the coin and then say the definition if it is heads and use the word in a sentence if it is tails. As with using dice, flipping coins seems to add an element of fun and inject energy into what might otherwise be a rather ordinary practice activity.

Game Two: Make the Request	**Game Two: Answer the Request**	
1. _____ borrow some paper?	1. . . . borrow some paper?	
	(yes)	(no)
2. _____ sit here?	2. . . . sit here?	
	(yes)	(no)
3. _____ use your ruler?	3. . . . use your ruler?	
	(yes)	(no)
4. _____ have a cookie?	4. . . . have a cookie?	
	(yes)	(no)
5. _____ borrow your book?	5. . . . borrow your book?	
	(yes)	(no)

Figure 9. Making Requests Game Cards

TIC-TAC-TOE

Overview

Tic-Tac-Toe is yet another engaging way to have students practice with new vocabulary. In the following example, students will make true sentences about their classroom using the target vocabulary of prepositions. This game can be played in two ways—either the nice way in which students help each other if one cannot remember what the word in the square means, or the cut-throat way in which students lose their turn if they get the vocabulary wrong.

Materials

- a tic-tac-toe handout for each pair of students (see Figure 10).

Content: Preposition Practice

Beginning students need practice to master prepositions of place in English. Instead of having them make sentences about something they see in a picture, such as *The ball is on the box*, have them make true sentences about what they see around them in the classroom. The fact that it is a contest makes students all the more eager to choose a square, make a sentence, and then place their *X* or *O* on the grid.

Procedures

1. Draw the tic-tac-toe grid on the board (see Figure 10).

2. Demonstrate with the class by making true sentences about the classroom out of the prepositions. For example, for the word *under*, ostentatiously look around the classroom and point out something that is under something else. Then make a sentence such as *The trash can is under the table.*

behind	on	next to
under	in	in front of
above	between	near

Figure 10. Tic-Tac-Toe Grid With Prepositions

3. Have two volunteers play the tic-tac-toe game on the board. Have one use *X* and one use *O*. The student who goes first should pick a square and make his *X* or *O* in it. Then that student has to make a sentence about the classroom. For this example game, encourage other students to help out. Then the other student chooses a square and puts the *X* or *O* in it. Continue until one student has won the game with three squares in a row or the game is a tie.

4. Put students into pairs and give one tic-tac-toe grid to each pair.

5. Have students decide who will use *X* and who will use *O*.

6. Have them play the game until all nine squares have a mark in them.

7. When finished, have students switch partners, get a new tic-tac-toe grid, and play again.

Variations

For extra support: If desired, put students into groups of three. The third student who is not playing can be the judge who decides if the sentence made is correct or not. Alternately, the third student could help either player form sentences.

With a different playing grid: After playing a few games with the tic-tac-toe grid and prepositions, distribute a new grid that has the name of an item in the classroom in each square. Then students can make sentences about the location of that item using prepositions.

With other structures: The tic-tac-toe activity can be used to practice many different structures. The grid can contain vocabulary words that students have to give the definition of or use in a sentence. The grid can contain adjectives and students can say the opposite. The game can also contain questions that students have to answer before making their mark.

ROLL THE DIE

Overview

Students cannot help having fun when they get to use dice in class. They will happily and tirelessly form questions or sentences based on a roll of the die. The use of a six-sided die works out nicely for the six traditional *wh-* question words.

Materials

- dice (enough for one per pair)

- a copy of the question word dice chart written on the board or copied and distributed to students (see Figure 11)

Content: *Wh-* Questions

Questions that begin with *who, what, when, where, why,* and *how* often can confuse students. Even though these words are essential for carrying on conversations, making small talk, and getting information, students struggle with them. This game is a fun review for students who have been studying the uses of these question words.

Procedures

1. Review the meanings of the six *wh-* question words.

2. Divide students into pairs.

3. Display the question word dice chart (see Figure 11) on the board or give students copies.

4. Choose a fun way to select which student starts. For instance, say that the student with the shortest hair or the student whose birthday is earliest in the year should go first.

5. Have the first student roll the die, and then ask a *wh-* question according to the number rolled. For example, if a three is rolled, the first student asks a *when* question.

6. The partner answers it and then continues the game by rolling the die.

7. If variety is desired after this has gone on for a few minutes, have students switch partners.

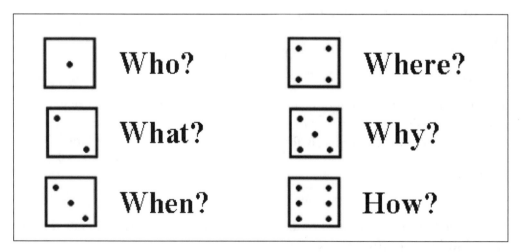

Figure 11. Question Word Dice Chart

Variations

For focused *wh*- questions: Assign themes such as sports, entertainment, food, or weather for the questions.

For other dice activities: The roll the die concept can work for other activities also. Each number could be given a different vocabulary word that students could make into sentences, or each number could be given a different task, such as *1) Name a kind of fruit, 2) Name a sport,* or *3) Name a famous actor.*

VOCABULARY BINGO

Overview

The classroom version of bingo is another way for students to practice recognizing vocabulary. In addition, students get practice writing the target vocabulary as they make their own bingo cards.

Materials

- vocabulary bingo page (one per student; see Figure 12)
- one copy of the vocabulary words cut into slips of paper and put in a bowl or cup.

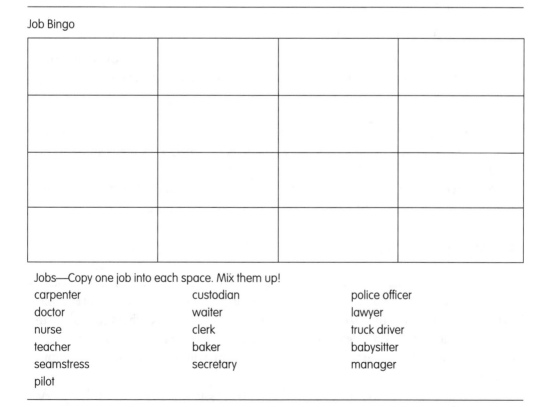

Job Bingo

Jobs—Copy one job into each space. Mix them up!

carpenter	custodian	police officer
doctor	waiter	lawyer
nurse	clerk	truck driver
teacher	baker	babysitter
seamstress	secretary	manager
pilot		

Figure 12. Vocabulary Bingo Page

Content: Job Names—Vocabulary

Students in intermediate ESL classes as well as preworkplace literacy classes often study the names of jobs and careers in English. This activity shows a way to indicate mastery of those job names, but it can be used for many different kinds of vocabulary.

Procedures

1. Review vocabulary for job names with students.

2. Hand out the vocabulary bingo page to each student (see Figure 12).

3. Have students write job names into the squares of the bingo card. They should mix up the order by putting the words randomly in the squares. They can cross out the word on the list below once they have copied it so that they do not use the same word twice. Encourage them to print neatly and copy the words correctly.

4. When everyone is finished, explain how to play.

5. Begin by pulling a slip of paper with a job name randomly out of the cup or bowl. Tell the responsibilities of the person who does that work without saying the name of the job. For example, if the word is *pilot*, say "This person flies an airplane."

6. Students find the word on their card and make an *X* across it.

7. The first person to get bingo (four squares in a row—up, down, or diagonally) wins and can be given piece of candy or small prize if desired.

Variations

For lower level students: Instead of a description, just say the name of the job several times and have students find it on their bingo card. This helps students connect what they hear with what they read on the page.

   For other vocabulary words: With other vocabulary items besides jobs, give a definition of the word and have students find it on their bingo card.

REFLECTIONS

These eight games form a basis for a strong repertoire of activities that are both energizing and educational. Because they can be adapted in terms of content and level, they can be used in dozens of different ways, allowing teachers to make fun, interesting games that cover exactly the content their students need to practice. Before using any of the games, decide what content you will use and then adapt the game accordingly.

   Keep in mind that overusing any one activity or game is never a good idea. As with show business, "always leave them wanting more" is a good motto for games in the ESL classroom. Let a game run its course, but quit before it gets boring or old. In that way, students will get a fun, engaging game that provides exactly the kind of practice they need.

Karen Hilgeman is a professional development specialist at the Adult Learning Resource Center in Arlington Heights, Illinois, in the United States. She teaches ESL and citizenship preparation classes to adult students, presents regularly at TESOL conventions and other forums, and has conducted teacher training in the United States, Japan, and China.

CHAPTER 23

Do-It-Yourself Games

Susan Kelly

INTRODUCTION

Like many English language teachers, I see games as an excellent means of practicing and reinforcing language learning, particularly speaking and listening. I enjoy them when I am learning a language and try to build them into my lessons whenever I can. I have found that whatever setting I have found myself in—kindergarten, middle school, language academy, university, or corporation—learners enjoy games, and the majority of them understand that playing games promotes language skill development. Games are not a waste of time. Thus I have acquired several books containing many game ideas, and I have spent hours searching the Internet for more.

As a teacher who believes in student-centered education, I need to have the students create the games, not me (or, I should say, not always me). Because the textbook I am using, *Strategic Reading 2*, by Jack C. Richards and Samuela Eckstut, includes a unit on games, having students create the games we would play in class made sense.

Instilling an understanding of learner autonomy in students is important. They must learn to manage their own English education. If I do all the planning and make all the decisions for class activities, I inhibit their participation (e.g., see Scharle & Szabo, 2000). Thus I introduced a Do-It-Yourself Games Project in which students work in small groups of three or four to design games for the class. The objective for this approach is to build learner autonomy, encourage collaboration, and provide a fun, motivating way to practice the language structures learned in class.

CONTEXT

I designed this project while teaching at Sogang University in Seoul. The majority of my students were second-semester freshmen with an intermediate proficiency level. A few students may have studied abroad or gone to a foreign-language high school, but they represent less than 10% of a class of 30 students. Because most of the students' high school language instruction was focused on grammar and translation, my department emphasized a communicative approach. We strove to give our students as much time as possible in class for discussion, and my goal was minimal teacher talk. This project helped me achieve that goal.

Although this project was directly connected with the games unit in the class textbook, a teacher can also use this project by connecting it thematically to a curriculum. For example, one might require that students design a game related to the topic currently being covered, such as sports, travel, or film. Another approach is to require students to use the grammar or vocabulary that they are learning.

Based on my experience teaching middle school students in Japan and freshmen in Korea, I would try this project with younger or less advanced students. My main consideration would be whether the students can give directions in English. Students need to be able to give clear directions and apply what they have learned. Preteen and teenage students may not be able to hold outside planning sessions, so I suggest allowing in-class time for creating the games.

CURRICULUM, TASKS, MATERIALS

To implement this idea in the classroom, teachers should first help students understand the objectives for a well-designed game: (a) all students must participate, (b) all students need to speak in English using the grammar and vocabulary learned in class, and (c) each group member needs to speak for at least 2 minutes at one time while addressing the entire class. These objectives can be accomplished by having one person introduce the game, one person thank the class at the conclusion of the game, and the remaining students either explain the rules, act as judges, or ask quiz questions.

On the first day of the games unit, I introduce the project, explaining that students will be creating English games for the class. I then put students into groups, but it is possible to have students choose their own groups.

Because I want the students to do most of the thinking and creating, I offer only a few suggestions. To provide them with a starting point as they plan, I tell them that they can create board games, trivia games, dramatic games, games with music, or anything they can think of. I do not tell them about previous games designed by students because I do not want them to replicate past games, and because they are familiar with creating games for extracurricular clubs they do not need much explicit direction. I do remind them that I am available to answer any questions or offer direction should they encounter problems or confusion with the assignment.

I feel it is important to allow these students freedom in designing their projects because they have had a highly regimented high school experience. My main objective is that they use English and give their peers a chance to use English in conversation. In another setting, I might feel that specific language objectives should be reinforced, but in this setting for this project I want to give my students a chance to be creative and expressive with English. One of the strengths of this project is that it may be adjusted to meet a variety of objectives and needs.

If a group chooses, it can add writing or reading activities to the game. Groups can also reward prizes, but I never mention incentives because I am not a strong believer in extrinsic motivation, and I am satisfied that the project helps students develop intrinsic motivation. I do not want a group to think it must buy prizes.

Each week, I dedicate 20–30 minutes of class time for one of the groups to teach its game and help the class play it. The game leaders must explain the rules and facilitate the playing. They must adjudicate any questions of accuracy or scoring in a fair manner. At the end of class, the group gives me a written copy of the rules of the game, which I assess for grammar, clarity, and organization.

Student Response

My students have created a wide variety of engaging games, far more creative than many games I have found in books or that I might create myself. Students have led games based on the traditional Korean board game *yut*, on modern game shows, and games from Italy, Japan, and the United States. Sometimes a game celebrates an upcoming holiday or sports event such as the World Cup. Sometimes the games heighten awareness of social or school issues. Through these games, I have learned more about what my students consider essential to a good relationship with *seniors* (i.e., the older students who in Korean culture serve as mentors) or the protocol of a successful Korean blind date.

One of the more memorable class games was led during the 2004 Summer Olympics in Athens. A group created a series of short games, including the English 100-Meter Sprint, which called for reading sentences fast; Sentence Relay, which required teams to quickly link sentences that the previous player said; Word Shooting and Speed Game, two vocabulary games; and Ball Game, which resembled Whisper Down the Lane or Telephone, the old game where one person whispers a sentence to the person next to him and the message is whispered down the line until the last person announces the sentence, which has usually become completely different from the original.

Similar to this group, several other teams also have elected to lead two or three short games. By explaining the game's rules and leading the game, each student speaks more, which indicates, I think, that the students understand the importance of each person's chance to use English. They do not simply allow the student perceived to have the "best English" to lead, which otherwise may happen often.

Student Assessment

In addition to assessing the written rules of the game, as explained earlier, I inform students from the beginning that they will be assessed as a group for their level of organization (i.e., they are prepared with the game as scheduled;

they have the needed media, props, and aids), creativity (i.e., the game is different from those of their classmates), and design (i.e., the game ensures that all students participate in English). I also assess students' individual speaking (a total of 2 minutes minimum, but usually about 4) and presentation skills based on the following criteria: volume, body language, and fluency. I use the rubric shown in Figure 1, which is based on a scale from 1 (needs improvement) to 4 (excellent).

This rubric includes both the individual and group criteria. First, I assess each speaker individually for volume, body language, and fluency. When the students finish the game, I assess the group as a whole for organization, creativity, and game design. Each student gets an individual score for the first three categories, and the group members receive the same score for the last three criteria.

Variations

Many of the games are so well done that I use them in other settings, always acknowledging the game's creators. For my midterm oral assessment, I have pairs or triads meet me, and they play a board game that one group designed. Depending on what spot they land on, I ask them questions including, "Do you like Italian food?," "Can you describe Sogang University?," and "Do you think you need cosmetic surgery?" The last question is one I would never ask them myself, but one that students find quite reasonable and interesting in Korea. Such questions offer an opportunity for authentic teacher-student cultural exchange and are another benefit to having the students create a game or form discussion questions. They know what is popular, relevant, and socially acceptable. I don't have that same authority and take fewer risks.

REFLECTIONS

Although this has been an effective, successful project, I have experienced some troubles. One pitfall is that students sometimes are not prepared. They have forgotten that it is their day. Thus I am left to fill 20 minutes of class time and to find a day to reschedule the group. As time is often tight in a semester, I am forced to drop another activity. I realize emergencies arise, but I want to be reasonable as well as organized. Consequently, I allow students to reschedule their game without penalty by e-mailing me 24 hours in advance. If they do not meet their deadline, I deduct 3 points from their organization score. I could also e-mail groups a week in advance to remind them of their date. Even though that seems unnecessary at the college level, it probably would save some frustration.

The Do-It-Yourself Game Project builds community in the class early in the semester. Students become friends with each other while working together. Moreover, they coach and support each other as they prepare their games. Students practice their speaking, collaborate on developing a new game, and consider how to engage their peers in using language, making this a project that promotes cooperation and autonomy while reinforcing language skills.

	Criteria			
	1	**2**	**3**	**4**
Volume	It was very hard to hear you.	Sometimes it was hard to hear you or you spoke too fast. Often monotone.	Usually, I could hear you and you spoke at a nice pace. Monotone at times.	I could always hear you and there was a lot of enthusiasm in your voice.
Body Language	Movements and posture distracted.	Frequent eye contact, posture suggests nervousness.	Good eye contact, posture usually indicates confidence.	Posture indicated confidence.
Fluency	Frequently hesitated. Speech was read from a paper.	Some hesitation and speech seemed memorized.	Occasional hesitation. Some control of pace.	Little hesitation. Pacing was well controlled.
Organization	Was not able to lead game as scheduled. Did not contact teacher.	Fairly organized, but started late or forgot needed tools.	Well organized, but experienced some technical difficulties.	Extremely well organized. Anticipated and prevented mishaps.
Creativity	Identical to an earlier game.	Very similar to games the class has seen.	Fresh, with many new elements.	Unlike any earlier games.
Game Design	Many students could not participate or the game was far too easy.	Some students could not participate and group did not fix the problem.	Most students could participate and they used a lot of English.	All could participate (since the group helped those who did not understand the rules or needed additional vocabulary, etc.)

Figure 1. Rubric to Assess Individual Speakers and Groups (Adapted from Oral Expression Rubric, 2007)

REFERENCES

Oral expression rubric. (2007). Retrieved September 27, 2007, from http://www.teach-nology.com/cgi-bin/oralex.cgi

Scharle, A., & Szabo, A. (2000). *Learner autonomy: A guide to developing learner responsibility.* Cambridge: Cambridge University Press.

Susan Kelly has been an English Language Fellow with the Regional English Language Office in Indonesia and has taught in Japan, Korea, Indonesia, and Los Angeles, in the United States. Her teaching interests include content-based instruction, writing, and integrating technology into the classroom. She has a Masters of Education from Lesley University.

PART 2: Beyond Skills

B. Get Acquainted

CHAPTER 24

BINGO: Building Interest and Negotiation Through Games From the Outset

Mary E. Hillis

INTRODUCTION

Bingo is a great game for the language classroom because it *builds interest and negotiation through games from the outset.* However, some teachers tend not to use bingo games because of the teacher preparation time involved. Forget copying individual bingo grids for each student, forget cutting out markers for the bingo boards, and forget the teacher being responsible for all the preparation and creation of the game. This bingo is different.

In this version of bingo, students create their own cards and are actively involved in all facets of the game, while teacher talk time is minimized. First, students fill in the squares on their grids with questions they would like to ask their classmates. Then, they move about the classroom, asking and answering each other's questions. Finally, students share the information they learned from their classmates and mark off squares on their boards until someone gets a bingo.

CONTEXT

Because of the amount of free conversation involved, this activity works well for high school, junior college, and university students who are at the pre-intermediate level or above. This bingo is ideal for a first-day-of-class activity, and if used as an icebreaker, will most likely take one full class period to complete because the teacher will want to allow adequate time for something to be shared about each student. On the other hand, the bingo game also can be adapted for use at any point during a language course, and by following the variations below it can be transformed to focus on a discrete grammar point or unit themes.

Whenever the game is used, it will get students talking and establish an active, participatory classroom environment.

CURRICULUM, TASKS, MATERIALS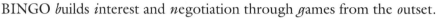

BINGO *b*uilds *i*nterest and *n*egotiation through *g*ames from the *o*utset.

Building: As a language teacher, building on what students already know and building on their individual strengths is a great way to get students more involved in the learning process. This version of bingo is based upon student-generated questions; therefore, it builds on their areas of knowledge. For instance, if students are interested in food, they could ask related questions, such as "What is your favorite food?" or "What was your most memorable meal?"

Interest: Language teachers are looking for ways to interest students in the class and the topics being studied. This game generates fun and interest in the course, not only because students ask the questions that interest them, but also because the game gives them a chance to use English for authentic communication. Finding out information from others is a useful skill both inside and outside of the classroom.

Negotiation: While participating in the game, students are negotiating meaning with their peers. As they complete their bingo boards, they exchange stories and experiences.

Games: Bingo is a popular game that most students are likely to be familiar with, and, although it is a game, this version has an educational purpose. When using games in the classroom, it is important that students know that they are practicing useful facets of English. In particular, this game focuses on question formation and can easily be adapted to focus on other grammatical areas or themed topics of study.

Outset: Even from the outset of a language course, games can be used to establish a participatory and open classroom environment. If used as an ice-breaker, the game gives the teacher and students a chance to get to know each other better, which could lower anxiety levels and spur communication among the various members of the class.

Procedures

First, introduce the bingo game to the students. If the teacher thinks students will have difficulty writing original questions on their own, reviewing question formation and/or brainstorming questions as a class may be necessary.

1. Copy and distribute the bingo board or have students create their own on a piece of paper (see Appendix). Instruct the students to write a different question within each square. Encourage students to be creative and ask interesting and engaging questions. Allow students time to write the eight questions needed for the activity. Also, let the students know that

their answers may be shared with the rest of the class, and that they may politely decline to answer a question if they consider it too personal.

2. Once all students have finished writing their questions, instruct them to stand up and ask one of their questions to another student. They should pose their questions and record their classmates' answers and names. Encourage the students to ask their classmates follow-up questions and ask the teacher questions as well. After students have finished with the first partner, they mingle around the classroom, asking their questions of other students. By the time this step is finished, each student should have talked to eight different students. Students should sit down once they have finished.

3. To wrap up the activity, the students will play bingo. The teacher calls out the name of one student in the class. All students who have that person's name on their bingo card raise their hands and mark the corresponding square on their bingo cards. Those students should then share one thing they learned about that person. A student will get a bingo when all of the squares on his board have been crossed off. Depending on the class size, you may wish to continue playing until everyone's name has been called and all students have been introduced or to stop playing after a few students get a bingo. Alternatively, having students share one thing they learned about the student whose name is called out may be omitted if the class is too large or there is not adequate time.

   There are many ways to vary this bingo game. For instance, the types of questions on the students' bingo board could be limited to a certain question type (all yes–no questions, for example) or to certain themes the class is studying (all questions about the current course theme of travel, for example), or to specific grammar points the class is studying (all questions written using the past tense, for example).

REFLECTIONS

After the game is finished, the teacher may want to correct some of the more common errors with question formation. In addition, the class could use this game as a springboard to a discussion about which questions are and are not appropriate for certain situations. Finally, to encourage students to remember their classmates, a fun follow-up quiz could be created with the information generated during this game.

   Although this game works well in a variety of contexts, some particular aspects of the game could be challenging for students. First, some students may have trouble thinking of eight original questions to fill in their bingo boards. In order to give students more assistance in forming questions, the teacher may wish to brainstorm questions as a class, or to allow individual questions to be repeated.

Second, because students' answers are shared with the rest of the class, there is a risk that someone might be embarrassed; therefore, be certain to remind students that their answers may be shared and that they can always politely refuse to answer a question if they consider it too personal or embarrassing.

Build interest and **n**egotiation through **g**ames from the **o**utset of language courses. Using this bingo game will enliven the first day of classes, motivate students to use English for authentic communication, and allow the students and teacher an opportunity to get to know each other.

ACKNOWLEDGMENT

I first learned of this game from Inez Schaecterle at Bowling Green State University in Ohio, in the United States.

Mary E. Hillis is an assistant professor of teaching English as a foreign language at Kansai Gaidai University, Japan. Since earning her master's degree in teaching English as a second language, she has worked with college and university students, business people, community members, and migrant farm workers. She is enthusiastic about language teaching and actively participates in professional organizations and communities of practice.

APPENDIX: BINGO BOARD

Directions: You will write questions to ask your classmates. Write a different question in each of the eight boxes below. Then, stand up and ask one question of eight different people in the class. Make sure to write down their names and answers.

Question 1: Name: Answer:	Question 2: Name: Answer:	Question 3: Name: Answer:
Question 4: Name: Answer:	FREE SPACE	Question 5: Name: Answer:
Question 6: Name: Answer:	Question 7: Name: Answer:	Question 8: Name: Answer:

CHAPTER 25

Flags of Ourselves: Using Student-Generated Props in the Classroom

Chad Kallauner

INTRODUCTION

I used to receive comments from students at the end of each semester that they wished they had had more opportunities to get to know their classmates. These comments motivated me to incorporate the activity described here. A game has been described as "an activity which is entertaining and engaging, often challenging, and an activity in which the learners play and usually interact with others" (Wright, Betteridge, & Buckby, 2006, p. 1). Flags of Ourselves helps students express themselves and become better acquainted.

In this game, students are given the opportunity to create flags symbolizing various aspects of their lives, such as their interests, backgrounds, goals, and personalities. In doing so, students from completely different backgrounds, cultures, and language families work together to learn a second language. English is the only common ground, and it is the only means with which students can communicate information and ideas. The activity represents the world as a sea of colorful banners coming together in unity. It is a wonderful sight when two students become friends due to their persistence in overcoming language hurdles. The reward for a teacher is seeing how friendships can be formed in this way.

CONTEXT

I always use this activity on the first day of class. It is appropriate for any level of language ability (beginning to advanced) and in almost any type of class (from speaking and listening to writing and grammar). Students are curious about one another, especially at the beginning of the academic year when the class is composed of students who never have seen each other before. It is the perfect icebreaker for shy, self-conscious students. Unlike basic self-introductions, this activity gives students a crutch, something tangible that they can refer to while they are nervously trying to verbalize their English on the very first day of class.

CURRICULUM, TASKS, MATERIALS

Flags of Ourselves can be used in a series of classes, not just in the first class. The teacher is relieved of any preparation time or providing materials because everything is done by the students.

The activity is based on the colorful, artistic national flags of the world. To begin, students think of symbols that represent themselves for each of several categories that I identify (e.g., favorite food, hometown symbol, future dream, hobby). All four symbols are incorporated into the same flag. Students are free to draw and arrange their symbols on sheets of blank white paper to create flags with the option of adding colors with pens or markers. For favorite food, students may draw a picture of a hamburger, sushi roll, bowl of noodles, or piece of chocolate, for instance. The hometown symbol may be something famous in the student's hometown (i.e., a picture of Mount Fuji if the student is from that region in Japan, or a snowflake if the student is from Hokkaido). Examples of pictures of future dreams include dollar signs (meaning wealth), a picture of a bride and groom, or a stethoscope (doctor). Finally, hobbies may be represented by a picture of a soccer ball, a musical note, a shopping bag, or a book, for instance. Although I encourage the students to add colors, some are more apt to do this than others, and no one should feel pressured.

The categories do not all have to be pictures; students can use stripes or bands of colors to represent objects or concepts. For example, a green border around the flag could represent the student's future dream of becoming rich, or blue stripes in the background could represent the sea that is associated with the student's hometown. There is no limit to the creativity that students can bring to this activity. I always bring my own flag to class to show them as an example (while telling them not to imitate mine too much).

The activity continues when students gather in small groups in a sort of show-and-tell fashion. This is a great way for them to get to know each other, talk about themselves in English, ask questions in English, and write about each other. For an added writing component, I ask them write about one group member's flag and that person. To practice descriptions, the student can describe the flag (colors, symbols, layout, etc.). Of course, this description can also be done orally. These options can extend the activity into an entire class session or more, depending on how much time the teacher wants to spend.

REFLECTIONS

I have noticed that students who are shy and reticent can use this activity to their advantage. Students sometimes stay after class, long after the activity is over, and continue to speak to each other (in English) about the flags. After moving to a new country to learn a new language, they are eager to find others with whom they have something in common. One time, a student from a country in Asia got to know a student from Latin America as the result of this flag activity. Old stereotypes and images were broken down, and the students ended up as friends who eventually visited each others' countries.

The activity can easily set the tone for the rest of the semester. Students have a better understanding of their classmates and, as a result, take an interest in each other. To follow up, I try to incorporate activities based on students' countries. For example, during the Christmas season, I have students do a crossword puzzle based on Christmas greetings in different languages. For a speaking class, students prepare presentations on an aspect of their culture (weddings, food, etc.).

Each semester, students tell me how much they enjoy the flag activity. They say how much it gets them talking and involved with classmates. Every teacher loves to hear that!

REFERENCE

Wright, A., Betteridge, D., & Buckby, M. (2006). *Games for language learning.* Cambridge: Cambridge University Press.

Chad Kallauner taught English as a foreign language in Japan for 7 years. He has written articles for publications such as The Language Teacher *(Japan Association of Language Teachers),* Thought Currents in English Literature *(Aoyama Gakuin University), and* Hitotsubashi University Review of Arts & Sciences. *He currently teaches English as a second language at the University of Texas at Arlington, in the United States.*

PART 2: Beyond Skills

C. Content-Based Instruction

CHAPTER 26

Add, Mix, and Shake: Content, Vocabulary, and Games in the Language Classroom

Lan Hue Quach and Scott P. Kissau

INTRODUCTION

With a growing population of students, challenging curriculum, and increasing demands for teacher accountability, many English as a second language (ESL) teachers feel they no longer have the time or the justification to use games in the classroom. To abandon games, however, in order to focus on more traditional, teacher-centered instruction, ignores the benefits of using games as an instructional tool. Richard-Amato (2003) warns against overlooking the pedagogical value of games, particularly in second-language teaching. Furthering this notion, Silvers (1982) claims that many second-language teachers see games as mere time-fillers and thus fail to realize that in the relaxed atmosphere resulting from the use of games, learning occurs. In addition to creating a more relaxed and enjoyable classroom environment and thus decreasing the *affective filter* (Krashen, 1981), many cognitive and social benefits can be enjoyed by incorporating games in the ESL classroom.

Games can be used in a variety of ways to support English language development. They can foster a healthy classroom dynamic and create opportunities for interaction (e.g., see Ellis, 1994; Swain, 1995; van Lier, 1996). Games serve as excellent warm-up activities by getting students motivated and thinking in the target language. They can be used as icebreakers for students who have recently arrived in the country or who do not know their classmates. Games are useful for introducing new concepts; reinforcing content, vocabulary, or grammar; and concluding a lesson. Teachers who use games will find that there are many cognitive and affective benefits. For example, using games to review or preview content can change the classroom culture. Playing games immediately fosters an informal atmosphere that reduces anxiety, encourages creative and spontaneous use of language, and creates a student-centered classroom.

Students who perceive themselves to have some control in the classroom are more motivated than those who do not (Deci & Ryan, 2002). The use of games can give second-language students more control by encouraging teachers who may use a more traditional or direct method of teaching to assume a facilitator role. As a result, this interaction helps build classroom community and fosters participation. Games can be used in any classroom to support language learning and can be easily adjusted for age, proficiency level, interests, and needs. Once the materials are initially created, minimum preparation is needed for future modifications.

Through participation in the games described in this chapter, students can meet numerous learning objectives. They require students to listen and respond to questions on a variety of topics and use expanded vocabulary in social and academic settings. They also integrate core content subject matter and thus help students meet learning objectives in other subject areas. Too often, the second-language curriculum is designed and taught independently, and to the exclusion of content area curriculum (Curtain & Dahlberg, 2004). In fact, research shows that a nonintegrated approach hinders the success of English language learners (ELLs) in the mainstream classroom (e.g., see Collier, 1989; Richards & Hurley, 1990). Gibbons (2002) asserts that when language teaching is tied to content, there is reciprocal learning of both. She observes that the mainstream curriculum is an "obvious source" (p. 120) for language development. The integration of subject content provides a meaningful context for using the second language, allows students to build on prior knowledge, and offers greater legitimacy to an ESL program that can at times be viewed as a luxury in an overly crowded school timetable.

CONTEXT

The games proposed in this chapter target ELLs in Grades 4–6 at an intermediate level of language proficiency. Although we introduce the games in this context, they can be adapted or modified easily to meet the needs of novice or more advanced learners at all grade levels and in all content areas. Due to the interactive nature of the games, they are ideally played in a diverse ESL or integrated classroom where a large number of students have the opportunity to interact with one another. Although the games can be modified to address curriculum expectations in different content areas, the three games described are presented in the context of teaching students about animal habitats, a common unit of study in Grades 4–6 in the United States.

CURRICULUM, TASKS, MATERIALS

Overview

The first two games can be played at the beginning of the unit of study and require students to work in teams as they respond to a series of teacher-generated prompts. In Frogs Don't Like the Desert, students quickly become highly motivated as they are required to move around the room and orally express their understanding of the relationships between animals and their respective habitats using visual aids and cue cards. Red and Black is another student favorite that has children actively involved in answering a set of increasingly difficult questions related to animal habitats. The excitement and concentration rise as students are given bean bags for each correct answer that they toss at the black and red targets. Another kinesthetic activity, Identity is the culminating two-part game that is played to review all concepts covered in a unit. Again requiring that all students get actively involved in the general review, Identity requires students to walk around the room asking questions and interacting with their peers in English to determine the identity of the animal whose name is on their back or on their hat.

FROGS DON'T LIKE THE DESERT

Preparation

1. For the first game, Frogs Don't Like the Desert, the teacher needs to identify relevant vocabulary words, verbs, and nouns that students need to review. After identifying the vocabulary and other text, the teacher will prepare a series of cards. One set needs to include colorful images of different animals and habitats (e.g., a frog and a desert). Although this may seem time-consuming, teachers can find images easily using the Google Image Search search engine (http://images.google.com), which allows anyone to access photographs or drawings. Flashcards also can be made easily by printing pictures found in various clip art programs or cutting out pictures from magazines such as *National Geographic*.

   In addition to the picture cards, we recommend that teachers create additional cards with words or phrases to be used in this game (see Figure 1). The teacher should use the proficiency level of the students to determine whether to use only visual cards, only text cards, or a combination of both. Using both visuals and text cards can help support ELLs in multiage or multileveled classes construct their statements accurately. We also encourage teachers to have students help them prepare the materials. To increase the durability and lifespan of the flashcards, we recommend that the images be placed on cardstock and laminated.

Figure 1. Sample Cards

2. Before students begin the game, the teacher needs to organize the classroom into stations (see Figure 2). For example, all animal flashcards need to be displayed in one section of the classroom and all habitats in another location. As an additional visual cue, teachers can create large posters or signs to remind students of the stations in the room. (Materials list: laminated images, word cards, poster board to name stations.)

Procedures

To play Frogs Don't Like the Desert, the teacher must first create stations where all the flashcards are displayed. The animal flashcards should be displayed in one station and the habitat flashcards in another in a different area of the classroom. The path from one station to the other should be unobstructed, but the students must be reminded not to run between stations. Next, the students should be placed into mixed-ability groups. The number of groups depends on the number of students in the class and the number of students the teacher wishes to have moving about the class at a time. To give everyone a turn, groups or teams should have no more than five students. In a small class of 10 or fewer students, we recommend placing the students into two evenly divided teams.

When indicated by the teacher, the first person in each group must proceed to each station and select a flashcard (see Figure 3). The players must then walk to the front of the classroom, and using a predetermined signal, indicate when

Figure 2. Stations

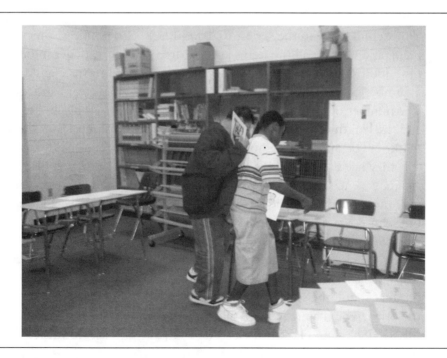

Figure 3. Playing Frogs Don't Like the Desert

they are ready to provide their answer. In our experience, the more outlandish the signal the better. Students, for example, love honking horns, ringing bells, or using fly swatters to indicate they are ready. Students even at the high school level usually respond well and responsibly with the use of props. The first person to signal must then display his or her flashcards to the other students and express the relationship between the animal and habitat depicted on the cards. For example, if a student picked flashcards with a picture of a frog and a desert, they should respond by saying, "Frogs don't like the desert."

Constructing this correct response shows that students (a) can name or call out the appropriate vocabulary words, (b) create a complete sentence using the words or visual prompts, and (c) understand or identify the general characteristics of the habitats or unit of study. Teachers can adjust the point values as necessary, but the first person to give a correct response usually wins 2 points. One point is also awarded to the other players if they are able to correctly establish the relationship between their chosen flashcards. Once the players all have had a chance to provide their answer, they return to their seats and the game continues in a similar fashion with the second player in each group. The game can end when all students have had a chance to play, when all flashcards have been used, or when the teacher feels the concepts have been adequately reviewed.

RED AND BLACK

Preparation

1. The second game in the series, Red and Black, also requires some initial preparation. Once all the items are prepared, however, they can be used time and time again with little effort. Teachers need to trace and cut out a number of circles on red and black construction paper or cardstock. The number of circles depends on the size of the group playing the game and the length of time the game is to be played. It is important, however, that there be an equal number of both colors. Once the circles have been cut, they need to be glued together. Glue each red circle to a black circle. Again, we encourage teachers to solicit help from their students to prepare these materials. Students who finish work early or have a little extra time can go to a teacher help station that is set up with all the materials ready for students to cut or glue. A very useful trick to consider before gluing the circles together is to place small, flat, inexpensive magnetic strips, which can be purchased at craft stores, between them. The final product should be several circles that are black on one side and red on the other. The magnetic strips allow the circles to stick to any metallic surface, including blackboards, so tape or stick tack are not necessary. We recommend that the circles be laminated.

2. The second and most important part of the teacher preparation is the creation of questions, which must be carefully constructed and prepared in advance. The teacher should create three questions related to the unit of study for each card. Teachers can handwrite all three questions on index cards; type, print, cut them out, and glue them on index cards; or print them out on cardstock and cut as needed. The three questions need to increase in difficulty. The first question should be relatively simple to ensure that all students experience success. Each student should be able to respond correctly to the first question. The second question should be slightly more difficult, and the third question even more challenging. The number of index cards with questions depends on the number of students who will participate.

3. Teachers should also purchase at least three beanbags for this game. An inexpensive alternative to buying beanbags is to fill small Ziploc bags with lentils, rice, or dried beans. Teachers making their own beanbags should ensure the bags are double-bagged and secured with tape so the beans do not fall out when students throw them. (Materials list: bean bags, red and black circles, magnetic strips, index cards.)

Procedures

Before playing Red and Black, the teacher needs to attach the colored circles to the chalkboard or wall in an alternating pattern (red, black, red, black). The design of the pattern and the space between circles is up to the teacher (see Figure 4 for examples). The teacher can create two mixed-ability teams (red and black), or allow students to select their own teams. Once ready to play, students from each team are chosen in turn to participate. Once chosen, a student is given an index card upon which are written three questions of increasing difficulty related to the unit of study. The student must read the first question aloud and then provide an answer. One bean bag is awarded for the correct response, and then the student proceeds to the next question. Upon answering the second question correctly, the student then moves on to the third and final question.

Each correct answer earns the student one bean bag and the opportunity to toss the bean bag(s) at the target (see Figures 5 and 6). A member of the red team, for example, would aim for a black target. If this player is successful in hitting a black target, the circle is flipped over, now revealing a red circle. On the other hand, if a player hits one of the team's own colored circles, that circle is also flipped, revealing the color of the opposing team. Placing a magnetic strip between the circles, as suggested earlier, facilitates the flipping of the circles on the chalkboard. At the end of the game, the team that has the most circles of its color showing wins. Although Red and Black can be played most easily as one

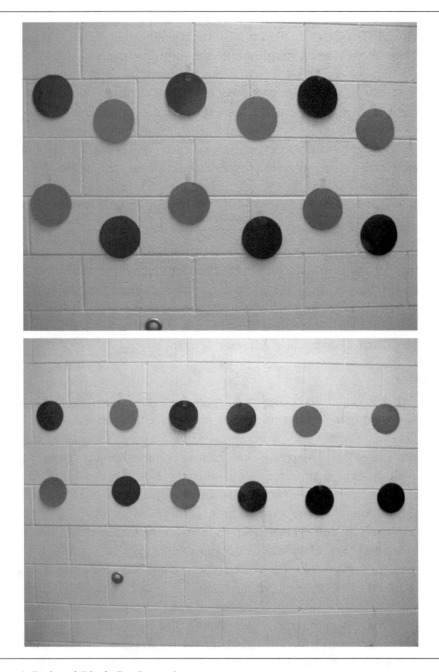

Figure 4. Red and Black Configurations

large group, having multiple games playing simultaneously around the classroom ensures that all students are actively involved. In such a situation, the teacher simply acts as a facilitator and walks around the room answering the occasional question about the accuracy of a response.

Figure 5. Sample Bean Bags

Figure 6. Playing Red and Black

IDENTITY

Preparation

The third and final game of the series requires the least amount of teacher preparation. To play Identity, the teacher simply needs to create cards on which the names of different animals discussed during the unit of study are written. This game has been widely used and called a variety of different names, including Who am I? What am I? or Name the Character (e.g., see Celce-Murcia & Larsen-Freeman, 1999). To prepare, teachers can handwrite the words on nametags, labels, or index cards. One card, or "identity," is needed for each student in the class. These words also can be printed on labels, which easily can be peeled and placed on the back of each student. If time or resources are an issue, teachers also can use tape, a safety pin, or long string to attach each card. If teachers have the resources, different colored foam or plastic hats can be purchased at a craft store (for usually $US1 or less). Teachers can then place the labels on the hats and ask students to wear the hats during the game. For the purposes of our unit review, the different identities that would be included are polar bear, lion, sea turtle, camel, and so forth. (Materials list: labels or cards with names of vocabulary to review, hats if available.)

Procedures

Identity is a culminating two-part game that is played to review all concepts covered in the unit. The name of an animal is attached to the back of each student. Students are instructed to walk around the room asking a variety of yes–no questions to their classmates in order to determine the identity of the animal. Teachers need to make sure they model the activity by choosing one of the animals as an example, reviewing how to create yes–no questions, and establishing the rules of the game. For more advanced students learning grammar, this activity can be used to teach grammar deductively. For example, when students complete the exercise, the class can generate the grammar rule by examining the role and position of the nouns and verbs. When the questions used in the exercise are written on the board and presented to the class, students can often see how the subject and objects are inverted. Upon correctly identifying their animal's identity, students are asked to assist other students in determining their identity.

Once all students have completed the task, they are put into groups based on habitat and given additional tasks to complete. For example, students can work in their respective habitat groups to compare and contrast the animals in their habitat with the others in the class. Students also can engage in a group writing activity by constructing a story using the animals in their habitats or creating a travel brochure using persuasive language to encourage others to visit their habitats. As another extension to this review, students could construct a diorama of their respective habitat with various supplies such as a shoe box, construction paper, markers, scissors, and glue. Following this hands-on activity, in which students of all proficiency levels can participate, the students present their dioramas to the class and discuss the role of each individual animal in the habitat. For more advanced level students, the class can engage in designing a zoo where each group is charged with the layout and content of the exhibits and information plaques. When using Identity as a review and grouping exercise, teachers can extend student learning using these suggested activities.

Variations

In the following sections, we offer ways for teachers to modify these games by considering classroom environment, cultural notes, and other relevant themes. We present these three games in the context of teaching habitats and animals in the science classroom. To adequately make these adjustments, teachers should first consider their own units of study. Gibbons (2002) provides teachers with practical steps in the integration of language and subject or content learning. She recommends that teachers first ask the following questions: (a) What are the language demands of the classroom? (b) What do the children currently know about language? (c) What are their language learning needs? These questions are intended to prompt teachers to think about programs and curriculum "through the lens of language, to help [teachers] hold language to the light, to look at it rather than through it" (p. 121). To modify these games for other units of study, we suggest that teachers first carefully consider the topics or units they are planning to teach and gather information based on these questions. By doing this assessment, teachers can identify where the missed opportunities for language development are and design the games based on the specific content that needs to be reinforced or reviewed.

Although the three games discussed in this chapter were presented in the context of a unit on animal habitats, they could be adapted to fit a variety of curriculum topics. The concept behind Frogs Don't Like the Desert lends itself, for example, to any number of mathematical concepts. Instead of choosing animals and habitats from different stations, students could select fractions, decimal numbers, and percentages and then compare the numbers. The questions asked in Red and Black could be changed to suit any topic of study, and rather than guessing the identity of an animal in a science class, students could ask a series of questions to determine the identity of a character in a novel read or a location studied. The possibilities are endless.

Classroom Environments

When the larger unit of study is considered, these three games can be easily adapted to address multiple age groups and levels of language proficiency. For instance, to make the game Frogs Don't Like the Desert more challenging and thus more appropriate for advanced language learners, the flashcards could be positioned face-down so that the students cannot choose those animals or habitats with which they are more familiar. Also, additional stations could be added to the game to increase the level of difficulty and integrate other concepts. For example, a station on reviewing adjectives could be added. The players would then have to incorporate the chosen adjective into their response, resulting in sentences such as "Purple rabbits don't like oceans" or "Alligators live in giant swamps." With a little creativity, one can imagine how different verb tenses, adverbs, prepositions, and a variety of other grammatical concepts could be incorporated into the game to challenge even the most advanced students.

Black and Red could be made to address different age groups and proficiency levels simply by adjusting the difficulty level of questions and the distance the bean bags are to be tossed. Cooperative learning strategies could be implemented in the game Identity to make it more suitable for less advanced ELLs. Students could work with a partner or in small groups to determine a given identity. They also could be allowed to ask questions other than just those that require a yes–no answer. To make the game more challenging, students could be discouraged from using specific words such as *animal* or *habitat*, thus forcing them to use alternate vocabulary or synonyms.

Cultural Notes

ELLs represent rich linguistic and cultural experiences and knowledge. When games are used to support the development of both language and content, all students benefit. In the words of Clegg (1996), "the language rich diet of an ESL group can turn out to be nourishing for the whole mainstream class. It can help all the children use language for learning in ways which were not previously available to them" (p. 15). Regardless of race, religion, or nationality, children and adolescents alike understand games. Furthermore, children from diverse backgrounds are familiar with and embrace the kinesthetic activities involved in the games shared in this chapter. The use of games thus offers a level of comfort and familiarity that many ELLs crave. In addition, the interaction with their mainstream English-speaking peers can support their second-language development.

Although we encourage the use of games in the classroom as a way to reinforce or review vocabulary, grammar, and content for ELLs, we also recognize that some students are uncomfortable in competitive or interactive situations. We encourage teachers to make the effort to understand the lives and backgrounds of students who have less experience working in groups or have anxiety about performing tasks in front of their peers. Over the course of many years of teaching second-language learners, we have encountered several students who are uncomfortable interacting and prefer to work individually or in less public spaces. Although we believe that it is important that such students be exposed to different learning environments, slight modifications can be made to the three games to help students gradually adjust. For example, the competitive nature of Frogs Don't Like Deserts could be eliminated, and students could simply be asked to formulate sentences based on their chosen flashcards. Red and Black could be played in smaller groups, and students playing Identity could write their questions on pieces of paper that they later exchange with partners. Once the answers to their questions have been provided, again in written form, the students could then guess their identity.

REFLECTIONS

We believe that second-language classrooms that support language development and foster communicative competence are noisy places of controlled chaos. These classrooms are energized, and students and teachers are engaged in the learning activities. The affective filter is low, and students are motivated. Students are encouraged to mill about the classroom interacting with their peers in meaningful contexts while using the target language. The three games proposed in this chapter can contribute to such an environment. Teachers can use these games in multiple content areas and modify them easily while reinforcing key concepts, vocabulary, and grammar.

Through many years of application in both the ESL and foreign language classroom, we have found these games (and others like them) to be highly engaging to second-language learners. They allow teachers to address planned learning objectives in nontraditional, student-centered ways. We have observed that most students participate and these games provide them with the opportunities to actively exchange meaningful information in a fun and relaxed setting. They often become so engrossed in expressing themselves in the second language that they forget that that are, in fact, learning. When language learning is fun and meaningful, teachers can be certain that students will retain newly acquired information.

As experienced second-language educators, we have come to realize that many effective second-language teaching strategies, such as the use of visuals, games, and social interaction in meaningful contexts, are not specific to the language classroom and are quite simply effective teaching strategies. The three games described in this chapter provide teachers with additional tools to use in the language or content area classroom. The minimal preparation, ease of adaptability for diverse groups of students and different content, and interactive nature of the games make them desirable to the busy classroom teacher. They not only provide opportunities for the exchange of meaningful information in social settings and thus espouse the characteristics of the communicative approach to learning languages, but also foster whole-class participation, develop class cohesion, address multiple learning styles, and are highly motivational. Furthermore, while allowing for the reinforcement, review, and extension of language concepts in an entertaining manner, these games lend themselves to the integration of other content-areas, such as science and math. All of these benefits can be observed when ESL and content-area teachers create opportunities for students to interact in meaningful, purposeful, and engaging ways. To start, simply add a little preparation and effort, mix with activities that make students active participants in their learning, and shake to create opportunities for students to interact with one another and their native-English-speaking peers. Let the games begin!

ACKNOWLEDGMENT

The inspiration for the game Red and Black came from a workshop presented by Mel Brown at the 2007 annual conference of the Ontario Modern Language Teachers Association.

REFERENCES

Celce-Murcia, M., & Larsen-Freeman, D. (1999). *The grammar book: An ESL/EFL teacher's course*. Boston, MA: Heinle & Heinle.

Clegg, J. (1996). *Mainstreaming ESL: Case studies in integrating ESL students into the mainstream curriculum*. Clevedon, England: Multilingual Matters.

Collier, V. (1989). How long? A synthesis of research in academic achievement in a second language. *TESOL Quarterly, 23*, 509–531.

Curtain, H., & Dahlberg, C. (2004). *Languages and children: Making the match* (3rd ed.). New York: Pearson Education.

Deci, E. L., & Ryan, R. M. (2002). *Intrinsic motivation and self-determination*. Rochester, NY: University of Rochester Press.

Ellis, R. (1994). *The study of language acquisition*. Oxford: Oxford University Press.

Gibbons, P. (2002). *Scaffolding language, scaffolding learning: Teaching second language learners in the mainstream classroom*. Portsmouth, NH: Heinemann.

Krashen, S. (1981). *Second language acquisition and second language learning*. Oxford: Pergamon Press.

Richard-Amato, P. (2003). *Making it happen: From interaction to participatory language teaching* (3rd ed.). White Plains, NY: Longman.

Richards, J., & Hurley, R. (1990). Language and content: Approaches to curriculum alignment. In J. Richards (Ed.), *The language teaching matrix* (pp. 144–165). Cambridge: Cambridge University Press.

Silvers, S. M. (1982). Games for the classroom and the English-speaking club. *English Teaching Forum, 20*(2), 29–33.

Swain, M. (1995). Three functions of output in second language learning. In G. Cook & B. Seidlehofer (Eds.), *Principle, practice in applied linguistics: Studies in honour of H.G. Widdowson* (pp. 125–144). Oxford: Oxford University Press.

van Lier, L. (1996). *Interaction in the language curriculum: Awareness, autonomy, and authenticity*. London: Longman.

Additional Resources

Carr, J., & Pauwels, A. (2006). *Boys and foreign language learning: Real boys don't do languages.* New York: Palgrave MacMillan.

Pavy, S. (2006). Boys learning languages—the myth busted. *Babel, 41*(1), 2–9.

Lan Hue Quach is an assistant professor of TESOL at the University of North Carolina at Charlotte, in the United States, where she is the coordinator of the Masters of Arts in Teaching in ESL Program. Her research interests are in multicultural teacher education and second-language–identity development of English language learners.

Scott P. Kissau is an assistant professor at the University of North Carolina at Charlotte, where he is the coordinator of the Masters of Arts in Teaching Foreign Languages Program. As a former French teacher, his research interests relate to the underrepresentation of boys in second-language programs.

CHAPTER 27

Using Common Language Games in a Science and Technology Curriculum

Lindsay Miller and Samuel Wu

INTRODUCTION

There are several definitions of what a language learning game is, or should be. These definitions contain the ideas that games should be competitions or that learners need to cooperate with each other to play the game. By some definitions, games have to have communicative elements, or they need to be group activities. Many definitions highlight the idea that special materials are needed for language learning games. We do not believe that games need to be defined too specifically, however. By placing a tight definition on what a language game is, we may reject activities that learners enjoy and that motivate them to learn.

In considering how we identify classroom activities that we consider games, we would suggest the following defining characteristics: (a) a game is an activity that both the teacher and students enjoy and have fun playing, (b) everyone in the class needs to be part of the activity for it to succeed (the role of the teacher is just as important to the success of a language game as that of the student), and (c) the main objective is not to compete or reach the end of an activity, but to motivate the learners in a relaxed atmosphere and encourage them to use the target language in creative ways.

Many well-known language games can be integrated into the curriculum to enliven the classroom atmosphere and enrich the learning experiences of the learners. It is important to consider how to introduce games to learners, however. Although games are well established and most language teachers use them, some learners may be resistant to playing language games in their lessons because they do not see this as "serious learning" (Miller, 1993, p. 38), especially in an English for science and technology context. This resistance is often the case with tertiary-level learners who are studying in degree programs.

CONTEXT

We teach at City University of Hong Kong (CityU). CityU is a large English-medium university with an emphasis on science and technology. Although most classes at CityU are conducted in English, the student population is predominantly local Chinese who use Cantonese as their mother tongue. These students come to the university from mostly secondary schools where the medium of instruction is Chinese. In the academic year 2006–2007, more than 6,000 full- and part-time students were admitted to the Faculty of Science and Engineering. Students entering the engineering programs at CityU generally have low English scores on their public examinations and the equivalent to 450 on the paper-based Test of English as a Foreign Language. Given this situation, most of our students need to take English for academic purposes or English for specific purposes (ESP) courses in their first year of study.

CURRICULUM, TASKS, MATERIALS

One of the ESP courses at CityU is a writing course for 1st-year engineering students that meets 3 hours per week for one semester. The course aims to develop students' fluency and accuracy in written and spoken English for professional communication and to provide a variety of experiences in technical communication. By taking this course, students develop the skills that enable them to write clear, concise reports in engineering. They also are required to talk about their reports and give oral presentations. The curriculum for the course includes learning to

- describe the processes, structure, and function of technical devices

- write technical reports by conducting and documenting research and using appropriate structure, format, and language

- give oral presentations that demonstrate audience awareness, effective verbal and nonverbal delivery skills, the ability to interpret graphical representations, and the ability to self-evaluate

The Games

The following games are well known to most language teachers. Our aim is to illustrate how such games can be integrated into a language curriculum developed for engineering students. We believe that ESP courses can and should incorporate such games.

Crossword Puzzles for Technical Writing

Good technical writing involves the ability to clearly define specialist terminology as well as properly describe technical objects or processes. To motivate students to review the various concepts of good technical writing, we created a fun and simple crossword puzzle to test their understanding of key terminology and highlight common language errors typical in Hong Kong (see Figure 1).

Original crossword puzzles can be generated easily using software available online (e.g., Crossword Weaver, n.d.). In our crossword puzzle, the clues are written with blanks, testing the students' understanding of the concepts of writing good definitions and technical descriptions. For instance, clue #5 across reviews the concept that technical descriptions should be systematically written in chronological order.

Technical Writing: Concepts & Grammar

ACROSS

2 _____ : Technical words only specialists will understand.
5 Repeating words being defined in the definitions are considered _____.
6 "I created a virus" is a(n) _____ sentence.
9 Formal definitions require a term, a _____, and distinguishing information.
10 This attractive mobile phone has a great _____.

DOWN

1 "The robotic arm was created by us" is a _____ sentence.
3 Technical description are best written in a _____ order.
4 I like this new laptop, _____ it is very expensive.
7 A thermometer is an _____ that measures temperature.
8 The IT repairman could not repair the computer because he did not bring sufficient _____.

Note: For a fee, you can use Crossword Weaver to print a nice copy of this puzzle (one that doesn't look like a web page). You can check it out for free by downloading the demo from www.CrosswordWeaver.com .

Continued on p. 242

Technical Writing: Concepts & Grammar

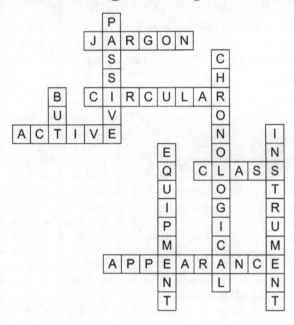

Figure 1. Example of Puzzle and Answer Key for Using Crossword Puzzles to Review Technical Writing Concepts

This exercise could have been an ordinary gap-fill activity; however, when designed as a crossword puzzle, it becomes a fun language game. Furthermore, unlike some gap-fill activities that accept synonyms as answers, answers for crossword puzzles need to be precise based on the number of available boxes provided. Students thus are required to practice thinking creatively and searching through a few possible words before arriving at the right answer.

When designed properly, crossword puzzles can stimulate learning, and in the milieu of science and technology—traditionally regarded by English as a second language (ESL) learners as "boring" ESP courses—they create an enjoyable, relaxed, yet purposeful learning environment.

Hangman Vocabulary Game

To prepare for a particular lesson in class, students are expected to read a relevant technical report. In order to review vocabulary, especially difficult words or jargon, a hangman-type language game can be employed.

First, the class is divided into four or five groups with three or four students per group. Paper men, which represent each group, are fastened to a whiteboard in a single starting position. Three additional positions are drawn on the board leading toward a cliff (a simple line can be drawn to represent the cliff). At the bottom of the cliff, the teacher draws the sea, where a huge shark with open jaws and sharp teeth is waiting. A long line is drawn across the bottom of the entire picture to represent the ground (see Figure 2).

Next, the teacher selects particular words from the readings to test the students. A word is represented by a number of blanks drawn on the board (similar to hangman), and each group can call out a letter to guess the word. If a group provides a correct letter, its paper man does not move and is safe from the jaws of death. Conversely, if a group is wrong, its paper man moves one step or position closer to the edge. All groups have three chances before their paper man advances too near the edge of the cliff and falls into the shark's open jaws, which signifies disqualification. When the winning group guesses the word correctly, the teacher elicits their understanding of the word. A point system can be employed to encourage students to beat the opposing groups (e.g., 3 points are given to the group that guesses the word correctly, and an additional 3 points are given for an accurate definition of the term).

This language game is extremely effective for getting students to actively participate to prevent their paper man from certain death, and the desire to win creates positive competitiveness, as evidenced when students can be seen busily flipping through the readings to decipher the mystery word on the board. It also generates much laughter and excitement—a simple, fun, creative learning environment that breaks the monotony of vocabulary learning.

Oral Presentation Games

In the final part of the course, students are required to perform oral presentations of their project work. One of the errors learners commonly make is to read aloud a prepared written script. In their attempt to perform well, they fail to realize that spoken texts and written texts are quite different (e.g., see Flowerdew & Miller, 2005).

In this language game, students are given a passage that introduces a fictitious instructional technology (IT) consultancy firm before proceeding to propose a system to solve a client's need. Long sentences of formal written English comprise the passage. In pairs, students have to change the passage into spoken English that is concise and easy to understand,without changing its meaning. The sample text follows:

> Formulated in 1980, CyberTech is a world-class, award-winning IT consultancy firm with a large portfolio of numerous accounts—ranging from small businesses to large conglomerates. Satisfied clients include McDennys, SportsWorld, AXPNetworks, and Marcus & Spence. In light of the limitations and requirements of your company, we will customize an operational system to meet your current needs, whatever they may be. The reason for proposing the CyberTech operational system is that it can maximize work efficiency as well as minimize operational costs of a company. Your staff

START
TEAMS
1-4

Position
1

Position
2

Position
3

J _ R _ _ _

P E S

(Ans: JARGON)

Scores:
TEAM 1
TEAM 2
TEAM 3
TEAM 4

Figure 2. Hangman Vocabulary Learning

will also be provided with training so that they can easily adapt to the new system. Besides, the experts of CyberTech are always available to offer assistance and support to ensure the smooth operation of the customized system designed for your company. Thus, it is assured that benefits and profits will be brought to your company by making use of the CyberTech system. (Wu, 2006)

For example, the following sentence from the text has complex grammatical structure: *The reason for proposing the CyberTech operational system is that it can maximize work efficiency as well as minimize operational costs of a company.* To change the sentence into concise, spoken English that is easy to understand, students typically revise it as: *You should use this system because it'll maximize efficiency and minimize costs for your company.*

Upon completion of the task, each pair is invited to orally present its revised passage (without notes), and the entire class votes on the pair with the best spoken version. In order to help the students vote for the best presentation, we ask them to consider the following questions: (a) Is the presentation easy to understand? (b) Is the presentation complete? (c) Is the speaker friendly and engaging with the audience? Students are asked to rate each other's performance on a scale from 1 to 5 with 1 being *dreadful* and 5 representing *wonderful.*

This language game encourages students to cooperate in pairs to consider how to best present the information orally and then compete with other pairs to make the best presentation. It also generates a great deal of class discussion about the best ways to present technical and semitechnical information.

REFLECTIONS

We both have taught English to science and technology students and believe that games can be successfully integrated into the curriculum. To introduce games into academic contexts such as a science and technology course, we recommend the following guidelines:

- Keep the game simple so that students can get involved as soon as possible.

- Do not introduce too many games, so that students will not think that they are wasting their time and those who are unused to interactive learning will not be too overwhelmed.

- Select games carefully. Although some games may look interesting or fun, they need to be integrated into the curriculum so that learners see the rationale for using the game to enhance their language learning.

- Identify certain activities to your learners as games and encourage them to have some fun. In a serious learning context such as a university course, some learners may not appreciate that learning can be fun.

- Be flexible with the rules and how the language games are played. If learners feel that they can play the game in a more interesting way or want to change the rules, then encourage them to do so. They will not be tested using the games, and the purpose is for them to enjoy their learning.

- Pilot the games even if you think that they are suitable for your learners. There are often management problems or time constraints that affect using the game (e.g., explaining and checking comprehension of the rules may be more time consuming than expected).

REFERENCES

Crossword weaver [computer software]. (n.d.). Retrieved September 3, 2007, from http://www.crosswordweaver.com/

Flowerdew, J., & Miller, L. (2005). *Second language listening: Theory to practice.* New York: Cambridge University Press.

Miller, L. (1993). Using games in an EST Class. *TESOL Journal, 2*(2), 38–39.

Wu, S. (2006). *Student Manual for Report Writing for Engineering.* (Available from City University of Hong Kong Press, Tat Chee Avenue, Kowloon Tong, Kowloon, Hong Kong.)

Additional Resources

Harmer, J. (1991). *The practice of English language teaching.* Harlow, England: Longman.

Houston, H. (2007). *The creative classroom: Teaching language outside the box.* Vancouver, Canada: Lynx Publishing.

Howard-Williams, D., & Herd, C. (1998). *Word games with English: Teachers' resource book.* Oxford, England: MacMillan Heinemann.

Rinvolucri, M., & Davis, P. (2005). *More grammar games.* Cambridge: Cambridge University Press.

Rivers, W. M., & Temperley, M. S. (1978). *A practical guide to the teaching of English.* New York: Oxford University Press.

Shameem, N., & Tickoo, M. (1997). *New ways in using communicative games in language teaching.* Alexandria, VA: TESOL.

Lindsay Miller is an associate professor at the City University of Hong Kong, where he teaches courses in self-access learning, materials development, and critical pedagogy. His publications include Second Language Listening (with John Flowerdew, Cambridge University Press, 2005) and Establishing Self Access: From Theory to Practice (with David Gardner, Cambridge University Press, 1999).

Samuel Wu is an instructor in the Department of English and Communication at City University of Hong Kong, where he teaches technical, business, and intercultural communication. He graduated with a Masters of Philosophy from the National University of Singapore, with research interests in the confluence of language, prosody, sexuality, and gender.

CHAPTER 28

The Business Apprentice

Kimberly S. Rodriguez and Susan M. Barone

INTRODUCTION

Current simulation and gaming theory supports active learning as a motivation stimulus (Cummins, 2000). Simulation and gaming theory, which was started as a mathematical method of interactive decision making, may be used in language learning contexts where the language of negotiation and decision making is sought. It is commonly used as a type of competition where the ultimate response or best product is desired. In the language learning environment, it is a good tool for encouraging and motivating students to put their best foot forward.

One of many avenues to promote active learning, The Business Apprentice game is based on the use of current reality television programming to inspire and motivate participants to compete for the best marketing presentation of an every-day consumer item. The main purpose of the game is to focus on presentation skills. Additional benefits include cross-cultural comparisons of group dynamics and exposure to idiomatic language.

Learning Objectives

- Negotiate in groups to determine a product and create a marketing and advertising scheme.

- Create presentations and develop necessary language functions and vocabulary to make a presentation.

- Become aware of pronunciation skills within the context of a real-world presentation.

CONTEXT

The authors' teaching environment is a graduate business school with students in their early 20s and older. The learner level is typically intermediate to advanced or near native. This is in an English as a second language (ESL) setting at a private university in the southeastern region of the United States.

CURRICULUM, TASKS, MATERIALS

Getting Started

Inspired by the popular American reality television show *The Apprentice*, this game provides students with an opportunity to be creative, practice team dynamics, and hone presentation skills. Students are asked to create a marketing and advertising campaign for a product and present their concept using production techniques such as video and audio recordings, slideshow presentations, and personal presentations. Students are given 1–3 weeks to complete their project. Depending upon class time, several episode clips from *The Apprentice* are used throughout the course to provide listening comprehension and a context for the task. We use the following clips from the first season of *The Apprentice*:

- The beginning of the opening episode, "Meet the Billionaire," which depicts the concept of the game, the organization of teams, and execution of the first task. This clip introduces the idea and provides a backdrop for the game, although we do not tell students about the game details until later.

- The final part of "Sex, Lies and Altitude," where each team presents its marketing campaign for an airline. This clip is the basis for the task the students are to prepare.

This activity is ideally suited to undergraduate and graduate business students with at least high-intermediate language proficiency. It has been used as a capping activity after students have done several previous assignments aimed at improving their presentation skills and building vocabulary. Students work in teams of 3–6, depending on class size. Each team chooses a team leader and a team name.

The assignment is to create a marketing and advertising concept for a product to be marketed by a corporation. The team must define a target audience, distribution channels, and price point; select a brand name; and produce a 30-second television advertisement and a print advertisement (see sample assignment sheet in Appendix A). Each team has 10 minutes to present its concept, during which each member of the team must have a meaningful speaking part. The presentations are judged by a panel of business school professors, and the winning team is awarded a prize.

This game encourages students to work in the team format, which is a mainstay of business programs. Students also practice valuable language used in negotiation, argument, expressing opinion, compromise, agreement, and disagreement. This task also provides students with an opportunity to research a product, determine an advertising message, and present their concept in a creative framework.

This has been a very popular activity with both students and judges and allows mastery of language skills within a realistic business context. It also allows participants to explore cross-cultural comparisons of team dynamics, especially those related to leadership.

Before Game Day

1. Students are given the assignment. If accessible, an episode from *The Apprentice*, in which teams present marketing concepts, can be used for reference. Each team chooses a team leader and picks a team name.

2. Each team selects a product and begins the process of determining the concept for marketing. The only restrictions are that it must be a tangible product, it cannot be a product or service from any of the television episodes, and it must be a completely original marketing concept.

3. Presentation skills and public speaking skills should be reviewed and practiced to help students master their techniques. If time allows, teams can also be given an opportunity to present before a nonjudging instructor for feedback on presentation skills, language structures, and pronunciation.

Game Day

For large classes, it may be necessary to run several preliminary rounds of presentations to narrow the number of teams down for a final competition. Presentations, which are made to the class and a panel of judges, are judged based upon presentation skills, use of language, and creativity (see Appendix B). It is important that access to more advanced production techniques not be a factor in judging; thus students without access to video cameras can present a concept in storyboard format and not be penalized.

Variations

The activity can be limited to a specific product or opened up to allow students to select the product. Depending upon the time and scope of the class, a number of expansions on this activity are possible. For example, students can analyze and discuss popular current advertising campaigns, make comparisons of advertising in different cultures, or research and discuss advertising bloopers. Teachers may even wish to invite guest lectures from business school professors on marketing- and advertising-related topics. We have had a great deal of success with this game and its alternate uses and expansions.

REFLECTIONS

The students' feedback on this activity has been overwhelmingly positive. This game provides a relevant and authentic business theme for language mastery set against the backdrop of a popular reality television show.

The process of negotiating a team concept and a team name alone is a valuable exercise in preparing the students for the American classroom culture and dynamics. Even the students with the least advanced language skills in the group are incorporated into the final presentation, often boosting their own confidence in their ability to perform favorably in another language. Students learn valuable visual as well as audio presentation skills and use them in a real-life scenario.

Students learn important skills for making their own presentations and, possibly more importantly, they gain valuable experience in group dynamics and peer critique (giving and receiving). By working with their peers, students are vested in the entire presentation and not just their own parts of it. They begin to master many of the subtleties of transition and organization. Because they must present their concept in a set timeframe, they also learn techniques for concise, clear communication.

This game provides a challenging but achievable task for students across various language levels. The resulting presentations build language and presentation skills as well as confidence and never cease to impress the students themselves as well as the judging panel. The activity has become a highlight of the business school, with various faculty and staff requesting to be included in the final judging each year. Because of the wide range of language skills and presentation skills employed, as well as the authenticity of the task, this activity prepares students for success in their classes.

REFERENCE

Cummins, J. (2000). Academic language learning, transformative pedagogy, and information technology: Towards a critical balance. *TESOL Quarterly, 34,* 537–548.

Additional Resources

Burns, A. C., & Gentry, J. W. (1998). Motivating students to engage in experiential learning: A tension-to-learn theory. *Simulation & Gaming, 29,* 133–151.

Christopher, E., & Smith, L. (1991). *Negotiation training through gaming: Strategies, tactics, and maneuvers.* East Brunswick, NJ: Nichols/GP Pub.

Curland, S., & Fawcett, S. (2001). Using simulation and gaming to develop financial skills in undergraduates. *International Journal of Contemporary Hospitality Management, 13*(3), 116–119.

Jones, K. (1998). Simulations and communication skills in secondary schools. *Simulation & Gaming, 29,* 321–325.

Kristian, K. (2007). Foundation for problem-based gaming. *British Journal of Educational Technology, 38*(3), 546–547.

Peters, V., Vissers, G., & Heijne, G. (1998). The validity of games. *Simulation & Gaming, 29,* 20–30.

Rettberg, S. (2004). Games/gaming/simulation in a new media (literature) classroom. *On the Horizon, 12*(1), 31–35.

Tsuda, K., Terano, T., Kuno, Y., Shirai, H., & Suzuki, H. (2002). A compiler for business simulations: Toward business model development by yourselves. *Information Sciences, 143*(1), 99–114.

White, C. (1985). Citizen decision making, reflective thinking, and simulation gaming: A marriage of purpose, method, and strategy [Monograph]. *Journal of Social Studies Research, 9*(2), 1–50.

Kimberly S. Rodriguez teaches at the English Language Training Institute at the University of North Carolina–Charlotte, in the United States. After a 20-year career in international business, she decided to pursue her interest in ESL in the university setting. With a bachelor's degree in linguistics, a master's degree in international business, and a teaching ESL certificate, she has experience in academic ESL, business ESL, curriculum development, and ESL teacher training.

Susan M. Barone is a sociolinguist whose research focuses on interactional language in professional settings. She has created discipline-specific programs in business, law, engineering, nursing, and medicine at the Vanderbilt University English Language Center, in Nashville, Tennessee, in the United States, where she is currently director.

APPENDIX A: SAMPLE STUDENT ASSIGNMENT SHEET

The Business Apprentice Project   **Due Date:** _____

The Business Apprentice Project is one in which you and your team members will be given the opportunity to practice the language structures and functions of negotiation, decision making, and presentation. This task is based on a popular U.S. television program where an apprentice is selected for a high-level position in a company. Your team is to select a product to add to the consumer product repertoire of a corporation and create an original and compelling advertising campaign for the corporate marketing advisors.

Your team will present its proposal on the last day of class in a 10-minute presentation that should include:

1. A marketing concept

   a. What is the product and why is it good for the corporation's product portfolio?

   b. Who is the target market and what are the key points of distribution?

2. Price

3. A sample print advertisement

4. A sample TV advertisement (either on video or a slideshow storyboard)

Time will be closely monitored and you will not be allowed to exceed 10 minutes. All members of your team must participate equally in the presentation, both in terms of time and substance. A panel of faculty judges will evaluate your final presentations, and the winning team will receive a prize. The judges will evaluate the following factors:

- presentation skills

- originality of your concept

- quality of the peripheral materials (easy to read, grammatical accuracy, professional appearance)

You must turn in a copy of your slideshow or video as well as a hard copy of any written materials that accompany your presentation.

Be creative! Be original! Enjoy! Good Luck!

APPENDIX B: SAMPLE EVALUATION RUBRIC

Apprentice Task Presentation

Team Name_____   Product: _____

Presentation Skills:

• Effective Speaking :	1	2	3	4	5 (BEST)
• Smooth Transitions/Flow:	1	2	3	4	5
• Organization:	1	2	3	4	5
• Overall Effectiveness/ Time management	1	2	3	4	5

Subtotal (20) _____

Concept/Content:

• Creativity :	1	2	3	4	5 (BEST)
• Print Ad:	1	2	3	4	5
• TV Ad:	1	2	3	4	5
• Overall Impact	1	2	3	4	5

Subtotal (20) _____

Total Score (40): _____

PART 2: Beyond Skills

D. Critical Thinking

CHAPTER 29

Logical Use of Logic Puzzles

Kurtis McDonald

INTRODUCTION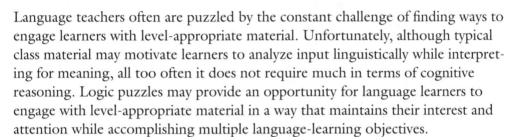

Language teachers often are puzzled by the constant challenge of finding ways to engage learners with level-appropriate material. Unfortunately, although typical class material may motivate learners to analyze input linguistically while interpreting for meaning, all too often it does not require much in terms of cognitive reasoning. Logic puzzles may provide an opportunity for language learners to engage with level-appropriate material in a way that maintains their interest and attention while accomplishing multiple language-learning objectives.

Logic puzzles, also known as logic problems, are word or story problems that offer a scenario and goal to be deduced through careful analysis of the information presented in clues. Although generally intended for native-speaking math students to foster logical thinking skills, or for puzzle enthusiasts for the fun of a mental challenge, logic puzzles can readily offer these and numerous other pedagogical benefits to language learners as well (Danesi, 1979; Danesi & Mollica, 1994; Raizen, 1999). Their inherent appeal also seems to go well beyond dedicated math students and pure puzzle enthusiasts; even those who claim to dislike math are often enthralled with logic puzzles (Smullyan, 1982). Indeed, it has been argued that humans may in fact possess a kind of instinct or desire to solve puzzles so basic that it is comparable to a sense of humor (Danesi, 2002). Not only does it seem that most people enjoy the challenge of a good puzzle, but language learners are most likely already familiar with solving puzzles in their native language and may be motivated by them as a change of pace in a language class (Danesi, 1979; Jewinski, 1980; Raizen, 1999).

Although logic puzzles encourage the use of many reading skills and strategies now widely believed to be important for second- and foreign-language learners, they are perhaps most directly related to introducing, reinforcing, and reviewing vocabulary presented in specific contexts. As learners are exposed to vocabulary in the well-defined contexts of logic puzzles, they are uniquely able to maintain focus on negotiating the meaning of the clues while making inferences, testing assumptions, and drawing logical conclusions (Danesi & Mollica, 1994).

Because each logic puzzle has only one correct solution attainable from the clues presented, learners can immediately test their comprehension of the material and make appropriate adjustments to their interpretations in ways that most types of reading do not allow.

Many of the benefits of logic puzzles for language learning have been outlined in the limited body of literature available on the topic to date. Most notably, articles by Danesi (1979) and Danesi and Mollica (1994) provide a foundation that serves to legitimize the general language learning benefits offered by the use of logic puzzles. Danesi presents a threefold rationale to support the use of logic puzzles for language teaching: (a) Most people like solving puzzles that do not require specific technical skill, (b) most language learners have prior experience solving puzzles in their native language and can take advantage of this background knowledge when asked to complete puzzles in the target language, and (c) students in language classes may appreciate the change of pace offered by logic puzzles. Later, Danesi and Mollica (1994), after completing a survey of previous research on the use of logic puzzles for language learning, found three benefits to be generally consistent across all of the relevant studies: (a) cognitive engagement with the material, (b) heightened focus on meaning, and (c) assimilation of the meaning-to-form relations employed in the puzzle.

Although logic puzzles have been shown to be of great potential benefit to language learners, the use of logic puzzles for language teaching and learning today remains largely overlooked and untapped. Clearly logic puzzles have many unique advantages to offer classroom teachers and their learners and should be more widely and thoroughly explored.

CONTEXT

Logic puzzles offer a great deal of adaptability in exactly how they are utilized in class. As the situational contexts of the scenarios can be almost endlessly adapted, the associated target grammatical constructions and vocabulary presented can be extremely flexible as well. Although nearly all widely available logic puzzles in print and on the Internet are intended for native speakers, the basic structure behind logic puzzles can be adapted in many ways to suit a wide range of proficiency levels, age groups, and teaching contexts. Obviously, the cultural situations and contexts, grammatical structures, and vocabulary presented in the logic puzzles used must be appropriate for the intended audience of learners. Simple logic puzzles presented with easily relatable situations could conceivably be used effectively with children through junior high school, although the teacher may have to be actively involved in leading the students through the logical deductions, especially at first. More sophisticated logic puzzles would be appropriate for high school learners through adults.

In my own teaching experiences, university students have been particularly receptive of logic puzzles. I have used logic puzzles with great success in my intermediate English as a foreign language (EFL) reading classes for 1st- and 2nd-year students at a large university's school of science and technology in Japan. In fact, on their course evaluations, students ranked logic puzzles the most favorably of all class activities done throughout the 2006 school year. Logic puzzles were used in class primarily as occasional reading comprehension and inferencing tasks with contextualized vocabulary introduction or recycling and focused exposure to the grammatical forms, meaning, and uses of relative clauses. They have served to achieve numerous objectives in these classes without demanding much class time or teacher preparation.

CURRICULUM, TASKS, MATERIALS

At the beginning of the course, students are introduced to logic puzzles in English through simple puzzles that review classroom phrases and vocabulary. Throughout the term, the difficulty of the logic puzzles increases and the vocabulary presented changes. Some of these puzzles are teacher-created and designed to include vocabulary that connects directly with the course work, and others are culled and adapted from numerous Internet sources freely available for educational use. Additionally, variations beyond simple reading-based puzzles have included knowledge-gap communicative logic puzzles in which the scenarios or clues are divided between students, as well as student-produced original logic puzzles for class members and the teacher to attempt. There is a seemingly endless array of effective uses of logic puzzles in class.

Materials

Logic puzzles do not require any special materials, although they should either be copied onto handouts for students, shown on a class projector, written on the board, or linked through a course Web site. The only material really essential is the logic puzzle itself. Although possibly intimidating at first, logic puzzles are not difficult to construct after the teacher becomes accustomed to the basic style of writing and design. Once the basic situational context and target vocabulary to be used in a logic puzzle have been decided, it is best to begin writing with the solution. After the solution is established, the clues should be written while tracking on a chart the information that is able to be deduced. Once enough clues have been presented to allow the solution to be logically deduced, the logic puzzle is complete. Of course, before using a newly created logic puzzle in class, it is best to test it out on a willing colleague.

Higher level learners may be ready to try logic puzzles originally intended for native speakers and, fortunately, numerous sources for logic puzzles are available both in print and on the Internet (see Appendix B). It should be noted that most logic puzzles found on the Internet are intended for native speakers and need to be adapted before being appropriate to most language levels and learning contexts.

Procedures

Depending on the level of the learners involved, the procedure for employing logic puzzles in class may range from simply handing students a copy of the puzzle and setting a time limit to working with the class step-by-step to solve the puzzle. Learners with previous experience working with logical deductions, such as high school students, university students, and adult learners, may quickly understand the task presented by a logic puzzle and be able to work independently to solve it. If such learners do have trouble solving a particular puzzle, allowing students to confer about the information presented in the clues, pointing out specific clues, or providing hints may be advisable. For learners who are not as practiced in logical deduction or those who may be hindered by low language proficiency, working through the solutions to the first puzzles presented in a class as a group may be necessary. The teacher may read through the puzzle scenario and clues while tracking the information presented on a chart for the students to see. As the task becomes clearer to the learners, student involvement in deducing the information can increase as the teacher becomes less involved. Ultimately, though, for logic puzzles to be most effective, learners must be mentally engaged with the material on their own to some degree. Some learners may never excel at solving logic puzzles, so it is recommended that they serve as a fun, occasional addition to class not tied to grades, although offering extra credit may provide a motivational stimulus to some learners.

REFLECTIONS

Although using logic puzzles in language teaching and learning is not entirely new, it is clear that all of the potential benefits have not yet been completely uncovered. Logic puzzles can meet many language-teaching objectives while keeping learner interest throughout the activity as well as in subsequent meetings over the course of a term or terms (Danesi, 1979; Danesi & Mollica, 1994; Raizen, 1999). University students—particularly those familiar with logical deduction, such as science, math, or engineering students—have demonstrated a keen interest in solving logic puzzles as an occasional warm-up activity in low-intermediate EFL reading classes at a large university in Japan. The appeal of puzzles among students learning English is undoubtedly as wide-ranging as the general public's interest in puzzles. The idea of using logic puzzles as a fun, mentally engaging way of teaching and learning language should be revisited by teachers in all contexts and utilized when appropriate to meet class objectives.

REFERENCES

Danesi, M. (1979). Puzzles in language teaching. *The Canadian Modern Language Review/La Revue canadienne des langues vivantes, 35,* 269–277.

Danesi, M. (2002). *The puzzle instinct: The meaning of puzzles in human life.* Bloomington, IN: Indiana University Press.

Danesi, M., & Mollica, A. (1994). Games and puzzles in the second-language classroom: A second look. *Mosaic, 2,* 13–22.

Jewinski, J. (1980). Logic and language learning through puzzles: From beginner to expert. *TESL Talk, 11*(2), 63–68.

Raizen, E. (1999). Liar or truth-teller? Logic puzzles in the foreign-language classroom. *Texas Papers in Foreign Language Education, 4,* 39–50.

Smullyan, R. (1982). *The lady or the tiger? and other logic puzzles.* New York: Times Books.

Kurtis McDonald is an instructor at Kwansei Gakuin University's School of Science and Technology in Japan, where he also serves as coordinator for educational technology. He has a master's degree in TESOL from Eastern Michigan University, in the United States, and more than 7 years of experience teaching English as a second language and EFL in the United States and Japan.

APPENDIX A: QUESTIONS DURING OFFICE HOURS: A SAMPLE LOGIC PUZZLE

Gyu Jin, Javier, Megumi, and Noora are all students in the same university English class. Of course, they are all hardworking, diligent students, so they often visit their instructor during office hours whenever they have a question or problem. Today all four students came to their instructor's office to get help. One student did not understand a homework assignment; another student was not sure how to pronounce a word. One student wanted to know how to improve her English vocabulary; another student just wanted the chance to practice speaking with the teacher. From the clues, determine the order that the students visited the instructor during office hours and the reason for each one's visit.

1. The first student to show up at the office had a quick question about pronunciation.

2. Both boys, Gyu Jin and Javier, came to the office sometime before the girl who wanted to practice speaking.

3. One of the girls, Noora, left the teacher's office just before Javier went in.

Order	Name	Reason
First		
Second		
Third		
Fourth		

A chart may be helpful to organize the information presented in the clues:

	Gyu Jin	Javier	Megumi	Noora	Homework	Pronunciation	Vocabulary	Speaking
First								
Second								
Third								
Fourth								
Homework								
Pronunciation								
Vocabulary								
Speaking								

Vocabulary Spotlight

What are some new vocabulary words or phrases presented in this logic puzzle? Can you guess the meaning of these words? Try to list at least five words or phrases and a basic definition to help you remember them.

Expansion Conversation

Now that you have figured out each student's reason for coming to the teacher's office hours, how would each student ask his or her question to the teacher? With your partner, take turns practicing an imaginary conversation between one of the students and the teacher.

Puzzle Solution

The completed table and chart for the Questions During Office Hours puzzle are shown below.

Order	Name	Reason
First	Gyu Jin	Wasn't sure how to pronounce a word
Second	Noora	Wanted to know how to improve her English vocabulary
Third	Javier	Didn't understand the homework assignment
Fourth	Megumi	Wanted to practice speaking with the teacher

	Gyu Jin	Javier	Megumi	Noora	Homework	Pronunciation	Vocabulary	Speaking
First	O	X	X	X	X	O	X	X
Second	X	X	X	O	X	X	O	X
Third	X	O	X	X	O	X	X	X
Fourth	X	X	O	X	X	X	X	O
Homework	X	O	X	X				
Pronunciation	O	X	X	X				
Vocabulary	X	X	X	O				
Speaking	X	X	O	X				

APPENDIX B: INTERNET RESOURCES

The following Web sites offer free logic puzzles of varying difficulties for educational use:

- Judy's Logic Problems: http://pages.prodigy.net/spencejk/yearlylps.html

- The Logic Zone: http://myweb.tiscali.co.uk/thelogiczone/

- Puzzles.com: http://www.puzzles.com/Projects/LogicProblems.html

- Anthony Atkielski's home page (*Who owns the fish* pdf files): http://www.atkielski.com/inlink.php?/ESLPublic/

Searching the Internet for "logic puzzles" or "logic problems" will result in many more examples.

CHAPTER 30

Three Games to Exercise the Brain

Alexander Sokol, Edgar Lasevich, and Marija Dobrovolska

INTRODUCTION

The three games presented in this chapter implicitly aim to develop learners' thinking skills along with their language skills. These games have been developed within the Thinking Approach to language teaching and learning (Sokol, 2007; Sokol, Khomenko, Sonntag, & Oget, 2008). This approach consists of a system of methods for implementing integrated learning of a foreign language and the development of thinking skills (see http://www.thinking-approach.org for more details on the theory behind the approach as well as practical examples for the classroom). Each game presented helps the learner master one or several thinking skills. For example, when playing Feature Constructor, learners focus on describing the different features or characteristics of objects. To Take Into My House helps them develop the skills for defining the different possible functions (uses or purposes) an object can have depending on the context in which it is used. One of the effects of The Most Useful Thing in the World is understanding that an object can have more than one function. In addition to the thinking focus, each game involves various aspects of language learning, such as learning and practicing vocabulary in Feature Constructor and The Most Useful Thing in the World, or speaking based on genuine communication in To Take Into My House.

CONTEXT

Although the games were initially designed for young learners with low levels of English proficiency, they can be adapted easily for older learners with higher proficiency levels. The games are suitable for both English as a foreign language (EFL) and English as a second language (ESL) contexts. The structure of all three games allows for modifications both in terms of content (e.g., vocabulary) and procedures (how they are implemented in the classroom), so it is easy to integrate them into various language-learning contexts. For example, when appropriate vocabulary is chosen, the game The Most Useful Thing in the World can even be used with adult English for specific purposes (ESP) learners, who often enjoy playing games. All three games can be used as entertaining activities outside the classroom.

ACTIVITY ONE: FEATURE CONSTRUCTOR

CURRICULUM, TASKS, MATERIALS

Getting Started

The teacher will need a copy of the worksheet for each learner (see Appendix A). Alternatively, teachers can choose to prepare their own worksheets (e.g., including different vocabulary) to adapt the game to their context.

Guidelines:

- Ask learners to describe ice cream as fast as they can and compare the answers.

- Divide the class into groups of 4–6 learners each.

- Randomly choose two features (i.e., adjectives)—one from each box—from the boxes on the worksheet (see Appendix A).

- Ask the groups to find an object that suits the description.

- Give a point to the groups that succeed. Give an additional point if they can think of more than one object.

- Choose new features for the next round.

Procedures

Teachers should ask learners to describe ice cream as fast as they can. Later, ask them to read their descriptions aloud. Discuss which features are the same, how many different features the class found, and what parameters these features describe (e.g., *cold* is for *temperature*, *white* is for *color*).

Option 1

1. Divide learners into groups of 4–6. Give each group two features chosen at random—one from each box on the worksheet (see Appendix A)—such as *cold* and *hard*.

2. Now in 2 minutes, groups are supposed to think of as many objects as possible that suit the given description. In our example, answers such as *ice, a metal safe, frozen vegetables*, and so forth, are possible. (Note: the number of minutes allowed can be varied.)

3. A group gets 1 point once it has given an example of an object that suits the description. The group that thinks of the most objects gets 2 points.

4. New features are given and a new round is played. The game can last for as long as the teacher decides, but it is better not to keep it going longer than five or six rounds.

Option 2

1. Divide learners into groups of 4–6.

2. One learner in a group chooses two features (adjectives) from the boxes and asks a partner on the right to name a possible object. That person should answer within 10 seconds and then choose two features for the next person.

3. (To make it more difficult, the teacher may ask learners to use one feature from the previous turn.)

4. A person unable to name an object is out of the game. (Objects, as well as pairs of features, cannot be repeated.)

5. The game is played until only one person remains in the group. Alternatively, the teacher may also set a time limit for this activity.

Variations

You can easily adapt the worksheet to make the game more appropriate to your context (see Appendix A). For example, a list of personal characteristics may be introduced to use the game as an activity to accompany work on a literary text (e.g., description of characters). Another option could be a list of features of companies or various types of business correspondence to make the game appropriate for business English purposes.

In addition, the game may also become an entertaining activity outside of the classroom. To make it even more interesting, features can be written on slips of paper and put in two boxes. In turn, each participant draws one from each box and should then immediately find an object that corresponds to the description. If a person fails to do so, his team can help. If no one comes up with an answer, the team loses the point.

Assessment

An average learner can easily name a couple of features of this or that object. It gets more difficult, though, when it is necessary to go from features to objects, especially when several features are given and learners must think of a possible option. At the same time, it is exactly this skill that often is required in real-life problem solving. Feature Constructor provides the context for developing this skill (going from features to objects) and allows learners to use vocabulary in a meaningful communicative context, thereby learning new vocabulary items and/or activating passive vocabulary.

Learners tend to enjoy the game because there are many possible answers and the actual procedure allows for variations that keep the game interesting for a long time. Also, the introduction of collaborative and competitive aspects in the game makes it attractive to various groups of learners.

REFLECTIONS

The game comprises both collaborative (learners working in a team) and competitive (teams playing against each other) aspects, which makes it attractive to various groups of learners. When playing the game, learners are involved in an open problem-solving task where multiple answers are possible, which supports both genuine communication and development of learners' thinking skills.

Traditionally, tasks dealing with description skills train learners to go from objects to their features. In this game, learners are involved in the reverse process, going from features of an object to possible objects that have these features. This skill is essential for problem solving in real life.

ACTIVITY TWO: TO TAKE INTO MY HOUSE

CURRICULUM, TASKS, MATERIALS

Getting Started

The teacher will need a copy of the worksheet for each learner (see Appendix B).

Guidelines:

1. Give a copy of the worksheet to each learner.

2. Ask learners to write down things (objects, substances, animals, etc.) they think it is not wise to take into their house (e.g., fire).

3. Get the learners to exchange their worksheets.

4. Learners explain to each other why they might need such a thing in the house.

5. Choose a leader. Ask the other learners to decide what object, substance, animal, etc. they want to be.

6. Learners come to the leader in turn and ask him to take them into the home. If the leader can say what this particular thing could do in a house, the person can enter.

Procedures

Pair work: Hand out copies of the worksheet (one for each learner). Give learners 2 minutes to write down various objects (one per line). An additional requirement may be that they should find objects/substances/animals that are not likely to be seen in their homes.

Learners exchange their worksheets: Then learners are asked to explain why they might want this object/substance/animal to be present in their homes. For example: a fire could cook food and heat the house in winter; a giraffe could help him get books from the upper shelf, etc.

Choose a leader (the teacher may play the leader part first). The leader comes in front of the classroom. He is going to furnish the house. Ask learners to choose what object/substance/animal they want to be. Learners come to the leader in turn. He asks them what object/substance/animal they are and must find a certain function for each character so that they can enter his house. The more characters the leader has gathered in the house, the more comfortable the house will be and the more points he will receive. For example:

Leader: What are you?

Learner 1: I'm fire!

Leader: Okay, you will be in the kitchen cooking food. And what are you?

Learner 2: I'm a giraffe!

Leader: Okay, you will be in the library and help me get books from the upper shelves!

The game is over if the leader cannot find a function for someone. The group's task is to choose things that are difficult to find a function for.

Variations

This game can be played in teams. Two teams are given some time to write down objects/substances/animals they are the least likely to take into their houses. Then, the worksheets are exchanged and the teams try to find useful functions for these objects/substances/animals. The first group to find at least one useful function for each object/substance/animal wins.

To make this game more teacher-centered, the teacher may choose to write down the objects/substances/animals for each learner. Then the worksheets are given to the learners, and they are invited to write down functions for each object/substance/animal. After that, a discussion may take place: Which was the most difficult to find a function for? The easiest? Which was left without a function? Which had the most functions?

Assessment

An average learner often thinks about one "correct" purpose of things (e.g., a chair is for sitting, an umbrella is for protecting from the rain). In reality, all things have many purposes depending on the particular contexts they are used in (see the following section, *The Most Useful Thing in the World*, for details). Although this game does not directly show how the context dictates the purpose, it can shift learners' stereotypes and help them go beyond the usual and think more broadly. This broader thinking can help learners overcome the mental inertia—accepting that something is the way we imagine it to be without even questioning if it is really so—which is often the main obstacle on the way to effective problem solving. In addition to developing their thinking skills by overcoming mental inertia and learning to define the function of objects in a certain context, learners also develop their language skills by being involved in writing, reading, listening, and speaking activities when performing a task.

REFLECTIONS

Mental inertia can significantly limit the contexts that learners consider when building solutions to problems. In many situations, learners deal with the so-called correct purpose of things. In this game, though, they must go beyond what is usually accepted—think outside the box—and find new functions various things may have in a certain context. Children like to make believe, and this game gives them the opportunity to do so. In addition, learners work on all four aspects of the language: writing (when listing objects/substances/animals), reading (after exchanging worksheets with their partners), listening, and speaking (when talking to the partner or the leader). Moving around during the game also makes it attractive to young learners.

ACTIVITY THREE: THE MOST USEFUL THING IN THE WORLD

CURRICULUM, TASKS, MATERIALS

Getting Started

The teacher will need a copy of the worksheet for each learner (see Appendix C).

Guidelines:

- Discuss with the class what one can or cannot do with a chair.

- Each learner chooses an object.

- Each learner gives features of the chosen object.

- Each learner writes down possible functions of their object based on the features defined.

- Learners compare their objects and find the most useful one in the group.

Procedures

Explain that today the class is going to play a detective game, and everyone will become a detective. The challenge is to find the most useful thing in the world.

1. Start with the whole class. Discuss how a chair can be used. Ask what one cannot do with a chair and why. It is important that every function (what an object can be used for) be based on one or several of its features. For example, one can stand on a chair because it is hard, stable, and has a flat surface of a certain size.

2. Ask each learner to choose an object. Tell them that it can be anything.

3. Ask learners to write down as many features of their object as possible. Explain that a list of features will make the next step easier. (If learners have difficulties finding features, the teacher may demonstrate how features of an object can be found through identifying parameters. For example, a tomato can be described using the following parameters: color, size, shape, type of plant, place of growth, and cooking methods. Each parameter can have certain values; for example, color includes red, yellow, and green, and cooking methods include frying, drying, and stewing).

4. Ask learners to fill in a table identifying the features and possible functions of the object (see Appendix C).

5. Get learners to compare their objects with those of their neighbors or groupmates. The learner who has formulated the most functions for his object has found the most useful object in the world. (The teacher may decide to allow learners to add functions after comparing the objects with classmates, which will increase the learning potential of the game.)

Variations

An alternative is to use this game as a speaking activity or a game outside the classroom. In this case, one object is chosen and the players in turn name a feature and characteristics of the object and define a possible function. The player unable to name a function is out.

In this variation, the game can be used with adult learners studying ESP. The teacher proposes one of the concepts to learners (e.g., a limited company in business English or bankruptcy in legal English) and asks them to think of various features or characteristics and then define a possible function. This activity could enable learners to go deeper into the meaning of concepts (and often explain them to the teacher), rather than just learning parallel lists of vocabulary.

Assessment

People often believe that functions are given once and for all and attached to objects forever (e.g., a book exists to provide information). In reality, the function is normally dictated by an immediate context where an object is used and is based on one or several of its characteristics. For example, if a child is playing with building blocks and constructing a town, books can become building materials (panels) thanks to such features as hard, flat, of a certain size, etc. When books are displayed in the living room of a house, their function may be a part of the interior design due to such features as being expensive or having a certain theme.

The ability to see these nontraditional features of objects is often associated with creative thinking. This game not only helps learners see more than one function of an object but also provides them with the methodology for doing so.

REFLECTIONS

This game can be seen as a typical task lying in what Vygotsky (1978) referred to as learners' zone of proximal development (ZPD) because most learners need scaffolding to do it well. In order to cope with the task, it is necessary to find features of a chosen object that do not seem obviously important in the beginning (e.g., the size of a book for the child's construction project, or its color for the purpose of interior design). The ability to identify these features represents an important part of learning. Moreover, when comparing objects with classmates, learners are involved in metacognitive thinking (Moseley et al., 2004; Palinscar & Brown, 1997; Perkins, Simmons, & Tishman, 1990). They have to consider their classmates' thinking when listing this or that function of an object and, at the same time, decide if any of the parameters their classmates identified could also apply to their objects. This process can also be seen as mediation.

REFERENCES

Moseley, D., Baumfield, V., Higgins, S., Lin, M., Miller, J., Newton, D., et al. (2004). *Thinking skills frameworks for post-16 learners: An evaluation. A research report for the learning and skills research centre*. Trowbridge, England: Cromwell Press. Retrieved October 16, 2007, from http://www.lsda.org.uk/files/pdf/1541 .pdf

Palinscar, A. S., & Brown, D. A. (1997). Enhancing instructional time through attention to metacognition. *Journal of Learning Disabilities, 20*(2), 66–75.

Perkins, D. N., Simmons, R., & Tishman, S. (1990). Teaching cognitive and metacognitive strategies. *Journal of Structural Learning, 10*(4), 285–303.

Sokol, A. (2007). *Development of inventive thinking in language education*. Unpublished doctoral dissertation, University of Latvia, Riga, and the University of

Louis Pasteur, Strasbourg, France. Retrieved April 14, 2008, from http://jlproj .org/new/index_.php?p=3&u=577

Sokol, A., Khomenko, N., Sonntag, M., & Oget, D. (2008). The development of inventive thinking skills in the upper secondary language classroom, *Thinking Skills and Creativity*, *3*(1), 34–46.

Vygotsky, L. S. (1978). *Mind in society*. Cambridge, MA: Harvard University Press.

Alexander Sokol completed his doctorate on the development of inventive thinking in language education. He is also the author and principal developer of the Thinking Approach to language teaching and learning (http://www.thinking-approach .org). Alexander works as a teacher, teacher trainer, researcher, and educational consultant.

Edgar Lasevich is a teacher, teacher trainer, and consultant. He is interested in various tools for the development of thinking skills of young learners.

Marija Dobrovolska is a teacher of English and German. She has been working in Germany for 2 years, piloting Thinking Approach ESP materials there and at the University Erlangen-Nürnberg. She is particularly interested in developing creative lexical tasks for young learners and adults.

APPENDIX A: FEATURE CONSTRUCTOR

As fast as you can, write five adjectives to describe:

ice cream
{
_____
_____
_____
_____
_____

How many common features do you have with your neighbor? In your group? In the class?

Choose two features (one from each box) and ask your partner to give you the name of an object that has both of these features:

WHITE

RED

YELLOW   GREY

BLACK

BLUE

GREEN   BROWN

WHITE ORANGE

VIOLET

LIGHT

CHEAP   HEAVY

EXPENSIVE

ROUND   SQUARE

HOT

COLD   SWEET

WARM

FROZEN   BITTER

TASTY

HARD METAL

SOFT

COZY

SOUR   WOODEN

GLASS   BEAUTIFUL

LARGE

SMALL   TALL   SHORT

BREAKABLE

BROWN AND
SWEET:
CHOCOLATE

WHITE AND
FROZEN:
ICE CREAM

ORANGE AND
TASTY: JELLY

SOFT AND
VIOLET:
BLANKET

APPENDIX B: TO TAKE INTO MY HOUSE

1. Write names of things (objects, substances, animals, etc.) that you think it
    is NOT wise to take to somebody's home:

```
┌─────────────────────┐
│                     │
│    _____      │
│                     │
└─────────────────────┘
```

```
┌─────────────────────┐     ┌─────────────────────┐
│                     │     │                     │
│   _____       │     │   _____       │
│                     │     │                     │
└─────────────────────┘     └─────────────────────┘
```

```
┌─────────────────────┐     ┌─────────────────────┐
│                     │     │                     │
│  _____        │     │   _____       │
│                     │     │                     │
└─────────────────────┘     └─────────────────────┘
```

```
┌─────────────────────┐     ┌─────────────────────┐
│                     │     │                     │
│  _____        │     │   _____       │
│                     │     │                     │
└─────────────────────┘     └─────────────────────┘
```

```
┌─────────────────────┐     ┌─────────────────────┐
│                     │     │                     │
│   _____       │     │   _____       │
│                     │     │                     │
└─────────────────────┘     └─────────────────────┘
```

```
┌─────────────────────┐
│                     │
│    _____      │
│                     │
└─────────────────────┘
```

2. Give the list to your neighbor.

APPENDIX C: THE MOST USEFUL THING IN THE WORLD

Say which of the following things you cannot do with a chair. Why?

- Sell it

- Put books on it

- Make a fire with it

- Decorate it

- Stand on it

- Sleep on it

Choose an object and write as many characteristics as you can imagine:

My object is _____

<table>
<tr><td colspan="2">Picture of my object:</td></tr>
<tr><td></td><td></td></tr>
</table>

It is:

Say what you can do with it because of each of its characteristics.

It is . . .	so I can use it to . . .

Compare your table with your friends' tables and decide which is the most useful object.

Index

Also Available from TESOL

Literature in Language Teaching and Learning
Amos Paran, Editor

More Than a Native Speaker:
An Introduction to Teaching English Abroad revised edition
Don Snow

Perspectives on Community College ESL Series
Craig Machado, Series Editor
Volume 1: Pedagogy, Programs, Curricula, and Assessment
Marilynn Spaventa, Editor
Volume 2: Students, Mission, and Advocacy
Amy Blumenthal, Editor
Volume 3: Faculty, Administration, and the Working Environment
Jose A.Carmona, Editor

Pre-K–12 English Language Proficiency Standards
Teachers of English to Speakers of Other Languages, Inc.

Planning and Teaching Creatively
within a Required Curriculum for School-Age Learners
Penny McKay, Editor

Professional Development of International Teaching Assistants
Dorit Kaufman and Barbara Brownworth, Editors

Revitalizing an Established Program for Adult Learners
Alison Rice, Editor

Teaching English as a Foreign Language in Primary School
Mary Lou McCloskey, Janet Orr, and Marlene Dolitsky, Editors
To order TESOL books:

Local phone: (240)646-7037
Toll-free: 1-888-891-0041
Fax: (301)206-9789
E-Mail: tesolpubs@brightkey.net
Mail Orders to TESOL, P.O. Box 79283, Baltimore, MD 21279-0283 USA

ORDER ONLINE at www.tesol.org and click on "Bookstore"